After
the
Internet:

ALIEN
INTELLIGENCE

After the Internet:

ALIEN INTELLIGENCE

James Martin

**CAPITAL
PRESS**
Washington, DC

Copyright © 2000 by James Martin

Library of Congress Cataloging-in-Publication Data

Martin, James, 1933–
After the internet : alien intelligence / James Martin.
p. cm.
ISBN 0-89526-280-0
1. Computers and civilization. 2. Artificial intelligence. 3. Internet
(Computer network) I. Title.

QA76.9.C66 M363 2000

303.48'34—dc21

00-034600

Published in the United States by
Capital Press
A Regnery Publishing Company
One Massachusetts Avenue, NW
Washington, DC 20001

Distributed to the trade by
National Book Network
4720-A Boston Way
Lanham, MD 20706

Printed on acid-free paper
Manufactured in the United States of America

10 9 8 7 6 5 4 3 2 1

BOOK DESIGN BY JULIE LAPPEN
SET IN BEBMO

Books are available in quantity for promotional or premium use.
Write to Director of Special Sales, Regnery Publishing, Inc.,
One Massachusetts Avenue, NW, Washington, DC 20001,
for information on discounts and terms or call (202) 216-0600.

Grateful acknowledgment is made to IBM Communications for
permission to reprint the image of a computer chip.

To Corinthia

Contents

Part III: Alien Technologies

Acknowledgments

I have learned much from the writings of, and from my interactions with, the following pioneers and thought leaders: Gordon Bell, Seymour Cray, Richard Dawkins, Hugo de Garis, Daniel C. Dennett, Doyne Farmer, Edward Feigenbaum, Jay Forrester, Robert Hecht-Neilsen, W. Daniel Hillis, Tony Hoare, John H. Holland, Kevin Kelly, Andrew Leonard, Robert Metcalfe, Marvin Minsky, Gordon Moore, Hans Moravec, James J. Odell, Richard Olsen, Roger Penrose, Tony Rutkowski, Sherry Turkle, Stephen Wolfram, and many others.

PART I
A New Beast in the E-Jungle

CHAPTER 1
The Sorcerer's Apprentice

Long, long ago, I was employed as a rocket scientist. A real rocket scientist. I did research on the rocket motors for the British Blue Streak missile. The attempt to create a rocket motor that was extremely powerful, but small, caused severe overheating problems that would sometimes melt the walls of the combustion chamber. Occasionally the motor would explode.

To try to understand what was happening, we built a laboratory device to simulate the heat transfer in the walls of the combustion chamber. The device consisted of a large vat of molten wax with electronic components set in it to simulate the heat flow. Readings from the test firings of the motor were manually fed to the heat-simulating gadget, and the rig was tinkered with endlessly in an attempt to make the motor run more smoothly.

One day it was announced that the Duke of Edinburgh was to visit the laboratory. Total panic ensued. The place was cleaned top to toe, and cynical bearded researchers were told to wear ties. To my horror

I found that the bath of wax had been unplugged and the wax had solidified, so I plugged in its heater. It took hours to remelt the wax and only the bottom part of it was liquid when Rolls-Royces started to arrive. Unfortunately the wax expanded as it melted, putting steadily growing pressure on the still-solid wax at the top. Suddenly, as the royal party was approaching, molten wax burst through the top and shot up like the geysers in Yellowstone Park. The entire room with all its equipment and research assistants was left dripping with hot wax.

That was the end of an era. Simulations started to be done on computers not in physical analogs. I decided to learn all I could about computing and joined IBM.

It is sometimes difficult to anticipate the effects of a new technology. By 1957 I was involved in data processing, but that year the editor in charge of business books for Prentice Hall wrote, "I have traveled the length and breadth of this country and talked with the best people, and I can assure you that data processing is a fad that won't last out the year." He was wrong. Data processing became the world's most successful growth industry. I was destined to write many books on it for Prentice Hall.

Those early beginnings were the start of something that would change society across the planet. Today we stand at the threshold of one of the most sweeping changes in history, brought about by digital technology.

■　■　■　■　■

At the start of this new century two revolutions are in progress, both destined to change our lives in fundamental ways. The first is the Internet, which is bringing an age of social connectivity to the planet. It brought e-commerce and ushered in an era of business reinvention. The second is the growth of radically new forms of computer-generated "intelligence." Many think that when computers are more advanced they will be able to replicate human intelligence. In fact we are discovering that the human mind is much more subtle and complex than we realized. Computers will not be like us. We are seeing the early stages of new forms of computer intelligence that are radically, totally, fundamentally different from human intelligence and, in narrowly focused areas, vastly more powerful.

Historians in the future may say that computing reached its infancy when, instead of merely following human logic in a sequence of basic steps, it began to exhibit an intelligence of its own, one very different from human intelligence. Software is already in use that can automatically evolve, "breed," or "learn" valuable behavior of its own. This does not make computers intelligent in the way people are. Instead, an alien type of intelligence is developing.

It is time to give up the twentieth-century notion that artificial intelligence is like human intelligence.

Some of the mechanisms of this alien intelligence can run largely under their own steam. A computer can execute logic millions of times faster than humans can, so, when we initiate a self-perpetuating computer process, interesting things can happen. The computerized "thought" that results is utterly different from human thought and so complex that we cannot follow its logic. It will change the nature of science. The challenge to business leaders is to harness this new capability.

Revolutions can be scary. Sir Peter Bonfield, the head of British Telecom, commented about today's business, "If you're not scared, you don't understand what's happening." The reinvention of business is radical. New companies with new thinking are racing ahead of blue-chip companies. Their stock market valuations often seem beyond reason. Electronic business is scary because it is a self-feeding chain reaction. The new computer intelligence will likewise become a self-feeding chain reaction—but it will ultimately become more scary because it will feed at electronic speed.

The revolutions of e-commerce and computer intelligence will support and amplify one another. Electronic commerce will become a fast-changing battlefield where great fortunes are made and lost, and computerized intelligence will become extremely important to this new commerce. The effectiveness of advertising, global marketing, learning about individual customers, and rapid adaptation to feedback will increasingly depend on the new forms of electronic intelligence. The new intelligence will affect investment, games, medicine, weapons and warfare, and science in general. It will change our lives.

> We are seeing the early stages of new forms of computer intelligence that are fundamentally different from human intelligence and vastly more powerful.

The mechanisms of the Internet were created two decades before the Internet took off on a large scale. The nonhuman intelligence we describe in this book may take a similar time to mature (although change is faster now). Its evolution is tracking about two decades behind the Internet's. However, some corporations are already using it, and some individuals are becoming masters of putting this new intelligence to work.

The marriage of the future Internet and the new automated intelligence will create a global chain reaction of immense consequences. With the possible exception of genetic engineering it is difficult to imagine a technology that will have a more profound effect on the human condition.

Technology once existed at the periphery of our culture. As alien intelligence spreads and feeds on itself, linked across the planet on a ubiquitous Internet, it will affect every aspect of our lives.

E-BUSINESS: A REVOLUTION BEGINS

Today's Internet is slow and crude. It is only beginning to have an effect on how most people live. But it has already caused a revolution in the way business is conducted. In 1995 business transactions on the Internet were almost zero. In 1999 most chief executives reacted to the Internet with great cynicism, saying, "Show me anyone who's made a profit with the Internet." In 2000 most chief executives were passing on a quote from Andy Grove, the head of Intel: "In a few years if you are not an Internet business you will not be in business." By 2003, according to Forrester Research, business-to-consumer Internet sales will grow to more than $100 billion, and business-to-business revenues will reach more than $3 trillion.[1] These figures represent a financial tsunami of a magnitude never before seen. By 2003 the rest of the world will be catching up and then fast surpassing the U.S. volume. Some individuals will make grand fortunes. Many traditional corporations will be swept away.

The Internet is not simply another distribution channel. It is not simply another way to get the same old marketing information to customers.

To make good use of the Internet, companies must fundamentally reinvent how they do business—their culture, their processes, their business models. Pioneers such as Dell, Cisco, and dot-com companies are setting new standards, inventing new capabilities, and insisting that their suppliers do the same. Traditional businesses must change—quickly—to avoid being destroyed by newcomers.

Most corporations look as though they are designed for an age that is gone. They need radically to transform if they are to remain competitive in an age of mercurial change. Transforming an old arthritic enterprise into a nimble corporation designed to evolve constantly and rapidly is a traumatic and risky quantum leap. *The Economist* says: "Recent experience suggests it takes little more than two years for a start-up to formulate an innovative business idea, establish a Web presence and begin to dominate its chosen sector. By then it may be too late for slow-moving traditional businesses to respond."[2]

THE GROWTH OF NONHUMAN INTELLIGENCE

The Internet's quantum leap in computer connectivity coincides with the growth of new types of intelligence in computing.

For half a century computing has been growing furiously. Only now, as it is reaching its infancy, can we begin to perceive what a precocious child we have created. That infancy in computing is beginning, as computers—rather than following human logic in a sequence of basic steps—*start to exhibit an intelligence of their own, fundamentally different from human intelligence.* We are now seeing the first baby steps of this new intelligence.

That is what this book is about. It is a very important subject because we will use this nonhuman intelligence to help run our world. As computers acquire this very different capability, they will use it to become ever more intelligent, creating a chain reaction of nonhuman intelligence that is becoming rapidly more powerful. The infant will grow up. It will become vitally important to business and will change basic methods in science.

When computing matures, artificial intelligence will be *nothing* like human intelligence. The human mind is diabolically complex and subtle; we will not get close to imitating it with computers. Machine intelligence will be a new type of intelligence—crude, at first, compared with the subtleties of the human mind but capable of improving its own power until it becomes awesome.

The vast majority of computing today is used to emulate human thought processes. But in the future, the primary value of computers will perhaps be to "think" in ways that humans cannot.

Software is coming into use that can automatically *evolve*, *"breed"* solutions, or *"learn"* valuable behavior of its own. Sometimes its behavior is completely unpredictable. When software is designed to evolve, it can do so fast. We can't follow its logic in detail, but we use it because it is very valuable. That is "alien intelligence."

We define alien intelligence as *processes executed on a computer that are so complex that a human can neither follow the logic step-by-step nor come to the same result by other means.* We couldn't write a conventional program to obtain the same result.

"Alien intelligence" refers to a growing family of techniques in use today that enable computers to recognize patterns that humans cannot recognize, "learn" behavior that humans cannot learn, explore data too vast for human exploration, "breed" programs that humans cannot write, assemble logical reasoning too complex for humans, evolve "brain mechanisms" that humans cannot design, and exhibit emergent properties that humans cannot anticipate. These things happen at electronic speed.

A computer can execute logic millions of times faster than humans can, so we initiate self-evolving computer processes that may become very complex.

Usually today we have to tell computers blow-by-blow what to do, so writing programs for them is a painfully slow process. Using alien-intelligence techniques we don't give the computer blow-by-blow instructions. Instead we give it a narrowly focused initiative of its own, very limited in its functionality but capable of extreme speed. *This is a fundamental break with the past—a quantum-leap change in capability.*

When software can be set up so that it "breeds," evolves, or in some way changes itself automatically, the changes take place fast. When the techniques become mature and widespread there will be a chain reaction of rapid iterations (even though most software will remain traditional for a long time to come). The change would be rapid even if the Internet didn't exist, but when hundreds of millions of computers are interconnected the potential for change is awesome. This potential for such rapid evolution of software (and, as we shall see, hardware) will be the rocket fuel for the human chain reaction of ideas about how to use the Internet.

The future of computing depends on the extent to which we are prepared to give up blow-by-blow control and let the machines race into unknown territory.

Where we can create electronic "life," it can mutate trillions of times faster than biological life. One might even wonder if it is part of nature's grand design that eventually evolution should occur in billions of machines linked by speed-of-light telecommunications.

When software "breeds" or evolves today, it does so in order to meet goals that humans specify. In the future we will want to set it up so that it improves its own goals. As machines race into unknown territory the question is: Can we control them? Are they bound, *ultimately*, to get out of control?

The twenty-first century will be a century of alien intelligence. As the century progresses, computers will become immensely more powerful than today—eventually billions of times more powerful—and there will be billions of machines interconnected by worldwide networks that transmit at the speed of light. Both software and hardware will "breed," "learn," and evolve, eventually at devastating speed.

For the next ten years our goal will be to light the fires of alien intelligence because of its great value to science, health care, entertainment, corporate efficiency, and moneymaking in general. Eventually the fires will be self-feeding. They will become a roaring forest fire around the planet. When this happens, we will become concerned about how to control the fire. Already we have "firewalls" to protect corporate computers, but they are designed for an age when software was easy to control.

The main concern now is how we light the fires. How do we put today's alien intelligence to work? That is what this book is mainly about. The last chapter discusses the future and its serious concerns. Is alien intelligence dangerous? Can we control the raging forest fires that we have started?

ALIEN INTELLIGENCE AT WORK

Alien intelligence is already in use today in diverse forms. Some organizations use it spectacularly; to others it sounds like science fiction. William Gibson, comments, "The future is already here; it's just unevenly distributed." When I see what's going on in some of the leading-edge laboratories and then go to traditional-minded organizations, it's clear that it is *very* unevenly distributed.

Alien intelligence techniques can be powerful because they enable computers to "learn." Some people object to the idea of computer learning because, they say, it is quite unlike the concept of human learning. When a computer "learns" it improves its knowledge, as a human does, but this is a mechanistic process. There is no cognizance involved; the computer merely becomes able to exploit better choices of action among an almost infinite number of possibilities. It can learn many thousands of times faster than a human learns but without the type of understanding that requires common sense.

> The twenty-first century will be the century of alien intelligence.

A computer can learn about you electronically and understand your needs in certain specific areas. Computers or electronic sensors can be relentless in monitoring and collecting information. Some people feel uncomfortable at the thought that computers can learn about them, but this will be part of the society we are creating. Machines can observe our behavior and update their knowledge about us. When I sign on to the Internet bookstore Amazon.com, the software greets me by saying, "Hello, James Martin. Here's a list of items we think you'll like." It has noted the books that I buy or examine in detail, and learned about my taste in books. Recently I bought a book at a real (nonelectronic) bookstore, and although I thought that this book was different from the types of books I find at Amazon, to my amazement the next time I signed on to Amazon it was recommending the very same title to me.

Just as Amazon learns about its customers' tastes in books and music, so all the processes of electronic commerce can be designed so that software can learn what customers are likely to buy, what changes they would like in the products, where to look for new customers, and so on. Clearly, having computers silently and relentlessly learning about customers has much commercial potential.

With alien intelligence techniques, computers can be trained to detect patterns that humans couldn't possibly recognize. They can be put to work analyzing, trying to make sense of overwhelming quantities of data, and taking action on the basis of knowledge acquired from the process. They can forage through masses of data, learning about customers, sales patterns, fraud, the spread of epidemics, and numerous other subjects.

Perhaps somewhat more alarming, HNC Software, Inc., uses alien intelligence technology to predict when individuals or organizations might go bankrupt. Such a prediction is useful to banks that issue credit cards. The software often flags cardholders who eventually do go bankrupt months before it is clear to humans that bankruptcy is inevitable. HNC encourages credit card issuers to join its "bankruptcy consortium." It is then able to collect an increasingly large body of historical data from many organizations about bankruptcies. The software makes itself able to detect the telltale patterns that may warn about bankruptcies.

John Deere improved its business by allowing farmers a great diversity of options in the products they order. Some farmers want four row planters, others want twenty-four row planters, and some want something in between. Planters can apply liquid fertilizer, dry fertilizer, or no fertilizer. John Deere offers over a million such permutations.

While such a rich set of choices is great for marketing, it can cause severe headaches in manufacturing. At John Deere, half-assembled machines were bunched up at one workstation while another workstation remained idle. It was difficult to control inventory.[3] A solution was found that employed alien intelligence. Software learned to "breed" factory schedules, different each day, far better than humans could produce. Planters now flow smoothly through the production line, with monthly output up sharply. We will soon see diverse examples of "breeding" software or procedures that we wouldn't ourselves be able to design.

Electronic devices have been built that can recognize people's faces. One such product from the Miros Corporation is being used as a security measure in some ATMs. In another security application, a door may open only if it recognizes your face.

In some countries the police use automated cameras to record the license plates of cars exceeding the speed limit. It is equally possible to record your face. Suppose you have a number of unpaid parking tickets, enough so that the police would arrest you if they could. You go to an ATM to withdraw money. As usual the security cameras record you. But now alien intelligence can match the image of your face with the one on your driver's license and transmit your location to the cops on patrol in your neighborhood.

Similarly, machines have been built that can recognize human emotions. A television set, or computer, will watch its viewers and detect their emotional response to advertisements. Marketers will use them to make multiple variants of advertisements, gauge the impact of each, and be able to display the ones that evoke the most positive responses from individual viewers. Computers have been designed that read human body language better than humans do.

Systems can be equipped with electronic senses that are constantly alert and intelligent. Embedded alien intelligence gives computers the ability continuously to analyze masses of data from sensors and act on the information when desirable. Sensors in your car, like sensors everywhere, will gather data continuously. Chips can analyze these data to prevent accidents. They can recognize if you are driving erratically. Insurance companies may lower your premium if your car sensors continually send a good report. A father may know if his teenage son is driving like a maniac.

Walter Wriston, the former chairman of Citibank, wrote in *Foreign Affairs*: "The attraction and management of intellectual capital will determine which institutions and nations will survive and prosper, and which will not.... The rules, customs, skills and talents necessary to uncover, capture, produce, preserve and exploit information are now one of humankind's most important assets." The ability to extract actionable knowledge from a vast mass of data will become critical to the pursuit of wealth. This used to be done by humans scanning the data. Computers, sometimes using the Internet and sometimes using automated sensors, will create an overwhelming deluge of data. As this grows, computers will be needed automatically to spot patterns and search for insights. Long ago we needed a genius like Kepler to look at the volumes of data about planetary positions and derive Kepler's laws of planetary motion. But that took Kepler most of his lifetime, and there are few Keplers around. Today, turning a deluge of data into actionable insight requires intricate computing. The key to unlocking valuable insights in science and business will be achieving the right combination of human intelligence and computer intelligence, and recognizing that these are fundamentally different.

Increasingly, corporations will confront one another with computerized systems. Electronic complexity is increasing and reaction times are decreasing as computerized systems become more advanced. The ultimate consequence of computerized competition is that the battle between the corporations becomes ever faster and more automated with deep alien intelligence. The methods that have served business well for many decades will be replaced with methods appropriate for real-time intelligent-Web interaction.

CHAIN REACTIONS

The Internet and alien intelligence both have immense potential power because, as noted, they become chain reactions. In a chain reaction one event causes other events; each of these, in turn, causes yet other events, and so on. Unless something slows down or interrupts a chain reaction, explosive growth occurs.

The Internet's success is the reason success can continue. Each generation of new ideas provides better capability for designing the next generation. The high market cap of the Internet companies causes extreme aggression. Advances lead to further advances.

As computers become intelligent, this chain reaction will inevitably occur. Once computer intelligence can improve its own capability automatically, the potential is there for machines to become more intelligent at a geometrically increasing rate.

The World Wide Web spread its capabilities worldwide almost immediately because it used the Internet. Web addresses now appear on television ads in most of the world. The applications of alien intelligence techniques will also spread worldwide. When alien intelligence and the Internet are teamed up, they reinforce one another. Machines will transmit their capabilities to other machines. With fiber optics, the circuits that connect computers will expand like floodgates opening. Computers will be able to exchange software, mine worldwide data warehouses, use intelligent search engines, and feed each other with fast-growing bodies of knowledge. New corporations, wanting to go public, will race to master the new methods. As the Internet becomes intelligent its new methods will spread like a brushfire.

> Technology once existed at the periphery of our culture. As alien intelligence spreads on a ubiquitous Internet, it will affect every aspect of our lives.

The rate of change is likely to continue to increase geometrically, not linearly, because there is positive feedback in research and development. Good ideas feed on themselves, and the Internet makes the feedback worldwide.

As its chain reaction develops, the Net's evolution will grow geometrically faster. However fast the Internet's rate of change is today, the Web is still only at the beginning of its true potential. It will soon be accessible to the public everywhere via television sets and cellular phones. It will use software and agents designed to learn at a rapid pace. Data in vast data warehouses will be designed for use by computers, rather than by people, to produce automated results. Search mechanisms will become more capable. But perhaps most important, the Internet will harness the new capabilities of alien intelligence. The pace of change may seem fast today, but it will become much faster when self-evolving software adds fuel to the Internet.

Driving these linked chain reactions is likely to be a main occupation of commerce for many years ahead. When will it stop? Not before our individual lives and all of society have been changed in inexorable ways.

STAGES OF GROWTH

When an industry is radically transformed it usually happens in three stages.

First, frameworks used for new facilities tend to copy the old. Mankind always wants to augment the past rather than break free from it. Early movies often looked like stage plays that had been filmed. It took decades to invent the rapid editing, special effects, and visual storytelling of today's films. Technology with radical potential for change has used words like "horseless carriage," "wireless telegraphy," and "paperless office." Eventually it became clear that cars changed the world in a way that "carriages" did not, and broadcasting changed the world in ways that telegraphy could not. Similarly, an enterprise well designed for cyberspace has no resemblance to one with paper-based offices. It is time for computers to break free from automating the past just as "wireless" needed to break free from "telegraphy."

Second, a new but fairly simple framework is developed. Instead of paper catalogues, corporations set up Web pages and use Web catalogues. Purchase orders and trading documents are sent electronically, computer-to-computer, instead of by snail-mail. Price auctions are used. Virtual operations are set up. This doesn't require rocket science. Any company can do it.

Third, big winners emerge who have learned to play the new games with great skill. At first the main competitive advantage comes from being the first to market; later competitive advantage and survival come from playing the game more and more intelligently. The mechanisms of e-business will evolve from procedures that are simple to procedures that use intricate forms of computerized intelligence. In the world we will describe there will be spectacular winners; the also-ran corporations will be far less profitable than the winners. The phrase "winner-takes-most" describes it well. The winner will have better information and better ways of deriving insight from that information. In the third stage, the mighty tumble. New corporations master the new ideas, while traditional executives are left desperate.

A few new corporations try to go straight to stage three. Cisco perceived that the world's telecommunications switching and routing equipment was obsolete, optimized for continuous voice channels. It needed to be replaced by a "new world" of high-speed computerized packet-switching. Knowing that such technology would change rapidly, Cisco decided to outsource all manufacturing so as never to be stuck with obsolete plants. If it didn't manufacture anything, it could change as fast as the technology changed. Cisco grew fast by buying companies in this business. It used the Web to communicate with both its suppliers and its customers. Suppliers constantly do real-time bidding for contracts. At the time of this writing 80 percent of Cisco's sales come from the Web. Fifty-five percent of orders are untouched by human hands. The savings from using the Web contribute $500 million to Cisco's $1.5 billion in overall earnings—a third of its earnings.

THE ELECTRONIC JUNGLE

The Internet has no master plan; it just grows like a jungle—constantly, amorphously, and unpredictably. Nobody is explicitly managing the Internet. Instead, millions of people contribute to its content in creative and fundamentally different ways. Each does his or her own thing, steadily adding to a common electronic resource. Different communities in the jungle have radically different cultures, but they coexist, often stimulating one another. As the Internet becomes vigorous in China and the non-Western world, it will develop understanding and appreciation of other forms of culture (for example, Chinese medicine). The Net puts many cultures into close proximity, and so they learn from each other.

This electronic jungle is far more broad and grand in scope than anything created by IBM, ATT, or the International Standards Organization. No corporation could have invented New York or Shanghai or the Internet. Electronics has its own worldwide ecosystem with intricate relationships among its members.

The Internet jungle, like nature's jungles, is a vast tangle of complex components interacting in unpredictable ways. It is becoming populated with an immense diversity of software creatures and intelligent systems. Alien intelligence technologies will enable these e-critters to "breed" and "evolve" and "learn." This crucible of human intelligence and software intelligence will produce wonderfully unpredictable results.

The electronic jungle will grow very rapidly in transmission speed, computing power, knowledge storage capacity, and alien intelligence. As alien intelligence takes root in the Internet, it will spread, establishing its role in the jungle. The Net evolves and grows like society grows, but at a lightning pace. The technologies I describe in this book will push the evolution of the Net into hyperdrive.

Although the Internet has junglelike characteristics, it is different from nature's jungles. A jungle has inertia because it is physical; the Net is a world of bits moving at the speed of electronics. The physical jungle is mature and stable in its overall behavior. The Net is not; it will change at great speed, twisting unpredictably.

ELECTRONIC HERDS

Thomas Friedman, in his wonderful book about globalism, *The Lexus and the Olive Tree*,[4] describes how the investors of the world have become linked in their knowledge and behavior into what he refers to as an "Electronic Herd." The Electronic Herd consists of vast numbers of often-anonymous stock, bond, currency, and multinational investors connected by screens and networks. Nobody is in charge of the herd. It has its own behavior.

Friedman comments: "The basic truth about globalization is this: No one is in charge—not George Soros, not 'Great Powers'.... I know that's hard to accept. It's like telling people there's no God. We all want to believe that somebody is in charge and responsible.... Democracies vote about a government's policies once every two or four years. But the Electronic Herd votes every minute of every hour of every day."

Analysts track the herd's movements all day on their Bloomberg screens. The herd analogy came from Merrill Lynch, which used to be the largest broker and advertised itself with spectacular images of a "Thundering Herd." In the new world the herd doesn't thunder but is far more devastating in its speed and magnitude.

Friedman's Electronic Herd relates to investment, but the Net has numerous herds. It has manufacturers of car parts wanting to attract the attention of the giant car companies and linking to global car-industry "exchanges" to buy car parts. It has herds of people wanting to buy a used copy of John Grisham's latest bestseller at a low price. When the Internet became popular with hackers, teenagers, and university students, it became a wild, uncontrolled resource, constantly evolving in new directions. Since it connected millions of creative and playful people across the planet, it became a live thing with new ideas raging across it.

Millions of people react to what the Internet can do. People's choices have impact on the future behavior of systems. The *software* or its owners respond to the greed, obsessions, berserkness, and power-lusts of the Internet herds, and the Web becomes a wild evolving organism.

Net users react to new fashions, marketing thrusts, and technologies, and can stampede on a grand scale. Gold rush fever can strike at a moment's notice. One little company, EarthWeb, went public in 1998. Despite revenues in the first half of 1998 of less than a million dollars and a loss of three million dollars in that time period, the company quickly acquired a market capitalization of $400 million. The Internet company eToys.com went public in 1999, with tiny sales, but its market capitalization was greater than that of Toys "R" Us, which had sales over $7 billion. In the week of April 10, 2000, however, many such gold rush companies lost most of their value when their stock prices plummeted; the market in tech stocks has proved volatile.

Computerized marketing mechanisms identify the winners and amplify their success. Millions of individual decisions to buy or not to buy reinforce each other, creating a boom or collapse, which in turn feeds back to shape the buying conditions that produced it. Virtually everything and everybody is caught up in a vast, non-linear web of incentives, constraints, and connections.

Corporations, whether they like it or not, exist and compete in this fast-changing jungle. The total reinvention of the nature of work will require new organizational structures and new human-technology partnerships. The change in the nature of corporations will cause economic changes with wrenching political implications. The evolution of cyberspace has gone far enough for us to know that it will drastically change society around the planet. Some countries will want to resist it, but to do so is to wreck their economy. By 2005 hundreds of billions of dollars a day of consumers' electronic cash will race across national frontiers, resulting in a growing separation of economy and state. The cyberspace economy will be worldwide.

OUTSIDERS

Throughout the history of computing, evolving from the massive isolated machines to the wild world of cyberspace, some of the most critical developments have come entirely from outsiders. Kids in garages created the personal computer industry. A college dropout produced the operating system for the IBM personal computer. The chip industry was spawned by a gaggle of start-up companies. A scientist in Europe's nuclear lab, CERN, invented the World Wide Web. Amazingly, no telecommunications company was involved in the birth or early growth of the Internet.

The future of knowledge technology will be dominated by global giants in the computer, software, and telecommunications industries, but, as in the past, many of the key new ideas will come from newcomers. The venture capital industry plays a critical role in trying to recognize these future winners and provide them with funding. This is one the world's grandest crap games, where untold millions are lost and won. People who wouldn't invest a dollar at Las Vegas, because the odds are against you, mortgage their house (as I did) and gamble the money on a start-up they believe in.

> As machines race into unknown territory, the question is: Can we control them? Are they bound, ultimately, to get out of control?

The casino is spreading from Silicon Valley to cyberspace. Conversations of college kids around the world today are about how they might make a fortune with a high-tech start-up.

This is an explosive mixture: cyberspace permeating our planet, electronic commerce becoming huge (soon trillions of dollars a year), entrepreneurs everywhere struggling to make the next fortune, an electronic jungle connecting the planet's people and machines, and now, perhaps most potent of all, the chain reaction growth of a new type of intelligence.

A BILLION KIDS IN CYBERSPACE

There will soon be almost two billion teenagers on the planet. About half of them will soon have access to television sets or inexpensive gadgets connected to the Internet. A billion kids in cyberspace constitute a youth culture that will develop furiously and surprise us in many ways. It is the planet's first global culture—and a force to be reckoned with.

They are a huge market accessible in remarkably focused ways. The Internet is so popular that it has brought de facto standards to an industry that could never agree about standards. For similar reasons it will bring to mankind a common second language—an English of diverse dialects. Esperanto never caught on; the Internet did. Two to three billion people around the planet are now trying to learn or improve their English because it is the language of mass-delivered entertainment, most pop songs, global news, and most of the interesting stuff on the Internet. Having a common second language is an ever more vital factor in the growing unity of mankind.

In the 1990s the Internet spread at an astonishing rate from a U.S. academic community to ordinary people around the planet. While computer-phobic commentators in aging country clubs were resisting the changes, hordes of young tigers plunged into the excitement of the Web, generating sky-high stock prices. Teenagers in Delhi and Penang chatter on the Internet to virtual friends around the planet. The wild fantasies of multiuser games on the Net are preparing teenagers for the computerized work environment of the future. Third World students, to their amazement, discover that doing research on the Net is often better than doing it in the great libraries of the rich countries.

Internet television will become a major instrument of commerce, used for shopping, advertising, games, news, e-mail, education, and exploring the ever-richer diversity of the Web. In Beijing almost every teenager in McDonald's has a cell phone; soon such devices will be linked to the Internet. Soon there will be hundreds of millions of pocket wireless devices in use. Except in deprived areas, children around the planet will grow up with the Internet, sending jokes to one another, making friends they will never meet, and playing the Web's seductive games with the fickle energy of childhood.

SORCERER'S APPRENTICES

The power of the microchip is doubling every eighteen months. The speed of fiber optics is doubling every year. It is like driving a car whose speed is increasing exponentially.

Rather than being firmly in control, we seem to be like the sorcerer's apprentice, having started something on a grand scale that we can barely steer. We're not able to pull the plug because our welfare, corporate profits, and defense are now too dependent on technology. A big question is: How can we drive the vehicle we are in as its velocity becomes exponentially faster?

As machines become ultraintelligent and "alien," will we be swept away by a tide of cultural change? Or will we employ the machines to evolve and improve our own culture? Some people will go along with the ride and love it. Others will hang on by their fingernails. Many people will be out of their depth, looking for cover. To masses of underprivileged people it will be a time of opportunity when rules are rewritten. Society and its traditional institutions will be shaken to their core.

In the story of the sorcerer's apprentice there was a sorcerer. Here we are all apprentices.

RIDING THE TIGER

We have started a fast-moving tiger, a process of inventing a global civilization. Some corporations will ride the beast, achieving spectacular results, fully realizing that they cannot get off lest they be eaten. Many *will* be eaten because they don't know how to ride the tiger.

This book will show you the sort of tiger that's about to be unleashed. It is an extraordinary story to tell. We'll start by explaining what alien intelligence is and how it will change thinking processes. Next we'll discuss how it fits in with the pervasive growth of the Internet. We can then talk about how it will change corporations and jobs, creating intense competition where the winner in each area tends to take most of the profits

> As new corporations master the new ideas, traditional executives are left desperate. The mighty tumble.

and everyone else struggles. To become a winner takes reinvention. A vital question for managers in traditional corporations will be: Can you change *fast enough*?

The first part of this book introduces alien intelligence. Part II describes how the masters of the new ideas will change our world. Part III explains alien-intelligence techniques in more detail, and the last chapter addresses the fascinating question of whether we can control machines that become highly intelligent in far different ways than ourselves.

The megarich of ten years from now will not be maharajas, great military conquerors, railroad robber barons, or oil sheiks. They will be gutsy, risk-taking iconoclasts who are masters of putting alien intelligence to work. They may be great adventurers, but not like Cecil Rhodes. Today's college kids should reflect that great wealth will not be dug out of the ground or conquered with armies, as in the past; it will come from the mind.

CHAPTER 2
Alien Intelligence

A BBC television program curiously entitled *The Soul* showed a sweet-looking scientist, Hans Moravec, explaining that in a few decades computers will become as intelligent as we are, and that once this happens they will use their intelligence to reprogram themselves to become more intelligent. They will, he said, improve their intelligence at electronic speed, immensely surpassing the human race.

Moravec, the director of the Mobile Robot Laboratory of Carnegie Mellon University, has made major contributions to the science of computerized robots. He writes in a serious and clearly argued book that intelligent machines will have superseded humans by about the year 2030, displacing us from existence.[1] He says: "I'm not as alarmed as many by [that] possibility, since I consider these future machines our progeny... ourselves in more potent form.... It behooves us to give them every advantage and to bow out when we can no longer contribute."[2] MIT computer scientist Ed Fredkin became known for his more optimistic view that future computers will keep us as pets.

Many researchers, entrepreneurs, weapons designers, and would-be moneymakers want computers to be *intelligent* as opposed to merely doing the accounting. But the attempts to create machine intelligence have had a rough passage so far.

One of the most notable aspects of artificial intelligence research has been its failure to deliver on its promises. In 1965 one of the great pioneers of artificial intelligence, Herbert Simon, wrote: "Within twenty years machines will be capable of doing any work a man can do." Ten years later Marvin Minsky, cofounder of MIT's Artificial Intelligence Lab, apparently unfazed by any timetable slippage, wrote: "Within a generation the problem of creating artificial intelligence will be substantially solved." After more than four decades of intense big-budget research, the computer's ability to demonstrate humanlike intelligence is largely absent. In spite of its enormous sales, the grammar checker built into Microsoft Office is unable to understand even our basic use of English plurals.

Most of the popular predictions about computing assume that computer intelligence will be like human intelligence, and robots will be like the ones we see in the movies. This is hopelessly wrong. Computers' "brains" are a million times faster than the human brain—and will soon be a billion times faster. They can be absolutely accurate, unlike the often wooly human brain. They will be interconnected worldwide at the speed of light. And they will have access to unimaginable quantities of data, which they can store and retrieve with absolute accuracy. The human brain, for its part, is awesomely complex and subtle. It is capable of all manner of types of thinking that computers will not emulate in the foreseeable future. The human mind is a world of dreams, imagination, chicanery, poetry, love, ingenuity, and storytelling. Not only do computers lack the poetry; they also don't have the common sense of a dog.

What the human brain is good at is utterly and completely different from what computers will be good at.

The vigorous but unsuccessful attempts to make machines emulate human intelligence eventually made it clear that human brain processes were much more intricate and complex than anyone had realized. In the last two decades different areas of science have demonstrated that we had drastically under-estimated the complexities of nature. Our mind and body, medicine, immune systems, the ecosystems of the fields and woods, virus evolution, and the intricate interactions of the planet's ecology are of extraordinary complexity. The tangled webs of nature are far more intricate and elaborately interwoven than we had ever imagined.

The pervasive view that artificial intelligence is human-like can be very harmful. It prevents thinking about the true partnership between people and machines. Machine intelligence should be thought of as having almost nothing in common with human intelligence. The goal should be for machines to do things that humans can't do, rather than merely mimic human intelligence. When nonhuman intelligence matures it will be formidable, immensely fast, deep, accurate, worldwide, and self-improving.

BEYOND PROGRAMMING

Without computers we execute manual instructions which mustn't be too complex for our limited brains. An employee can add to or adjust instructions on the basis of experience, but often these changes are lost and forgotten when the employee leaves. When mankind started to program computers it acquired the capability to create long collections of instructions and accumulate them indefinitely. But computer programs were merely the automation of *human* thought processes—step-by-step programs that prepare invoices, design a house, or buy or sell stocks. Computers, it was thought, do what we tell them to do.

The idea that computers meticulously obey orders has always been attractive. Humans feel safe if they think the machines do only what we tell them to do. Computers have to follow human-written programs instruction by instruction. A payroll program always does the same thing; it never forgets to pay someone. This gives a comfortable feeling that we are in control. Each sequence of instructions is a logical set of statements that a human could follow. If software has "bugs," these errors are there because humans were careless in writing the sequence of instructions. If we stepped through the logic carefully enough, we could find the error.

> When computers are as powerful as the human brain, they won't be doing what the human brain does. They will have deep, unfathomable forms of alien intelligence, vastly beyond human intelligence.

It would appear that the software can't have free will, any more than a pocket calculator can have free will. However, we can program computers to do things that are unpredictable. They can generate random numbers and adjust their behavior depending on what the numbers are. Computer systems can read data from many sources and take action based on those data. They can search or analyze data in ways far too complex for humans, and can be programmed to learn from what they find—all at speeds far outstripping human capability. They may be programmed to produce insights that executives would not have found on their own, or science that would have eluded traditional methods.

When a computer generates its own unique behavior, it may be programmed to do so with a particular purpose in mind. It may, for example, try to maximize the performance of investments or protect a plane from missiles in an air battle. It may judge or constrain its own actions. A personal computer connected to the Internet might be programmed to try constantly to please (and surprise) its owner.

THE GAME OF LIFE

The first hint that alien intelligence was possible might have come when computers started to execute runaway sequences of instructions so lengthy that humans couldn't guess what the result would be. Programs could loop or modify their own instructions. When different sequences of instructions are executed simultaneously, on computers with multiple processors, it is not possible to follow step-by-step what is happening.

Programmer James Conway produced a program he called the "Game of Life" in which patterns on a screen seemed to take on a life of their own. He programmed simplistic little creatures, rather like biological cells, all of which followed a simple set of rules. The computer screen is divided into an array of checkerboard-like squares, called *cells*. At the tick of an imaginary clock each cell may change its color depending on the color of its four neighbors. The cells may follow very simple rules, but the patterns that evolve can be spectacular. There may be dancing patterns of color and shifting abstract shapes, or armies of strange patterns that parade across the computer screen, reproducing themselves or mutating into different forms.

It has often been said that computers cannot create anything. In fact, they can be startlingly creative. Software can do things that humans cannot do and can be made intelligent in unanticipatable ways.

Even though Conway's cells followed very simple rules, sometimes their behavior was astonishingly complex, even to Conway. His simplistic programs took on a life of their own. Often his life fizzled out on the screen as it evolved, but sometimes it produced behavior that was interesting and completely unpredictable.

Conway's "life" is dumb. His cells have no flicker of intelligence. But a similar form of life can be given intelligence. It can be made to evolve in such a way that it seeks a specific goal. We then have something quite different from conventional programming. We are not telling the computer step-by-step what to do; we are setting up a process that is designed to evolve.

There are many different ways in which software can be set up so that it evolves. It may have to evolve through millions of stages before it produces something interesting, but computers are so fast that this is practical. The software may evolve so that it attempts to achieve a specific goal, or it may be designed to modify that goal.

In this new realm of computer "thought," our comfortable feeling of being in control goes away. We are no longer telling a computer what to do step-by-step. We have moved beyond programming in its conventional form. We are learning how to create computer programs that have no relation to human thought.

EXPLORING AN UNKNOWN LAND

Software critters like those of Conway evolve on their own, without human intervention. A different type of evolution can be designed to include human intervention.

Richard Dawkins, the Oxford biologist who writes beautiful books about evolution, created a program to achieve *evolution* of tree-like shapes on a computer screen. The program could take a line, add different numbers of branches to it with different angles and lengths, add branches to the branches, and so on. Each step in the evolution process produced eight new diagrams that were displayed, along with the original diagram, on a computer screen divided into nine windows. Dawkins could select which of these nine diagrams he liked best, and the one he chose would immediately mutate into another eight diagrams. He picked one of those and again it mutated. In this way he could progress quickly through many mutation cycles.

When Dawkins first ran his program, he was amazed at its behavior. "I never imagined it would evolve anything but tree-like shapes. I had hoped for weeping willows, poplars, and cedars of Lebanon." However, the branching structures began to cross back over themselves, filling in areas until they sometimes congealed into a solid mass. They formed little bodies, and branches sprouted from those bodies looking like legs and wings. The drawings evolved, totally unexpectedly, into weird bugs and butterflies. Dawkins, far too fascinated to eat, sat at his screen discovering amazingly complex water spiders, scorpions, and other shapes. He commented: "I was almost feverish with excitement. Nothing in my biologist's background, nothing in my twenty years of programming computers, and nothing in my wildest dreams, prepared me for what actually emerged on the screen."[3]

Dawkins couldn't sleep that night. He feverishly explored the startling world he had created, which he called Biomorph Land. Dawkins hunted for nonplant shapes in Biomorph Land, trying to compare the evolution he had studied and written about for many years with the unpredictable evolution in his computer. In the months ahead he discovered "fairy shrimps, Aztec temples, Gothic church widows, and aboriginal drawings of kangaroos."

GODLIKE INTERVENTION

Dawkins's "Biomorph Land" contains a vast number of drawings that could possibly be discovered, most of them uninteresting. To make them more interesting, Dawkins experimented with the use of "genes" that act like a formula that controls how the drawings evolve. A string of such genes can be used to automate aspects of the evolution, and by modifying the genes Dawkins could experiment with the evolution of his creatures in faster and more interesting ways.

When "genes" are used to control the evolution of artificial life, a higher level of evolution becomes possible: *the genes themselves can evolve, not just the creatures.* In first-order evolution the creatures evolve; in second-order evolution the genes evolve. Genes can be selected that produce the most interesting sequences of evolution, or that traverse interesting territory at high speed.

In these forms of computerized evolution a human plays God. In first-order evolution he selects a creature from the collection of creatures on the screen (as in Dawkins's nine windows), and this becomes the basis for the next round of mutation. But in second-order evolution the human chooses not from *static creatures* but from *sequences of evolution* displayed rapidly on the screen. Genes control these sequences of evolution, so the person is choosing genes rather than just creatures to be the basis for the next stage of evolution. When Dawkins evolved only creatures he was surprised at the results; when he evolved genes the surprises came faster and were even less predictable.

Dawkins is the god of this biomorph world, but the god was scratching his head in astonishment at what his creations were doing.

THE SOFTWARE STRAITJACKET

Manual programming puts corporations in a straitjacket. Software written in traditional ways can be very difficult to modify, because it casts *human* procedures into concrete. The Y2K bug demonstrated this. It was a nightmare to correct the seemingly trivial problem of having a two-digit date routine. Changing the Year 2000 date routines cost the United States more than the Korean War had cost.

Corporations respond to the painful slowness of programming by buying application packages. This prewritten code allows the machines to work well, but it often prevents creative new uses of computers. In the whirlwind change of today's electronic-commerce world, the companies that use computers in new and innovative ways are those that make fortunes.

Since I first programmed computers thirty-five years ago, they have become ten million times faster. A large program then was a million lines of code, which took about two hundred people two years to write. Today a large program might be ten times larger—but it still takes about two hundred people two years to write it.

> Manual computer programming creates a crippling bottleneck. It is like pulling a Ferrari with a horse.

In the next thirty-five years computers will again become ten million times faster. If we had to create the software for such computers with human programming techniques, we wouldn't be able to take advantage of the hardware. Manual programming creates a crippling bottleneck. It is like pulling a Ferrari with a horse.

In the future, computers will become so powerful that we will not be able to handcraft software one line of code at a time. Automated intelligence will be needed to grow and evolve software, to generate code. We are now beginning to see corporations set up computers that can *learn* automatically about customers, *breed* efficient production schedules, use *neural-network* software to anticipate problems before they happen, *generate* software for new types of applications, and do *data mining* to extract insight from vast data warehouses. Such uses of computers are the beginning of a new type of innovation that will become essential because the winners in the new e-business world will be those corporations that innovate fastest.

Many corporations need to transform themselves faster than their critical software can change. There needs to be an emphasis on creating software that can be rapidly and easily changed. Better still is to create software that can change *itself*, constantly learning and adapting.

Today we see isolated examples of software programs that constantly adapt corporate processes, but this will become more and more prominent—and, eventually, essential to business success.

There will be a world of difference between rigid programs chipped out of rock and software designed for automatic (or, perhaps more often, semiautomatic) adaptation.

NEEDLES IN HAYSTACKS

When we write a program one instruction at a time, we occasionally make a mistake. With a small program it is usually easy to test the program, detect its malfunction, and fix the error. But if the program is large, it becomes disproportionately difficult to find and fix mistakes because there are so many combinations of instructions that can constitute an error.

Some would compare it to finding a needle in a haystack, but in fact the problem can be worse. The difficulty of finding a needle in a haystack is proportional to the number of straws in the haystack. The difficulty of finding a bug in a software haystack, however, may be proportional to the square of the square of the number of straws in the haystack because of the number of possible combinations. We can divide the haystack into small pieces and try to make each piece bug free. That helps enormously, but many subtle bugs have a knack of avoiding detection. It is almost impossible to make a handcrafted program of a million lines of code bug free.

Next time you fly you might reflect that software problems play a part in more than half of today's air crashes, and that the software on modern jets is handling more and more functions and is becoming increasingly complex.

There are limits to the complexity of software that we can create by hand. That is why the automation of software development is very important. In most software development so far, it has been a struggle to make something work and to debug it. There has been no thought about building software that can improve itself. On the contrary, programmers have employed rigid methodologies that try to ensure that the software's behavior is entirely repeatable.

Some types of software have been designed to evolve themselves constantly. Techniques for "breeding" software, or in some way growing it organically so that it evolves to execute precisely stated functions, are leading to automated or semiautomated evolution of software. This is very different from chipping it out of the rock one instruction at a time. Such a process is contrary to the deeply embedded disciplines of software engineering.

Still, to evolve software with alien-intelligence techniques is an engineering discipline. A horse breeder carries out breeding with a firm goal in mind; a software breeder does the same. It is not evolution with random mutations but evolution with a precise, measurable target. Software evolution directs itself toward that target at electronic speed, often trying out thousands of variations as it progresses toward its goal. As described in Chapter 17, we will need "evolution engineers" who may work for an overall "architect" who specifies the functions of the components that need evolving. The evolution engineers may evolve business processes that are much higher level than software development. This is already done, for example, with the "breeding" of schedules that allow factories to produce a constantly changing mix of products.

EMERGENT PROPERTIES

With the new forms of intelligence we can examine each instruction and process used by a computer to reach a conclusion, but the overall behavior is much too complex for us to be able to pick apart its detailed logic. If a software system has many little "agents" operating in parallel, we can understand the behavior of each agent, but we cannot predict the behavior of the system when the agents work together. We can study in meticulous detail the behavior of an ant but still not be able to predict the behavior of the ant colony—there is no correlation between the two. Some alien-intelligence techniques use software ants (called "cellular automata"). As with an ant colony, many of them scurry around doing their own thing; the combined activities of their working together can produce valuable results that are in some cases completely unpredictable.

When many units interact with one another they can form a "complex adaptive system," which has been a focus of much recent study. Such systems often exhibit what are known as *emergent properties*. An emergent property is a property that emerges as a byproduct of other forms of behavior. When many units team up to give a combined result, as in an ant colony, a lynch mob, or an Internet community, the association exhibits properties of its own, quite different from the properties of the individual units. The ant colony has properties that emerge because of the behavior of the ants. These properties persist even when the ants are replaced by new ants.

Computing techniques described in Chapter 15 have led to a new understanding of complex adaptive systems. They show that a complex adaptive system's emergent properties would not be revealed by an inspection of the components of the system and the rules they obey. Emergent properties are often surprising and not predictable either by mathematics, or philosophy, or by any scientific method.

Society's interaction with cyberspace is one of the most complex of complex adaptive systems. It will have powerful emergent properties, but it is too early yet to know what they are. Just as you could delete many ants in an ant colony, you could remove many Internet users and you would not change the emergent properties. They are characteristics of the system, not the individuals.

As the world races into the age of cyberspace, driven by the huge money-making potential of global electronic business, the evolution will be turbulent and wild, interlinking hundreds of millions (soon billions) of computers. We have created a live, tornado-like, unpredictable creature with powerful emergent properties.

Marshall McLuhan popularized the term "global village," but the Internet is not a global village because in a village everybody knows what everybody else does. The Internet is a global city. Nobody in the global city can know what most other people do. It has vast numbers of separate communities with radically different cultures, but they coexist, sharing the same streets, often stimulating one another, sometimes antagonistic to one another. It is a worldwide melting pot, which grows like society grows, but at a lightning pace. We can no longer doubt that it will reinvent civilization around the planet.

The Internet had no master plan; it just grew. It is a global city with no mayor. It spreads like pondweed—an amorphous worldwide city, with no city center and no city planner. It may seem amazing that nobody is managing the World Wide Web, but this is a common property of complex adaptive systems. It is because it has had no manager that it has become so diverse and hence so valuable. Many millions of people do their own thing, contributing to a common electronic community. Different contributors, worldwide, are creative in fundamentally different ways, so the Net evolves rapidly like an unpredictable chemical reaction.

Stirred into this chemical reaction is a new ingredient—alien intelligence.

BREEDING TIME

We can run self-evolving software on a personal computer and obtain fascinating results, like those of Dawkins. Often when people don't use their computer it runs a useless "screen saver" with moving patterns or tropical fish. Instead it could be spending its idle time breeding software. It could be linked to a network of software breeders on the Internet, exchanging code, sharing genes, or jointly participating in a large breeding operation.

Much self-evolving software runs on PCs, but it could evolve much faster on parallel computers—computers with multiple processors operating simultaneously and independently. These multiple processors have generally been in one machine, but they could be separate computers scattered across the Internet. Distributed computers would exchange and broadcast genetically evolved code.

When software is grown organically, we do not necessarily know what to expect. It is not like growing seeds from a packet. Software breeding can be an organic process that runs wild and creates unexpected properties. Unlike nature it can run wild at extreme speed. The results can be made available anywhere on the Internet.

The challenge is how to create self-evolving applications that are important to business or science. The future of computing depends on the extent to which we can direct self-evolving software so that we can extract the most value from it.

SELF-EVOLVING TECHNOLOGY

God didn't design nature as a software engineer would have. The processes in nature are designed to evolve, adapt, learn, and constantly improve themselves. In a similar way much future technology will be designed to evolve, adapt, learn, and constantly improve itself. Because the processes of nature evolve and improve over a very long period of time, they become awesomely complex. Self-evolving technology will also become complex where necessary.

As we shall see, chips as well as software have been designed for high-speed evolution. We have powerful *field programmable* chips. (More about them later.) But if we design what they do by hand, it is a painfully slow process by which we lose most of the benefits. Again, it is like pulling a Ferrari with a horse.

When computer processes are designed to evolve they do so at electronic speed. On earth it took a billion years for single-cell life to evolve, and several billion years for multi-cell life to evolve into dinosaurs, orchids, whales, and eventually man. It took three centuries to evolve from the first Industrial Revolution machines to today's industrial society. The evolution of the Web will be extraordinary after only thirty years. Self-evolving software, hardware, and networks will produce extraordinary results after thirty weeks, and

The processes in nature are designed to:

Evolve

Adapt

Learn

Constantly improve themselves

Many future processes in computing will be designed to:

Evolve

Adapt

Learn

Constantly improve themselves

the pace will continue to accelerate. In Chapter 17 we will see how a Japanese laboratory is breeding "brain" mechanisms on hardware chips at the rate of about one per second. As our self-evolving technology matures and uses the fiber-optical Internet, the evolution will proceed many billions of times faster than nature's evolution can. We will reach a time when digital technology will evolve of its own accord with minimal need for human intervention. The change that happened in nature in a billion years will happen in computer laboratories in a few years.

When it matures, evolution will occur at electronic speed in millions of machines linked by speed-of-light telecommunications.

TYPES OF ALIEN INTELLIGENCE

There are multiple techniques for creating computerized "thought" so different from human thought that humans cannot follow the logic or do the same thinking process. The vast number of steps, self-modification, and simultaneous processing on parallel machines defy step-by-step human checking. Nevertheless the process is logical. It is as precise as mathematics.

These alien thought processes take us into new types of business invention. They take science into realms that could not be tackled with traditional mathematics. They facilitate engineering with innovative sensors and controllers. They can provide philosophy (as we shall see) with new insights.

Alien intelligence is of immense potential value because it can achieve results that we couldn't program, and these results can have countless important applications. In some cases we have a self-evolving form of intelligence that can continue to evolve until it becomes a very deep capability in a highly focused area, such as foreign exchange investing, control of robots, or finding customers on the Web.

Although we think we know what we mean by the term "intelligence," it is surprisingly difficult to define—any definition would trigger arguments. We can, however, define "alien intelligence": processes executed on a computer that are so complex that a human can neither follow the logic step-by-step nor come to the same result by other means.

We use the term "alien intelligence" to refer to a growing family of techniques that have this capability. Each technique is easy to understand and is basic engineering. There is nothing science fiction–like about it, even when we can't follow the logic of the results it achieves. The techniques include:

- *Evolutionary* techniques, in which software is designed to evolve on the basis of results. Evolution may continue for a long time and take place at high speed.

- *Breeding* techniques, which help us *breed* programs or procedures as opposed to *writing* them. Breeding has a clear goal in mind, and software progresses toward this goal. This becomes interesting when it's possible to breed something that we couldn't design. Hardware, as well as software, can be bred (see Chapter 12).

- *Learning* techniques, with which software can learn, steadily improving its ability and often learning things at electronic speed that humans could not learn (see Chapter 13).

- *Neurocomputing,* in which neural networks are designed in software, emulating crudely the neural networks of our brain. They can be set up so that we can "train" them, for example, to recognize patterns in voluminous data, or constantly to adapt their behavior on the basis of feedback. Neural networks can be set up so that they learn and improve their own capability (see Chapter 14).

■ Techniques in which large numbers of small software objects (called *cellular automata*) execute rules of behavior independently. Complex and unpredictable results can emerge from this process. Many situations that we need to understand are "complex adaptive systems" that can be simulated with this technique (see Chapter 15).

■ *Inference* techniques, in which software links together many independent rules to derive inferences. Software can produce complex logic from an established collection of rules. The rules can be changed easily, which in turn changes the results (see Chapter 16).

■ Software that tries vast numbers of combinations in an attempt to find an optimum solution.

■ *Pattern recognition* techniques, other than neurocomputing, in which software can be trained to recognize patterns.

■ *Data-mining* techniques, such as those above, for deriving useful insight from data in a data warehouse.

Many such tools now exist, and doubtless many are yet to be invented. Some are useful because they go to work on the massive amounts of data that are now available, others because they explore endless combinations of possibilities.

Some of these mechanisms, once launched, can run largely under their own steam, executing logic millions of times faster than humans can, and, more important, developing computerized "thought" that goes far beyond human thought.

THE TURING TEST

The grand prize in the artificial-intelligence community goes to a machine that passes the Turing test.[4]

Alan Turing was an English mathematician and logician whose work laid the foundation of much modern computing. He was famous for helping crack the Nazi *Enigma* code early in World War II. Turing found that it is difficult to define machine intelligence, so he proposed the so-called Turing test, in which a judge engages in a free-ranging question-and-answer session with a computer and with another human. The three are in separate rooms and the judge communicates only via teletype machines; the object is to determine which participant is the computer. If the computer can fool the judge into thinking it is the human it passes the Turing test. In fact, no computer has passed the test.

> Like a horse breeder, a software breeder has a precise goal in mind. But software evolution directs itself toward that target at electronic speed, trying out millions of variations.

Some software has succeeded in passing itself off as human in Internet chatrooms. On occasions sex-desperate hackers have flirted with someone they thought was a woman without realizing that they were chatting up a chunk of software. Most attempts to claim the Turing prize are similar: ingenious conjuring. If a machine *appears* to pass the Turing test, it's a sign that some trickery is going on.

Suppose an alien in *Star Trek* is capable of coming to the most brilliant conclusions. The crew of the *Enterprise* is suspicious of him because he can't understand human feelings, has no sense of time, and gets lost when walking around the ship. He seems to exhibit the highest level of intelligence but often can't explain how he comes to conclusions. He has alien thought processes but completely lacks common sense. How would we define intelligence for such an alien? He would definitely not pass the Turing test. We would have to define intelligence in terms of nonhuman thinking.

It's generally a lost cause to make machines imitate human intelligence. The constant preoccupation with the Turing test seems like a desperate effort to have a line to the dock of humanness rather than be cast adrift from human thought.

Turing dreamed up his test because any other attempt to define intelligence seemed to run into problems. Later he came to the conclusion that it is pointless trying to define intelligence at all. But we *can* define alien intelligence because in doing so we do not fall into the trap of thinking in terms of human thought. Remember, alien intelligence by definition is a process that a human can neither follow nor replicate by other means.

A favorite definition of intelligence is that of Haneef Fatmi and R.W. Young: "that faculty of mind by which order is perceived in a situation previously considered disordered."[5] In many of our examples a computing process *discovers order where humans had not perceived order.* Such clarification, sometimes derived from "data-mining" processes, can be critical in competitive business situations.

Another definition says that something intelligent should be able to improve its own processes. Many of our illustrations are of processes that improve themselves automatically until they achieve a level of capability far beyond human capability.

Alien intelligence does not pass the Turing test because it is clearly not humanlike thinking. If we accept that the interesting aspects of machine intelligence are those that humans cannot come close to, then the Turing test becomes almost completely irrelevant.

IDIOT SAVANTS

Once computers can improve their own capability automatically, and transmit that capability to other machines, we have the potential for a chain reaction of machines becoming more capable at a formidable rate. The future of computing and, related to that, the future of e-business depend on the degree to which we are prepared to harness this nonhumanlike intelligence.

But however formidable computerized intelligence, computers are idiot savants. They are brilliant at specific computations but have no flicker of broader intelligence. Human intelligence is very broad, while machine intelligence is highly focused and narrow. But human intelligence is a few feet deep, while machine intelligence can be miles deep. As alien intelligence techniques deepen, computers will become more idiot and more savant. They will acquire a self-improving capability for specific tasks, so deep that humans cannot comprehend it, but have no understanding of things that to humans are common sense. A human idiot savant can at least feed himself and enjoy television.

A KNOWLEDGE ACCUMULATOR

Computers act as an accumulator of knowledge. A computer, or the Internet, can accumulate more and more knowledge, expertise, and software. As we agree on standard ways of encoding it, a formidable body of knowledge will become accessible to computers. One computer in one place accumulates knowledge, but when computers are linked worldwide they can access each other's knowledge. The amount of knowledge indexed on the Internet grew at chain-reaction speed and created new needs for filtering, grading, and processing knowledge.

The ability to do worldwide searches on the Internet arrived with astonishing speed. It was one of those explosive chain reactions of which the computer industry is capable. We can search documents stored around the planet because they are in English (or some other human language) and computers can relentlessly build indices of their contents. But however impressive the deluge that results from a search, the computers are carrying out a dumb operation. They do not understand the contents of the documents they produce.

Most of the information on the Internet is encoded so that *humans* can use it. A major quantum leap in capability occurs when the information is designed for *computer* consumption rather than *human* consumption. Computers can understand and process information that they can find worldwide. For this to happen they need to be looking for data, not just text, and the data items need to be precisely defined. Whereas the words in an English dictionary are standardized across the planet, most data are not.

> The comfortable feeling of being in control goes away. We are no longer telling a computer what to do step-by-step.

If a computer can search the World Wide Web for knowledge and process the knowledge it finds, vast new horizons open up in the capability of computers. Increasingly knowledge needs to be encoded so that *machines can use it automatically.* We need standard objects, databases with data represented in standard ways, and knowledge represented in rules so that programs can make deductions with it. Computers will download software from the Internet (or private corporate networks) and use that software to carry out all manner of activities. Once appropriate standards are set,[6] computer-processable knowledge will become available in vast quantities for tackling specific types of problems.

In many fields, organizations understand the need for world-wide standardization of data and are now taking steps to achieve it. In some cases global organizations such as MasterCard have established global warehouses, which require standardization. We have already seen how HNC Software has established a "bankruptcy consortium." In some fields governments have passed laws intended to lead to standardization. The U.S. Health Care Portability and Accountability Act of 1996, for example, called for standard representations of health care data so that computers can analyze the data, search for patterns, and understand the spread of diseases and the medical history of individuals. Software will find early-warning signs of problems and ways to cure given symptoms. Partly because of this, a grand vision is now emerging in medicine—to change medical practice so that its goal is mainly to *prevent* illness rather than to *cure* illness after it has become a problem. Today, serious illness is often not detected early enough and then is difficult to cure. The new types of computer intelligence can help both the prevention of illness and its earliest detection.

There is a move now to standardize data formats for a variety of industries. This will be critical as electronic commerce matures. For instance, the software giants Microsoft and SAP are jointly defining schemas for exchanging business information (for use with the Web language XML).

In many fields, machine-processable pools of knowledge are starting to come into existence, requiring de facto standards to be accepted by an industry. Various alien-intelligence techniques can be applied to standard forms of data.

ELECTRONIC-SPEED LEARNING

Long ago Arthur Samuel wrote a famous software program for playing checkers that learned how to play better based on observations of its own games. It evolved quickly from playing a poor game to being unbeatable, at least by Samuel. There are a variety of techniques for making software learn. Software neural networks, for example, are designed to go through millions of trial-and-error attempts at something, repeatedly adjusting their behavior. They can quickly learn a behavior that we cannot program by any normal means.

If computers can learn, they learn fast—lightning fast compared with the painful struggles of human learning. If the learning process works, it can be pursued relentlessly, with the software endlessly striving to improve its performance. Making computers intelligent and making them learn will often go hand in hand. As we strive to create software that is intelligent, we will often try to make that intelligence self-improving. Self-improving software will polish its performance to a degree far beyond that of most humans.

Automated learning will be extremely valuable where it can be achieved. It will have endless applications in electronic commerce. It is being used in the design of investment trading systems. Money managers will be only too keen to have systems that might improve their performance. For every attempt to make an intelligent missile defense system there will be a corresponding effort to make missiles intelligent enough to penetrate it, and then an attempt to defend against these new missiles, and so on. In a similar way we will see grand capitalist battles to improve machine intelligence and use it to beat the competition.

THE LAW OF BASIC ENGINEERING

Throughout the history of engineering it has often been the case that *great engineering is simple engineering*. Ideas that become too cumbersome and entangled die on the vine. Sometimes they are replaced with conceptually cleaner ideas, often aesthetic in their simplicity. Computer scientist Ed Dijkstra comments, "All through history, simplifications have had a much greater long-range scientific impact than individual feats of ingenuity."[7] When a programmer's block diagram looks like spaghetti, the time has come to rethink the entire program.

We might contrast *basic engineering* with *convoluted systems*. By *basic engineering* we mean engineering that is straightforward and has an elegant simplicity about it. By *convoluted systems* we mean systems with an entanglement of human-made complexity. *Basic engineering* may be massive, like the telephone system, because it replicates or grows organically using basic rules or standard components. *Convoluted systems* are a human-made mess, ultimately limited because maintenance is so difficult. A fundamental difference between *basic engineering* and *convoluted systems* is that systems with basic engineering can grow and evolve relatively painlessly, whereas convoluted systems become very difficult to change; they strangle themselves in their own spaghetti.

When basic engineering creates useful products or services, they can spread fast in the marketplace. The Internet uses *simple* mechanisms that work on standard computers and telephone lines. Once it was working, it could be replicated everywhere. When it reached critical mass, it took off like a rocket. The World Wide Web grew from nothing to massive acceptance in two years. The pointers that made the Web possible were *simple* mechanisms implemented in a standard way. Once the Web was in place, numerous researchers, universities, entrepreneurs, and corporations put it to use to interlink a vast amount of information. It spread around the planet, soon becoming very impressive because its search engines made so much information accessible.

As we look at each of the exciting potentials described in this book, it is important to ask, "Is it basic engineering or will it get snarled in its own complexities?" If it is straightforward engineering that is easy to implement and valuable, it can spread fast, attracting much money to enhance it. If it is deeply convoluted and difficult to define, it will probably not spread. We can make the mistake of becoming enamored of things that fall into the latter category.

One might state a Law of Basic Engineering: *Technology that is basic engineering will spread rapidly if it is useful. Technology that is convoluted and entangled will have difficulty spreading.*

> Alien intelligence is of immense potential value in such highly focused areas as foreign exchange investing or finding customers on the Web.

An example of basic engineering that will have a massive impact is fiber-optic telecommunications. Optical fibers are essentially simple, but because they transmit light they can, in principle, handle staggering bit rates. The technology for routing and switching this deluge of bits can be made simple, so that mass-produced chips handle all types of traffic—voice, data, television, fax, software, virtual reality. With such essentially simple networks it is not worth billing different amounts for different distances—that adds unnecessary complexity. So people and computers across the planet will be wired together with switched circuits of massive capacity. This will have more profound social consequences than most other aspects of knowledge technology.

It pays to search for simplicity and ease-of-use in computing even though it needs more memory, computer power, and bandwidth, because memory, computer power, and bandwidth will quickly drop in cost.

Our genes have long sections of dead code abandoned millions of years ago, but nevertheless they work and replicate. Similarly when software "breeds" or evolves using the techniques we describe, it can produce structures that we cannot understand but that also work and replicate. If they are easy to use they fall into the category of "basic engineering."

We need computers to do some very complex things, but we can often achieve the appearance of simplicity by hiding the complexity in mass-produced modules that have a standard, easy-to-use interface. The global telephone network is diabolically complex, but its complexity is entirely hidden from the telephone user. Intel processor chips are immensely complex internally but can be used with a simple standard instruction set. They can then be mass-produced like newsprint.

ALIEN-INTELLIGENCE BILLIONAIRES

The Internet took years to mature but suddenly, like a desert blooming in spring, it gave rise to a frenzied new mega-rich class—geeks without girlfriends but with a billion in stock. Alien intelligence will do the same. Like the Internet it will sooner or later produce a chain reaction. It is too early to know for sure when this chain reaction will happen.

What types of alien intelligence will spread? We should apply the Law of Basic Engineering to it. If it is a practical basic-engineering discipline that can grow and multiply, it can have a long way to go. If it is convoluted engineering that ties us in Gordian knots, it will soon be forgotten.

Some fortunes will be made with mass-produced components such as chips that recognize human faces, security devices, devices that help prevent car crashes, toys that learn like a puppy, monitors that prevent heart attacks, and numerous devices that we couldn't imagine today.

When computers reach a certain level of intelligence, they will use that intelligence to make themselves more intelligent. We will design systems that improve their intelligence at electronic speed. They will immensely surpass human capability in areas as narrowly focused as chess playing. Some of these areas are directly concerned with making money. There are software tools for financial trading, for example. Like chess, money management has its own Grand Masters. Soon, as computer power increases, the best chess-playing machine will be far superior to a grand master, and the same will probably be true in foreign exchange trading. In all areas of investing the grand masters will make their numbers because they tightly couple human intelligence and automated intelligence.

The Internet will become immensely faster because of fiber optics and new architectures, and ubiquitous because of wireless devices. It will start to use numerous types of self-evolving agents and other software designed to learn at a rapid pace. It will use far more intelligent search engines and vast data warehouses. Data will be designed to be used by computers, rather than people, and to produce automated results. Software designed for breeding and rapid evolution will flood through the Web. Because millions of such resources will be connected to it across the planet, competing for attention and supremacy, the Internet will be constantly evolving every day. Although changes today seem to come alarmingly fast, the marriage of the Internet and alien intelligence will make it clear that we have as yet barely hit the accelerator.

Skilled investors looked for aspects of the Internet that would have fast self-feeding growth. Yahoo!, eBay, and America Online, for instance, spread across the planet like pondweed. Some business-to-business exchanges will grow very fast, reaching huge financial volume. Fortunes can be made seeking out these chain-reaction investments. Some types of alien intelligence will have a chain-reaction growth in capability. In Chapter 17 we discuss a technique for "breeding" brain modules. The father of this technique believes it will give rise to a trillion-dollar industry worldwide by 2018.[8]

Alien intelligence can race far beyond human intelligence when we set up autonomous mechanisms that evolve, grow, breed, or relentlessly seek some goal. Such mechanisms can lead to results that are new and powerful, and often surprise us. It will be a constant challenge for scientists and business leaders to harness them in effective ways. As we shall see, many mechanisms for alien intelligence fall into the category of basic engineering. They will be expanded, amplified, and replicated in spectacular ways.

And like the Internet, when they reach critical mass, they will go forth and multiply at breathtaking speed.

Hans Moravec, writing about future computers, says, "It behooves us to give them every advantage and to bow out when we can no longer contribute."[9] The best entrepreneurs are not likely to bow out. They'll lock into the chain reactions and go for wilder rides than today's dot-com kids could ever dream of.

CHAPTER 3
Not Like the Movies

The 1979 movie *Alien*, when it first came out, seemed like a breakthrough in science fiction movies. It had a dramatic story about a freighter in deep space that seemed plausible until, toward the end, one of the interesting characters turned out to be an electronic machine, with crude-looking wires and chips in his skull. This cyborg was placed on board by the freighter company (of course) to keep tabs on the crew. When I saw the movie, a woman in the audience reacted to this sudden revelation that a crew member was a machine by shouting, "Oh, come on!" The movie originally had a different plot, designed for technical plausibility, and the crew member in question was fully human. However, before the movie was released the filmmakers converted the crew member into a cyborg because they thought that the plot twist would make the movie more exciting to the average moviegoer.

Despite the objections of certain moviegoers, like the woman sitting near me that evening, the makers of *Alien* were largely correct.

There is immense fascination with the idea that we will eventually build robots like humans and build a computer like the human brain. The public can comprehend that a machine might be like a human. Machine enthusiasts have always wanted to believe that we will build machines like humans. When Babbage created mechanical calculators at the end of the nineteenth century, a firm trying to sell this technology ran advertisements proclaiming "BRAINS OF STEEL."[1]

Still, this is mere mythology. We must get past thinking of computers in anthropomorphic terms and begin properly considering the significance of alien intelligence.

We have noted that when people first heard of radio they called it "wireless telegraphy." That made it an understandable notion, but tended to block the more important concept of "broadcasting." Similarly, thinking of computers as having an artificial version of human intelligence can make them appear to be understandable but blocks their more important uses: nonhuman intelligence.

DEBUNKING THE MYTH

We have reached an age when businesspeople and leaders everywhere need to understand what computers are capable of. Computers are fundamentally changing every institution. In today's electronic jungle the rewards go to those capable of radically reinventing their business. It is crippling to think of computers as glorified word processors, or to believe that a humanlike intelligence can be packaged in the machines. To think about how computers can make a business more competitive or improve health care, we need to downplay anthropomorphic thinking and come to terms with the computer's radically different capabilities. We damage our ability to understand computers if we think of their intelligence as being an automated form of our own intelligence.

"Artificial intelligence" was always a misleading term because it gives an unwary person the misguided impression that computers could be intelligent in the way humans are intelligent. Androids can look great in movies. The scientifically illiterate public (which includes many politicians, professors, and highly educated people) can be convinced by the magic of movies that we will have such machines, but in reality in the foreseeable future we will not come close to creating humanlike intelligence or robots like those in the movies. *What we will create is something far more interesting.*

Much of the future value of computing will, for corporations, lie in creating nonhuman intelligence rather than having computers imitate humans. Human intelligence will remain unique. Many processes in the electronic jungle will need both human intelligence and computer intelligence, and it is fortunate that they are so different.

As technology matures it escapes old patterns. For its first half century, computing has been used to emulate human thought processes. It will mature when we become confident and skilled at harnessing its alien thought processes. It will become extremely important to our new commerce in cyberspace, new weapons and warfare, investment, medicine, and science in general.

We must set the computer free to do what it can do well.

It has been easy to get research grants for trying to make computers imitate human intelligence because this is easy to describe. It grabs the imagination. Huge amounts of research money have gone into trying to make computers behave like people. To say that computer intelligence has no resemblance to human intelligence is more difficult to understand. But the largest value of computers will lie in their doing things that humans cannot do. Remember, alien intelligence is not only fundamentally different from human intelligence, it is also in certain areas incomparably more powerful.

CANALS ON MARS

It's decidedly unfashionable to say it, but the predictions that we will have robots like those in the movies are as quaint as the Victorian astronomers' pictures of canals on Mars.

Robots of the future will not look like the robots in the movies. They will not need humanoid bodies; in fact, humanoid shapes would be a severe disadvantage for most of the things they do. There is no need for them to clunk around like the robots in *Star Wars* or *Robocop*. They may be invisible; you may talk to them like talking to the wallpaper. They could consist, for example, of millions of mass-produced components the size of fleas, interconnected by radio. They can have a nervous system with all manner of sensors that can occupy an entire building, or city, or global corporation. When they do mechanical work they need visible components, but most of the time they do not. They can be network-connected, capable of light-speed interaction with computers or data warehouses anywhere on the planet. They will not have one single brain, but large numbers of tiny computers with special functions interacting with one another in diverse ways. They will not be an alternate life-form with their own philosophers and consciousness, but gadgets designed to carry out specific functions.

It is easy to portray computers as having humanlike behavior. How would one portray intelligence that is drastically nonhuman? Computers of the near future will know much more about your medical condition than your doctor and much more about your finances than your banker. But they will not look good on film.

THE HUMAN BRAIN

Our brain and central nervous system consist of about a hundred billion cells called *neurons*. Mental or sensory activities can cause a neuron to get excited. When it is sufficiently stimulated, it fires an electrical pulse that goes over a long, thin nerve called an *axon*. The nerve can split into thousands of branches going to other neurons. These neurons have contacts, called *synapses*. When the pulse arrives at these synapses it excites or inhibits the destination neuron. If that neuron is suffi-ciently stimulated, it fires, sending an elec-trical pulse down *its* axon.

> We must set the computer free to do what it can do well.

I am always awed by the statistic that your brain has as many neurons as there are stars in the galaxy. The brain is constantly active, with vast numbers of pulses circulat-ing. If you think of a pulse as being like a flash of light, the brain is like a vast galaxy ablaze with twinkling light, even during deep sleep. Often a chain of pulses among neurons causes a pulse to return to the originating neuron. This feedback can make loops of connec-tions reverberate, like ringing in a microphone-speaker system.

Some synapses are excitatory in nature and use neurotransmit-ter chemicals that tend to *enhance* the firing of the neuron. Other synapses are inhibitory, using neurotransmitter chemicals that tend to *inhibit* the firing of the neuron. If the right mix of pulses arrives within a short time, the neuron fires. When a baby learns, it is growing the nerve patterns between neurons and adjusting the synapses so that the influence of one neuron on another changes. This process continues throughout life, slowing down as our per-sonality and behavior patterns become more established.

Most of your brain consists of the wiring between neurons. Your brain and nervous system has a thousand trillion connections between neurons—about 100,000 kilometers of wiring in a skull twenty centimeters across.

The density of nerves in the brain is much greater than the den-sity of wires on the densest of microchips. The brain is a masterpiece

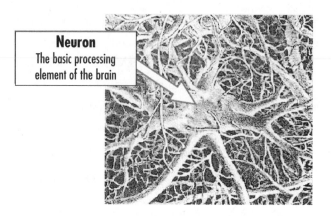

Neuron
The basic processing
element of the brain

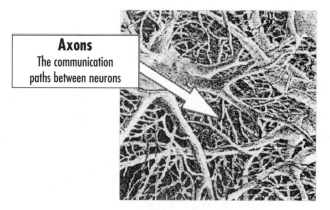

Axons
The communication
paths between neurons

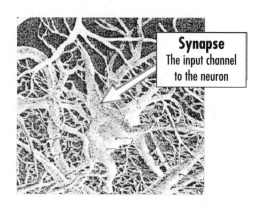

Synapse
The input channel
to the neuron

of miniaturization. When a neuron transmits a pulse down a nerve the pulse is in the form of ions, not electrons as in a computer. The density of ions in the axon is much less than the density of electrons in a wire on a microchip. This activity requires only a tiny fraction of the power required by similar activity in an electronic chip. Unlike a chip, the brain uses chemicals for communicating, as well as electrical pulses. Chemical transmission is much slower than electrical transmission, but can be used to broadcast messages throughout whole areas of the brain, as when we produce adrenaline or take mood-changing drugs.

The part of our brain where most of our thinking goes on is our cerebral cortex, heavily folded around the inside of our skull. If we stretched out the cortex, opening up all its folds and creases, it would be a sheet of meat about two millimeters thick and the size of four sheets of typing paper. A chimpanzee's cerebral cortex is the size of only one sheet of typing paper. A rat's cerebral cortex is the size of a postage stamp.

MOSQUITOES

Many writers state that our brain has about a hundred billion neurons and compare a neuron with a transistor. In the not-too-distant future, they say, we will have parallel computers with a hundred billion transistors, and then they will start to become brainlike.

This is an oversimplification that needs to be hooted off the stage. We have parallel super computers today with more than a hundred billion transistors, but in no sense are they brainlike. A neuron has on average around ten thousand synapses, so it is drastically more complex than a transistor.

Your cerebral cortex has ten thousand times as many neurons as a mosquito. I tried to explain to my ex-wife that she had the brainpower of ten thousand mosquitoes; it didn't go over too well. Both a swarm of ten thousand mosquitoes and my ex-wife have ten billion neurons, but there is all the difference in the world in how they use them. Suppose the ten thousand mosquito brains were all interconnected with high-capacity wireless links and that they had evolved like that for eons. They might be more annoying than my ex-wife, but they almost certainly wouldn't have intelligence like her.

A common argument holds that by such-and-such a year the personal computer will be as powerful as the human brain, and therefore will be capable of thinking as humans think. The problem lies not in hardware speed and capacity but in application complexity. In 1960, enthusiasm for "artificial intelligence" had reached fever pitch. If it could have been known then that a personal computer in the year 2000 would be a hundred times more powerful than the fastest supercomputer of 1960, there would have been spectacular predictions about how people would be using it. In reality most people are using it for word-processing, e-mail, and spreadsheets.

Ray Kurzwell a brilliant engineer who invented the Kurzwell reading machines and music synthesizers, writes that by 2020 your personal computer will have human-level brain capacity, and by 2048 it will have the brain power of the entire population of the United States.[2] In reality it won't get close to being able to think like you, let alone the entire U.S. population. But it will be able to have deep, formidable forms of alien intelligence.

In his wonderfully imaginative book *The Age of Spiritual Machines*, Kurzwell writes, "In the second decade of the 21st century, it will become increasingly difficult to draw any clear distinction between the capabilities of human and machine intelligence."[3] In reality alien intelligence will have many functions spectacularly beyond human intelligence. It will be able to access millions of other computers with such intelligence over speed-of-light networks. When we have computers as powerful as the human brain, they won't be doing what the human brain does. They will have deep, unfathomable forms of alien intelligence vastly beyond human intelligence.

COMPLEXITY

One transistor in a computer is typically connected to three or four other transistors, and rarely more than ten. One neuron in our brain is connected to about ten thousand other neurons, on average. Some neurons are connected to as many as eighty thousand other neurons. A neuron can "fire" and send a signal to thousands of other neurons because the nerve that carries the signal divides many times. Just as sap in a tree rises through many branches, so in our brain does the signal of a neuron firing travel through many branches to other neurons. But the complexity of this is staggering. The thousand trillion connections among neurons in our brain are exceedingly convoluted.

It would be virtually impossible to design a machine of this complexity and get it right. The human brain is so amazingly complex for two reasons. First, it has *evolved* for such a long time. Much of it started evolving long

> Many believe that in the near future parallel computers will become like the human brain. This is an oversimplification that needs to be hooted off the stage.

before there were forests or dinosaurs. Humans have lengthy DNA sequences in common with creatures that lived hundreds of millions of years ago. Second, it is designed to *learn* after we are born and constantly adjust its wiring. It grows its wiring very fast in the first years of life and continues learning and changing for a lifetime.

We can build computers and software that learn and evolve, and do so at electronic speed. The results will often be exciting.

Researchers in need of grants will say they want to create human-like intelligence in machines—that gets lots of press coverage. But most of the time what evolves will not be like human intelligence; it will be an intelligence of its own. Software will learn to achieve narrowly defined functions that humans couldn't possible achieve. A challenge for today is to specify what those functions could be.

ELECTRONIC ADVANTAGE

The computer has some massive advantages over the brain. It is a million times faster and will soon be a billion times faster because of the development of smaller, faster, more parallel chips, and speed-of-light channels. It is meticulously precise, whereas the brain is not. It can handle exceedingly complex calculations or logic with unerring accuracy. It can be connected to other computers around the planet and have access to vast quantities of precise data. When two humans talk, they might do so at a speed of two words per second. Two computers talking over a fiber-optic trunk could do so at two *million* words per second, and they might be a thousand miles apart. Computers can have infinite flexibility in software. The brain's knowledge disappears when it dies; a computer's knowledge doesn't. Furthermore, the brain has only one set of programming; a computer could have many.

Most of the nerves in our brain and nervous system are enclosed in a sheath—a fatty membrane of myelin. Small unsheathed nerves conduct impulses at only millimeters per second; large sheathed nerves transmit impulses at around 90 meters per second. An optical fiber transmits impulses at 300 *million* meters per second—three million times faster.

A neuron fires in about a thousandth of a second, a transistor can fire in less than a billionth of a second. What's more, optical components will have speeds far in excess of today's components, so computers of the future are likely to be built out of components a billion times faster than those of the brain. Furthermore, computers have a precision in timing that the brain doesn't have. There is much randomness, redundancy, and indirection in the workings of the brain, which helps give the brain its great flexibility and robustness, whereas electronics can be designed to carry out precise tasks at maximum speed. The electronics can be fast but brittle—if something fails, it's dead—whereas the brain is slow but malleable—if something fails, it finds an alternate way to work.

The extent to which a computer is faster than the brain depends on the degree to which parallel operations are built into the computer. Seymour Cray set out to build a supercomputer with a million fast processor chips running simultaneously. This machine was never completed, partly because it coincided with the passion for downsizing and personal workstations, but sooner or later such massively parallel supercomputers will be built.

The brain uses parallelism to run different processes simultaneously. A supercomputer can also use parallelism to run similar processes many times simultaneously and then to combine the results. A different form of parallelism is to split work into tasks that can be performed on many computers simultaneously. The world has hundreds of millions of personal computers, most of which are idle more than 90 percent of their time. Complex work may be designed so that tasks can be farmed out to vast numbers of computers on the Internet or university networks to be performed in idle moments. Networks will become massive parallel computers. Ultimately vast numbers of computers will cooperate to achieve specific results.

EXTREME DIFFERENCES

The potential capabilities of computers and fiber-optic circuits are utterly different from those of the brain. The brain is slow, forgetful, mortal, sometimes inaccurate, but of diabolical complexity. The computer is lightning fast, precise, and unforgetting, but simplistic compared with the brain.

A "thinking" machine could have thousands, even millions of tiny computers operating in parallel. It could interact with millions of computers around the planet at a fiber-optic speed. It can process vast quantities of data, searching for patterns incomprehensible to humans. It can be constantly alert and react instantaneously. If it has software designed to learn, it can learn at electronic speed. But it completely lacks human capabilities for common sense, compassion, intuition, and wisdom.

Given these extreme differences between humans and machines, it is folly to try to make machines behave like people. Machines should do their own thing. Almost the whole field of "artificial intelligence" has been concerned with making machines try to imitate human intelligence. Not only is this a lost cause, it is also an immense distraction from where the true value lies: making machines intelligent in ways that humans could not possibly emulate—unique and powerful ways.

In a sense, many of the advocates of artificial intelligence have been barking up the wrong tree. Theirs is a very seductive tree: to make computers exhibit humanlike intelligence. But the field of artificial intelligence has been characterized by false promises. What we have learned, painfully, is that the human mind is so wonderfully and extraordinarily subtle that it defies emulation by computers. Attempts to give computers humanlike intelligence either have not worked or have resulted in the ability to tackle a very narrow and specific problem, such as scheduling factory production or playing chess. General humanlike intelligence has constantly eluded the artificial-intelligence world because we grossly underestimated the complexity of the brain.

As it matures, *nonhuman intelligence* will become awesome. We can create software that operates in ways unimaginable for biological brains. It will handle operations that humans could not dream of handling.

FLAPPING WINGS

Trying to make a computer that thinks in a humanlike fashion is rather like trying to build an airliner with flapping wings and feathers. There is no resemblance between birds and jumbo jets. Nature's propulsion mechanisms will never be like those of jet engines. Likewise, the computer's talents are quite different from those of people. A human's thought processes will never be like a supercomputer's. Machinery is radically different from biology.

Trying to make machines behave like humans is somewhat ridiculous. The goal that has pervaded artificial intelligence—making machines imitate human intelligence—emasculates the entire subject. Machines will never be good at what we do well, and we will never be good at what machines do well. Once this is recognized we can set out to build a synergy between what computers are good at and what we are good at. Humans, when relieved from the chores of computer-like thinking, can be trained from an early age to develop those skills that are *uniquely* human.

The public has difficulty comprehending, or even thinking about, nonhuman intelligence. But much of the future of business and electronic commerce lies in harnessing and automating deep nonhuman intelligence.

NETWORKS OF NEURONS

When computer scientists began to understand the electrical activity in the brain, they concluded that one ought to be able to build similar mechanisms with electronics—the equivalent of neurons, axons, and synapses on a silicon chip. Alternatively, and easier for widespread implementation, these mechanisms could be simulated in software. This is a very exciting idea. The term *neural network* came into computer science to refer to hardware or software that emulated neurons, axons, and synapses.

If we could build electronic mechanisms that emulated biological brains, who knows what we might be able to train them to do.

> Trying to make a computer that thinks like a human is rather like trying to build a jumbo jet with flapping wings and feathers.

The prospect of being able to create this new type of computer generated much enthusiasm in research circles. But the journey from idea to full realization is long and difficult.

A computer that operates with neural networks is referred to as a *neurocomputer* (see Chapter 14). One day we will probably build a machine with as many neurons as our cerebral cortex. It will have a large number of separate *neurocomputers* all carrying out different functions.

The cerebral cortex is complex, but it is only a fraction of our brain. Far more neurons exist in our midbrain and sensory systems. They use neural networks to make sense of the deluge of data that constantly floods our eyes, ears, and nerve endings. The midbrain controls the basic functions that keep us alive, such as the heart, stomach, and lungs. This relatively primitive processing had to evolve before the higher-level functions of the cerebral cortex could develop.

A baby is born with a neural network, which rapidly grows as the child learns about the world he or she has been born into. Recently it has become clear that we could somewhat similarly grow neural networks with electronics. Because electronic machinery is millions of times faster than biological machinery, the speed of growth could be very fast. Unlike a human baby's neural network, the nonhumanlike results can be replicated and transmitted over the Internet. The potential of this is awesome.

MEMORY DIFFERENCES

Human memory is completely different from computer memory.

One of the most impressive aspects of our brain is how many memories it stores in such a small space. Do you remember the movie *Star Wars*? Do you recall the final battle? Do you remember Alec Guinness's voice saying to Luke Skywalker, "Use the Force, Luke"? You might say "yes" to those questions even though you last watched that movie twenty years ago. Our brain is full of a lifetime of memories like that, subtle memories of people, memories of our children growing up, detailed memories of the beautiful scenery when we visited Switzerland. A psychiatrist can drag out memories from childhood or even suppressed memories. A lifetime's memories are all inside a small skull.

Various science writers have compared the memory of our brain with the memory of computers. Our brain uses around thirty billion neurons to store memories. But Wal-Mart's data warehouse computer, at this writing, has about 168 trillion bits (21 trillion bytes) of storage. The information is organized so that it can be searched rapidly with data-mining techniques to obtain business insight. The capacity is growing rapidly.

Our brain's coding technique is clearly much more ingenious than that of Wal-Mart's data warehouse. Our brain seems to store ideas and assemble associations of ideas when we remember a past conversation or a sunset in some exotic locale. Your memory of the final scene from *Star Wars* is a string of ideas linked together to compose an image.

Computers store data with absolute accuracy. The memories in our brain are full of inaccuracies. We often believe that we remember something correctly when in fact our memory is false.

Think of a favorite scene from a movie that you haven't seen for many years. Try to remember it in as much detail as you can. Keep thinking about it until you believe you can remember it clearly. Then watch the actual film. You will normally find surprising and massive discrepancies between the movie and your memory of it. Your brain does not store a bit map, as a computer does; it somehow encodes ideas and links ideas together. It can easily add incorrect ideas or interlink ideas wrongly.

Moreover, when someone talks to you about what is being remembered, they can insert new ideas into your memory, sometimes distorting your own recollection. Take the sequence from the movie *Out of Africa*, for example, in which Meryl Streep first flew in an airplane with Robert Redford. A friend might say, "Do you remember how Robert Redford's yellow scarf flew behind him in the white plane, and how enchanted Meryl Streep was with the herds of giraffes that galloped away from the plane?" You may add many ideas like those to your memory, distorting it multiple times. In fact, Robert Redford wore no scarf, it was the plane that was yellow, and they were wildebeest, not giraffes.

Lawyers (most of whom seem to take joy in the perversion of justice rather than the promotion of justice) understand how to manipulate and even create false memories. False Memory Syndrome (FMS) is becoming better understood and documented. The FMS Foundation is concerned with how therapists generate false memories, of sexual abuse, for example, and how lawyers use or manipulate false memories. More than a million Americans claim to have memories of being abducted by aliens in spaceships.[4] Many of the abductees have sought psychiatric counsel. Studying this, psychologist Nicholas Spanos and his colleagues concluded that these memories are nonsensical, but that there are no obvious pathologies in most of those who claim to have been abducted.[5]

Computers have no such problems.

WHAT COMES NATURALLY IS HARD

A baby playing with building blocks can rearrange them to make towers or walls. The baby happily looks around for a block of a particular color or a long block to make an arch. In the 1970s the Stanford Research Institute had a famous robot called Shakey and tried to get it to do the same. Shakey was five feet tall and aptly named. It was remote-controlled by a very large computer that used programs designed to explore a machine's ability to reason. Shakey used a television camera to see the blocks. It could work only with simple, uniformly colored, flat-faced blocks in a room with clean, plain walls. The robot could not possible have recognized the blocks in the clutter that a baby lives with.

Shakey used a clever reasoning program developed at Stanford,[6] and also MIT's blocks-manipulating programs.[7] When Shakey tried to push blocks, the outcome was often not as expected. Each move took about an hour of computer time and had a high likelihood of failure. The films made of Shakey were heavily edited to make the robot appear much faster than it really was.[8] Shakey, and other robots, could not come close to a baby's capability at playing with blocks, or give any indication that this would be achieved in the near future.

A baby not only arranges blocks but learns how to do so by trial and error, steadily developing skills. What the baby does naturally with gurgling delight is extremely hard for a machine to do.

One university, realizing that to get yet more money for computer research from the Department of Defense it needed to think up something that the generals could understand, hit upon the idea of developing a machine that could play ping-pong. This would require the development of various robotic capabilities. The results would be clearly visible, and grants would be needed for many years to improve the robot's game. After some years of well-funded research a general paid a visit, perhaps hoping for a good game of ping-pong. He was horrified to find that all that was available was a hydraulic arm that could simply move a ping-pong paddle to intercept a ball carefully lobbed in the right place. The grant seekers had difficulty explaining that this was a major achievement.

> Only about 0.1 percent of our DNA is different from when we were cavemen. But that small increase in complexity eventually led to civilization as we now know it.

While we have difficulty making a computer do most of the things a baby can do, we can tell it to search through hundreds of millions of documents around the world on the Internet and find what papers are available on, say, X-ray crystallography applied to analysis of organic cell structures. Future search engines will do this with much less unwanted clutter than today. While computers are often hopeless at things humans are good at, they can be great at things humans can't do.

This difference in capability is explained by our evolution. Encoded in our brain is the result of more than a billion years of evolution, struggling to understand the world and compete for food, sex, and territory. If evolution is represented by a twenty-four–hour clock, all human history describes what happened in the last tenth of a second. Reasoning, reading, and what we call culture are a very thin veneer representing a few hundredths of a second out of the twenty-four hours. And a computer can cope with only a tiny fraction of this veneer.

CHIMPANZEE COMPUTING

There appears to be an enormous difference between ourselves and animals. Animals do not read, think deeply, or go to the movies. We assume that they do not have a soul or think about God. But their DNA is almost as complex as our own: the DNA of a chimpanzee contains about 98.4 percent of what is in human DNA.

Even a dim-witted cow has 90 percent of its DNA in common with humans. DNA has steadily grown in complexity since things first crawled out of the primeval slime. The 1.6 percent of our DNA that makes us different from chimps has evolved relatively recently. The ability to behave like a chimpanzee is remarkably difficult to emulate with computers.

Only about 0.1 percent of our DNA is different from when we were cavemen. This small increase in complexity gave rise to interesting emergent properties that led to civilization, consciousness, rock concerts, a vision of God, and the ability to invent machines. Ten thousand years ago the complexity of our DNA was on the threshold of being able to produce these properties.

SCIENCE BY PRESS RELEASE

The build-a-human-brain mythology turns up in many disguises. People want to believe it, so it can always generate press stories. A news report in 1996 described how scientists in British Telecom said they could create a "Soul Catcher" chip. This chip, the report said, would store memory and sensual sensations such as smell, sights, and sounds in the form of neuron pulses in the brain that could be downloaded into a computer. People would then be able to relive their own experiences and *transfer them to another person's brain.*

Dr. Chris Winter, head of the British Telecom artificial life team that developed the device, was quoted as saying: "This is the end of death—immortality in the truest sense.... By combining this information with a record of a person's genes, we could recreate a person physically, emotionally, and spiritually."[9] British Telecom, he said, had invested £20 million ($31 million) in the project. The chip would be available in less than thirty years.

The Institute for Atomic Scale Engineering is concerned with highly futuristic applications but commented on the ridiculousness of the British Telecom story. Forrest Bishop of this institute described how difficult it would be to capture the sensations of sight, smell, hearing, touch, and taste. The skin, for example, has sensors all over the body. Even then, these inputs don't constitute a person's experience. The mind constructs experience from these inputs along with prior experiences. You could in no way "recreate a person" from this kind of information and details of the person's genes. He described British Telecom's story as "science by press release."[10]

HUMAN VERSUS MACHINE INTELLIGENCE

Fortunately, perhaps, what we are good at machines are bad at, and vice versa. The following table contrasts the capabilities of the human brain with those of the computer.

	Human Brain	Computer
Speed	Slow	Many millions of times faster
Wiring	Exceedingly complex	Relatively simple
Precision	Makes mistakes	Absolutely accurate
Memory of facts	Limited	Vast data warehouses
Access to information	Data stored in the head	Data in systems worldwide
Associative memory	Many diverse associations	Limited

Location	One location	Worldwide connectivity
Communication	Slow, imprecise	Fast, accurate

Given this immense difference in properties of the brain and computers, the capabilities of people and machines are very different:

	Human	Machine
Common sense	*Yes*	No
Ability to set goals and to think about meaning and purpose	*Yes*	No
Ability to recognize patterns familiar to humans	*Yes*	Limited
Ability to recognize patterns unknown to humans	No	*Yes* (with neural networks)
Ability to draw analogies and associated diverse ideas	*Yes*	No
Very high speed logic	No	*Yes*
Ability to execute logical processes that humans understand	No	*Yes*

Accurate storage of a vast amount of data and rules	No	*Yes*
Ability to apply a vast number of rules with precision	No	*Yes*
Ability to do complex calculations	Limited	*Yes*
Absolute accuracy	No	*Yes*
Precise replication in many locations	No	*Yes*
Immediate communication with many locations	No	*Yes*
Immediate worldwide interlinkage	No	*Yes*
Precise cooperation with other machines, worldwide	No	*Yes*
Originality	*Yes*	No
Ability to inspire or lead other humans	*Yes*	No
Wisdom	Sometimes	No

Most processes in corporations need both the human and the computer. Some processes can be completely automated. Few processes can be optimally done by a human alone.

A key to creating efficient corporations is to achieve the best synergy between what machines do well and what humans do well. Many executives think of computers as automating human processes, but in fact computers can do things that no human could possibly do. Computers are so different from the brain that we should learn to take full advantage of the differences. It is more exciting to create thinking machines with completely *alien* capabilities than to try to emulate humans.

RESISTANCE TO NEW METHODS

In their early years new patterns of evolution try to emulate the old. The first motor cars were called "horseless carriages" and looked as though they were designed to be drawn by a horse. The new patterns are layered upon the old, but eventually new methods become so powerful that they dominate the old.

But the old often resists the new. For instance, René Descartes is often considered to be the father of modern philosophy, but in 1663 the Roman Catholic Church placed Descartes's works on the Index of Forbidden Books, and Oxford forbade teaching his doctrines. After Francis Bacon and then Descartes proposed a new

> The true power of the computer to extend science is immense, but radically new methods are needed to harness its power.

science of observation and experiment to replace the traditional Aristotelian science, the Parliament of Paris passed a decree forbidding attacks on Aristotle on pain of death. The Cartesian Method was fought on the grounds that "it turns away the young from the study of the old and true philosophy."[11]

When computers became practical, the easy and natural-seeming way to use them was to emulate the human capability for sequential thought. A computer program seemed like an automated representation of the equations and formal logic mathematicians had developed.

History's great mathematicians and scientists cast a long shadow. We bow to their authority rather than replace their type of thinking with a radically new approach. The methods of Newton and Einstein seemed too established to challenge. Mathematics done with equations is at the very core of scientific thought. The computer was a tool to build upon what was profoundly respectable.

Now we need to realize that the true power of the computer to extend science is immense, but that radically new methods are needed to harness its power.

NOT IN OUR OWN IMAGE

In recent decades, mankind's view of its own prestige has taken some body blows. The earth is not the center of the universe, as once thought. It is a planet of a minor sun toward the edge of a galaxy of four hundred billion suns in a universe with a hundred billion galaxies. Faraway planets probably have life much older and wiser than ours. Sheep can be cloned; humans could be cloned, too. Man's brain is millions of times slower than computers. We talk slowly, face to face; computers will communicate a billion times faster and can do so across the planet. When computers become intelligent, their intelligence will evolve at electronic speed.

Science can now restore much of this lost prestige. The nearest planets with intelligent life are tens of light years away, probably hundreds, so we can't have a dialogue with them. They're too far away to interfere with us; it won't be like the movie *Independence*

Day. Computers of the near future are unlikely to have awareness, feeling, or consciousness. We are in charge. They are just gadgets. We are alive; they are not. Computer intelligence will not be like human intelligence; it will be deeply impressive but fundamentally different—a lightning-speed alien intelligence.

Perhaps the passionate attempts to make computers think like ourselves are merely narcissistic. Humans have often thought of God as a perfected version of what they themselves wanted to be. Thomas Jefferson had a wonderfully integrated image of God as the great architect, landscaper, and social organizer—just what Jefferson himself strove to be. Jefferson's God created everything to perfection. There was no concept of evolution; to believe what Darwin later believed would have been to commit the heresy of saying that God created imperfect creatures. Charles Babbage's God created the world so perfectly that it ran its programmed course without His having to interfere with it. God was the ultimate software engineer—again, just what Babbage himself would have wanted to be. He believed that "the Creator who selected the present law must have foreseen the consequences of all other laws."[12] To the French astronomer and mathematician the Marquis de Laplace, God was a mathematical intellect—a super-Laplace: "...an intelligence which could comprehend all the forces by which nature is animated... and would embrace in the same formula both the movements of the largest bodies in the universe and those of the lightest atom."[13]

If we create God in our own image, perhaps we want to create godlike machines in our own image, also.

But alien intelligence is not in our image. That raises the interesting question: Who will be able to cope with thought processes so radically different?

CHAPTER 4
Alien Thought

magine a group of philosophers debating while a column of ants goes by. An ant stops and asks, "What are you discussing?" The philosophers realize that there is no way they could explain their conversation to the ant. They tell the ant that its brain could not even begin to comprehend. The ant, somewhat peeved, says, "Well, *we* do things that *you* probably couldn't understand."

Now imagine computers of the future busily interacting, transmitting hundreds of millions of bits per second to one another around the planet. A philosopher observes this and asks, "What are you discussing?" The computers realize that there is no way they could explain their dialogue to the philosopher. A computer tells the philosopher that his brain could not even begin to comprehend. The philosopher says, "Well, *we* do things that *you* probably couldn't understand."

It's important for anyone who needs to think about how to put computers to work, and especially perhaps for the new dot-com inventors, to know about the differences between computer "thought" and human thought—the processes that machines are good at and those that humans are good at. If you think that computers merely automate thought processes that humans are capable of, then you will fail to understand the potential of the machines. Alien intelligence will make fundamental changes in how science is done. In many cases scientists want bigger telescopes or better laboratories when they could obtain more value from putting the new forms of computing to work on data they already have.

CYBERTHOUGHT

The vast majority of what is programmed on computers today is human thought processes that are automated—the processing of invoices, production planning, engineering calculations, and so on. Computers execute them unimaginably faster than humans, but they are still human thought processes. In the future computers will be increasingly valuable for a different kind of "thought" that humans cannot do—"thought" that is quite alien to humans. We need a word for this: *cyberthought*.

We thus have three types of thinking:

■ Human thought processes.

■ Machine emulation of human thought processes.

■ Cyberthought.

Cyberthought employs the techniques we call alien intelligence, and because of this, humans can't follow it in detail. We can examine each instruction in the process the computer used to reach that result, but the overall process is much too complex for us to pick it apart. Sometimes, however, we can check the results to see if they are valid.

Cyberthought processes have various characteristics that cannot be emulated in human thought.

■ They may employ vast quantities of data, sometimes trillions of bytes, which would be overwhelming to humans. They never forget or distort data.

■ They may execute highly parallel procedures. Many procedures, each by itself simple, may be linked in ways that make the overall result complex. The behavior of the overall collection of procedures is different from and far more sophisticated than the behavior of the individual procedures. The results of the parallel processing may be surprising and completely unpredictable.

■ The formulations may be complex and sprawling. They may incorporate thousands of rules, or procedures, rather than the small number that are in diagrams or equations for human use.

■ The process may have feedback that modifies the process itself. It may examine its own results and adjust its own behavior so that it does a progressively better job. It may search systematically for alternate patterns of behavior.

■ The behavior of different components may be competitive, with each component competing to have more influence than the others.

■ Because the behavior is steadily adjusted on the basis of results, the process may, in effect, learn at electronic speed.

When behavior consists of sequential processes, we can understand it by understanding each process. But when behavior consists of multiple processes happening simultaneously, with interactions among the processes, then we cannot understand it merely by understanding each process. An aerospace company could perfect the design of each component of a jet fighter and still have a plane that is unfit to fly. It is the interaction among the components that matters, and that can be highly complex.

EVOLUTION AND LEARNING

A computer process may be set up to evolve. It is given a goal and after each iteration measures or estimates how close it is to meeting that goal. It adjusts its behavior in order to progress toward the goal. Remember, intelligence in nature is designed to *evolve, learn, adapt, and constantly improve itself;* if we are to compete with its complexity, we will need engineering that is designed to do all of those things.

One of the most powerful aspects of future computing is the building of systems that learn. Some software is designed to improve its own procedures, like a child exploring new types of behavior, but modifies itself thousands of times a second. It may improve its capability to carry out a specific function until it reaches a level of capability far beyond what its own human creator could have programmed.

A computer that learns does so very differently from how any human learns. Whereas we may modify our behavior over the course of weeks or months, computer programs may do so in seconds or milliseconds.

To keep up with the extreme rate of change in corporations today, much software must be designed so that it is easy to modify. Cyberthought routines may be designed to modify themselves and transmit their modifications to other computers.

A DELUGE OF DATA

In many areas of science and business today we are confronted with an overwhelming deluge of data. A chain store can collect data about every item bought by every customer in every shop. In order to maximize the chain's profits, computers can relate that data to advertising, packaging, the positioning of goods on the shelves, the local competition, demographics, and other factors.

Today's electronics generate an ocean of data. Space telescopes surveying the earth each produce a billion bytes of data per minute. Computers for foreign exchange trading give tick-by-tick details of every price change around the world.

> A very important question is how to achieve the most powerful synergy between what we are good at and what machines are good at.

Such data rapidly become too voluminous for human processing. We are already drowning in data, and in the near future immeasurably more data will become available because of the spread of ubiquitous microsystems and sensors. John Scully, when he was CEO of Apple Computers, lamented: "It is just not very useful to have these massive amounts of data. All we have done is to take the way that machines create data and scale it up. We are finding that it is *machine scaleable*, not *human scaleable*." But in reality these nonhuman-scaleable data contain information that would be exceedingly useful to executives like Scully if only they could mine it. A vital business question is, "How can computers process voluminous data in ways that provide insight for key decision-makers?"

Every word Shakespeare wrote in his lifetime can be recorded with about seventy million bits. We might use the term "shakespeare" as a measure (like a gallon) referring to seventy million bits of data. Consider: the machine on which I am writing this book has a main memory of about fourteen shakespeares and a disk capacity of about 570 shakespeares.

Traditionally data were first seen by humans, who collected the data, checked them, and organized them. Today most data go straight to a computer; humans never see them. Scientists of the past have looked through microscopes or telescopes and carefully recorded what they see. Market researchers have stood in supermarkets writing down the buying habits of customers. Today telescopes are operated remotely on icy mountaintops, in orbit, or on the far side of the moon, and their digital images go straight to computer files. Voluminous market data, untouched by humans, go straight to data warehouses. Traffic sensors, subatomic particle detectors, battlefield surveillance cameras, patient monitors—all carry on endless vigilance. Electronics under the ocean listen endlessly for enemy submarines. A hearing aid can be a medical sensor. Each can of beans in a supermarket has a bar code on it so that distant computers know when it is bought, and if the purchaser uses a credit card, the computers also know who bought it. Soon wireless smart cards in your wallet will be interrogated without your even knowing.

As Scully lamented, this deluge of data would be of little value to unaided humans. Computers are needed to look for trends, patterns, or correlations, or to derive some insight that is useful for human decision-makers. Increasingly, computers will be programmed to act automatically when certain conditions are detected.

THE BEER-AND-DIAPERS SYNDROME

Computers sometimes find relationships when they digest masses of data that at first seem ridiculous. According to one story (possibly apocryphal), the Wal-Mart computers discovered a correlation between the sale of beer and of babies' diapers. "Nonsense," said the retail executives. Unfazed, the machine went further, announcing that the correlation was stronger on a Friday evening than other times. How could that possibly be? The retailers eventually concluded that most American men are henpecked and that their wives send them out to get diapers on a Friday evening. To deal with this situation, the men buy six-packs of beer. Wal-Mart could increase sales by putting beer on the diaper shelves.

The *beer-and-diapers syndrome* became a term data-mining experts used to refer to situations where computers find correlations that humans would not find. In the great amorphous mass of medical data there are many potential beer-and-diapers opportunities. They might reveal side effects of drugs, unexpected causes of mental illness, or factors that delay the onset of Alzheimer's. Like a gardener detecting warning symptoms before a plant is really sick, a computer may detect that a person is heading for a heart attack or stroke in time to head off catastrophe. We've already seen how HNC uses software to detect early warning symptoms of companies that are headed toward bankruptcy.

ALIEN-INTELLIGENCE MATH

The vast number of steps, degree of parallelism, and self-modification of future computing will defy step-by-step human checking. Nevertheless, the process is logical. It is as precise as mathematics. It is in effect a new form of mathematics that goes far beyond conventional math equations. New computational processes will become very important because they can be applied to the messy deluge of data that the real world produces. As these techniques mature, they will fundamentally change engineering and science.

All manner of scientific data simply cannot be reduced to equations. Instead, with powerful computers, we have adopted a new approach to science: we store the masses of data and allow elaborate computational tools to explore them.

When we try to model complex adaptive processes with equations, we often fail. Equations are useless in designing a system that can play chess, to take just one example. But using an entirely different approach IBM's scientists designed a system, "Deep Blue," that beat the world's reigning chess champion, Garry Kasparov. Many aspects of science are as unyielding to traditional mathematics as chess is. They can be tackled with new computing techniques, not traditional math.

Some complex processes are modeled with equations, but in order to do so scientists distort the process into forms for which equations can be found.

There is an old story about a drunk looking for keys that he has dropped. He is looking under a lamppost, even though he dropped them some way away, because the only place where he can see is under the lamppost. We are surrounded by complex problems that cannot be solved with equations or algorithms, but scientists have been taught to work with mathematics. Equations and algorithms are what computers can handle. The history of computing has focused on problems where equations and algorithms can be used, because that is *under the lamppost*. Many of today's most important problems have barely been tackled because they don't yield to equation-based mathematics; they are not under the lamppost.

As we will see later in this book, new techniques will allow scientists to range far beyond the small patch of light under the lamppost.

THE CHANGE IN SCIENCE

Biology used to be a science that cultivated things in petri dishes and studied diverse species but that had little need for number crunching. Today biology, like almost every science, is drowning in data. A top genetics laboratory can easily produce ten thousand shakespeares a day. The amount of information stored in Genbank, the international repository of gene sequences, doubles every year (and the doubling time is shrinking). The data deluge will be larger when serious mapping of the brain becomes practical. Many challenges in biology, from gene analysis to drug discovery, have become challenges that need alien-intelligence techniques to discover patterns and test hypotheses. America's National Institutes of Health (NIH) issued a report in 1999 saying that there is "an alarming gap between the need for computation in biology and the skills and resources available to meet that need." This comment could be applied to most sciences.

High-energy physics uses grandly expensive particle accelerators to hurl atomic particles at each other at the highest speeds possible. The spectacular collisions produce a debris of fleeting subatomic particles. Occasionally, very rare particles appear for the minutest fraction of a second. Nuclear physicists have ever more exotic theories, far stranger than Alice in Wonderland. One of these was dependent on the existence of an ephemeral particle which physicists called *the top quark*. The Fermi Lab near Chicago set out to detect it. The computers had to comb through more than fifty million collisions between subatomic particles to find a handful of candidates. This involved three million shakespeares of data. Experiments in the next few years will produce far more data. CERN, the European Lab for Particle Physics, is planning experiments that will produce over a hundred million shakespeares per year.

Until recently most astronomers studied things that we can see through telescopes. Much of the universe, however, consists of dark matter that we can't see. Much of our own Milky Way is made up of nonluminous objects, such as brown dwarfs and suns that have died. Only occasionally do we get a clue that a dark star is out there because it moves into the light from a visible star. (Massive objects bend light rays slightly so the dark star may give away its presence by distorting the light from other stars.) This happens so rarely that it is necessary to monitor hundreds of millions of stars and galaxies for many years in order to detect the nonluminous objects. Computers sift through trillions of bytes of data, endlessly searching for anything unusual or interesting. Because these mountains of data require an enormous amount of computation, it makes sense to have computers in many locations chewing through the data. The same data may be reexamined many times as new computing techniques or new hypotheses develop.

Charles Alcock, an astronomer at the Lawrence Livermore Laboratory, comments, "Our ability to gather data is increasing rapidly, but our ability to make sense of it isn't keeping up."[1] Expensive spacecraft have explored space, but computers have not adequately explored the data they have collected.

> To think about future computers in anthropomorphic terms completely limits the ability to understand what they will be capable of.

The Sloan Digital Sky Survey is using one telescope to map half the northern sky in five wavelengths from ultraviolet to near infrared. It will produce digital information about more than two hundred million objects, totaling about five times as many bits as in the entire Library of Congress. Alexander Szalay, an astrophysicist investigator for the survey at Johns Hopkins University, remarks that unless we learn how to correlate this deluge of data with computers, it will be as useful as the pages of a twenty-volume encyclopedia that have been torn out and cut into one-inch squares.[2]

Carnegie Mellon University, funded by the National Science Foundation to create software to "patrol astrophysical data and make discoveries," also recognizes the problem. Andrew Moore of

Carnegie Mellon says there are trillions of high-order correlations, each requiring billions of computations. He states, "We are proposing to help automate the process of scientific discovery where there is too much information for a human being to even have the chance to spot patterns, regularities, and anomalies."[3]

Often astronomers who make interesting discoveries will be exploring the vast archives of data rather than exploring the skies. They need telescopes for the data warehouses, not telescopes for the sky. They need to be masters of alien intelligence.

The same can be said for most other sciences and other industries. What Moore wants to do with astrophysics, many other people want to do with e-commerce to determine where the highest profits can be made. Charles Alcock's comment that astronomers don't have the capability to use the masses of data they collect could just as easily apply to biologists, medical doctors, supermarkets, intelligence agencies, hedge funds, or physicists. Intelligence agencies, for example, are overwhelmed with data from intercepted phone calls, faxes, e-mails, surveillance cameras, and other instrumentation. And this deluge is growing because digital snooping devices are becoming cheap and ubiquitous. The National Security Agency produces so much data that it can analyze only a tiny fraction of it.

Our world today is flooded with data, but only in rare, isolated cases have we begun to extract the gems of knowledge buried in those data.

SEARCHING FOR OPTIMUM RESULTS

Many different algorithms can search for optimum results in a decision-making or design process. Consider the layout of wiring on complex chips. There are numerous ways in which transistors could be positioned on a chip and their interconnections laid out. Finding the best layout helps to pack many more transistors onto the chip, which is economically important. A computer processor chip has millions of transistors but many millions of interconnections. This wiring is immensely complex, often taking up 99 percent of the potential chip surface, leaving only 1 percent for the transistors that do the work.

Optimizing the physical layout of the chip involves moving the components around so that on average they are closer together, resulting in shorter wires that take up much less of the valuable chip space needed for transistors. It is an extraordinarily complex task that needs to be done by software. The software takes two linked transistors that are far apart, tries moving them close together, and reconnects the chip wiring. If this change saves space it keeps the change and repeats the process, steadily reducing the tangle of wires. It jiggles them hundreds of millions of times while searching for an optimum layout. In the beginning it moves transistors that are far apart; as the design progresses, it moves transistors that are closer together; eventually it can only swap transistors that are already adjacent. This process is referred to as *simulated annealing*.

The human brain would work much faster if this type of design optimization could be applied to it.

CYBERTHOUGHT VERSUS AUTOMATED HUMAN THOUGHT

In many fields we can distinguish between cyberthought and the automation of what are essentially human thought processes.

Most software for investing, for example, essentially automates what human investors do. A highly skilled money manager realizes that much of what he looks for when investing can be programmed, and that often it will be much more comprehensive or efficient if it is programmed. Some software tools used by investors operate automatically, but most of them contain a programmed version of human thought. Computers execute it much faster or more accurately than humans, but it is still human ideas in a machine.

While many programs for assistance in trading automate *human* thought processes, some are completely different. They use neural networks, genetic algorithms, or inference engines (all described later) to process information in ways that humans cannot. They may search for patterns that humans would not find.

Cyberthought can often produce surprising results. A person cannot check the results directly because the computer has executed millions, perhaps billions, of steps to produce the results. Sometimes, but not always, the results can be verified indirectly— one can check whether beer and diapers *really* sell together. In some cases a result gives a person new insight or helps a person to recognize previously unnoticed patterns.

The Santa Fe Institute is exploring the behavior of a wide diversity of complex adaptive systems. The stock market is one such system. In the past, theories about how the stock market rises and falls have been explored with equations, such as the complex econometric models used to try to understand the behavior of the economy. But equation-based models have not satisfactorily explained seemingly irrational movements that lead to speculative bubbles and crashes, so John Holland and Brian Arthur of the Santa Fe Institute set out to explore stock market behavior using software agents that genetically evolve their own buying and selling rules.

At first the behavior of these agents was placid and predictable. The agents initially tried such simple rules as: "IF the price is 40 or more THEN sell; IF the price is below 40 THEN buy."[4] However, after a while one of the agents learned to anticipate trends and discovered that it could make money by selling late in a rising market. Before long, other software agents learned to do the same. Their collective behavior made these trend projections self-fulfilling for a while. Like human traders, the agents tried to keep ahead of their competition by using trend projections in more aggressive ways. The behavior of the market became increasingly agitated, steadily leading to a speculative bubble. Eventually the bubble reached a level that couldn't be maintained, and a crash occurred. These humanlike agents eventually created a market characterized by boom-and-bust cycles. This behavior seemed to replicate what happens in real markets. Like real markets, the markets created by the software agents didn't settle down or even stay at quasi-equilibrium for long.

> Our world is flooded with data, but only in isolated cases have we begun to extract the gems of knowledge buried in those data.

Traditional mathematics and equation-based models do not predict this behavior. Stock market crashes usually catch us by surprise. Science and society have numerous other complex adaptive systems that equations cannot accurately represent. Some of these have been successfully modeled with cellular automata, genetic algorithms, and various forms of parallel computing.

The behavior of an integrated collection of processes is different from, and far more sophisticated than, the behavior of the individual processes. A process may have *feedback* that modifies itself, or it may have feedback that modifies other processes. It may examine the results and adjust its behavior to make the results progressively better. The behavior of different components may be *competitive*, with each node competing to have more influence than the other nodes.

BEST OF BOTH WORLDS

Because alien intelligence and human intelligence are radically different, formidable results can be achieved when the best of human intelligence works in tight partnership with the best of alien intelligence.

Many executives and decision makers of the future will be able to do their job well only if they work in partnership with machine intelligence. This will often be deep alien-intelligence processing with access to vast warehouses of data. The machine intelligence will help make decisions that humans alone cannot possibly make.

Computer-phobic managers will be swept away by managers working closely with computers.

Sometimes when alien intelligence is being used, humans have no idea how the data are being processed. They will merely see the results. The results, however, may demand a rapid response—from either the human or the alien partner. An online system may detect fraud. An invisible neutron-beam processor at an airport may detect explosives in a suitcase. An elevator may radio for preventive maintenance before it fails. A person's instrumentation may warn him that he's about to have a stroke. A jet pilot in battle may have to respond immediately to what his or her heads-up display says.

A very important question is how to achieve the most powerful synergy between what *we* are good at and what *machines* are good at.

For some applications the *machine* of the partnership may be a supercomputer and the *humans* may be a large team, perhaps each with his or her own computer. Such an arrangement is used in intelligence agencies for cracking ultrasecure cryptography or for examining billions of satellite images in search of covert activity. It may be used in police departments to track international finance crimes or in seismic laboratories to look for oil. Increasingly, teams of scientists will gather vast quantities of data and use alien supercomputing to deduce laws that underlie those data. Quantum chemists, rather than conducting laboratory experiments, as in traditional chemistry, run experiments in the simulated environment with intense computation, sometimes using cellular automata.

A PARTNERSHIP OF UNEQUALS

Much research and development has been done on "man–machine interaction," but it has usually dealt with the structure of the dialogue between humans and machines. Researchers have been concerned with screen design, syntax, mouse dialogues, graphical user interfaces, speech input to computers and, in general, how to make the machine as user-friendly as possible. At the outer limits the subject has included virtual reality in its various forms.

But there is a much deeper aspect of human–machine interaction, which addresses how human thinking and machine thinking should interrelate.

In a partnership between machine intelligence and human intelligence, what should the machine do and what should the human do? As alien intelligence evolves, how should its relationship with human intelligence evolve? The machine will often employ data or computer power elsewhere on the planet. How can an intelligent human–machine combination be designed to achieve the most powerful results?

To think about future computers in anthropomorphic terms completely limits the ability to understand what they will be capable of. We cannot make the common mistakes of thinking of computers as automating what humans do. This is exactly the wrong place to start. You wouldn't think of chemical plants in terms of how they can emulate humans, so why should you think of computers that way?

Computer intelligence is often very deep but quite narrowly focused. We can build a machine that plays good chess. We cannot build a machine that directs good movies. Good filmmaking can't be reduced to rules. To make a great movie requires sensitivity to numerous subjects so subtle that they are difficult to express—the style of photography, the building of suspense, the development of complex human character, the blend of story and music, convincing dialogue, beauty in lighting, acting that conveys conviction, the best camera motion. This type of intelligence will probably never be automated.

Life has an endless variety of delicate experiences—the smell of home cooking, falling in love, subconscious reaction to birdsong in spring, the appreciation of a clever idea, the feeling created by a baby's gaze, the skill of the clarinetist in a Mozart concerto. Computing, no matter how deeply intricate and complex, is a barbarian world, devoid of these sensations.

The alien thought of computers will become capable of appreciating other sensations, often more subtle, but quite different from what the human mind can appreciate. As sensors scan their environment or software forages through warehouses of data, machines can learn with electronic relentlessness to detect patterns that humans cannot recognize and nuances that humans cannot appreciate. We can "breed" silicon chips for complex functions where we cannot understand how the chip works (see Chapters 12 and 17). Our challenge will be to harness such alien capabilities so we can create a better lifestyle, or better corporations, and try to evolve to a world of preventive medicine, clean ecology, new levels of creativity, and war-free politics.

FARMERS OF DATA

Computers will absorb an ever-increasing amount of data. Managers need computerized imagery that enables them to *visualize* their fast-changing environment, digest its complexity, interact with it in real time, and make appropriate decisions. Complex data can be represented as colorful three-dimensional landscapes that computer users can fly through and explore. Colored charts may be designed with motion or animation. A decision maker familiar with imagery can quickly spot areas that need attention.

Alien intelligence might recognize patterns in data warehouses that humans would never detect. It is necessary to convert such information into charts that help human intuitive thinking. Visual representation of complex information will become increasingly important.

The human brain is designed to absorb and react to images. We can train ourselves to do this in an astonishingly sophisticated way. I was recently shown around a hydroponics farm with all manner of plants growing artificially, their roots visibly spreading in troughs of controlled liquid nutrients. The person tending the plants would note: "This strawberry plant is deficient in potassium. This one needs more light; we should move it over there. This has too much calcium...." I would ask, "How do you know?" She had learned to deduce complex information from the subtle coloring and growth of the leaves and the length of new shoots. She had acquired a feeling for what the plants needed and claimed that no digital system could replace the subtleties of that feeling.

> Alien intelligence can sometimes turn a black art into a science.

Just as a skilled gardener learns over the years to recognize when plants need attention by the appearance of their leaves, so does data-mining software train itself to recognize symptoms or patterns that may be important. This works only if there is a mass of data to train on, so the accumulation of such data is critical. The training takes place at electronic speed, and self-training software may quickly acquire a capability that humans cannot understand. The computer is like a science fiction gardener in a jungle of data trying to make sense of what it sees. It sees things that we don't see.

When we link alien intelligence's ability to detect patterns in complex data with our own human visual skills, we can grow powerful person–machine partnerships. BTT, an investment company in Zurich with a good track record of investing in technology, has a comprehensive data warehouse of present and past stock movements and characteristics. A full-time BTT employee monitors the visual representation of complex information extracted from the warehouse and explores using software packages that create different ingenious ways for humans to derive insight visually from complex multidimensional data.

Humans cope easily with some three-dimensional problems because we live in a three-dimensional world. We have much more difficulty with problems with more than three dimensions. A computer, however, can cope with many-dimensional problems and search for many-dimensional patterns. And fortunately, a computer can produce three-dimensional slices through multidimensional data and enable a human decision maker to view them with three-dimensional graphics—sometimes 3D landscapes that an intelligent decision maker can zoom into and explore.

Being able to digest the data computers collect could prove vital to corporations' success—indeed, to their very survival. In 1995 Britain's oldest and proudest merchant bank, Barings, crashed in flames with breathtaking suddenness. One day it was there, older than the United States, the next day it was gone, with almost no warning of problems. The bank's top management later revealed that Barings had been wrecked by a naive trader, Nick Leeson, a twenty-seven-year-old with no college education who had been refused a trading license in London. How could such a naive individual destroy, in a few weeks of trading, a venerable banking institution that had survived European mayhem for centuries? The bank's head office was drowning in computer data but not able to see what was going on. If management had been able to see the data visually, there would have been a red spike in Singapore that would have gone through the roof.

A Bank of England postmortem on Barings commented that many other banks might have similar problems. As we increasingly operate in a jungle with herds that can rampage electronically, the risks and opportunities are amplified. Banks and corporations will need excellent visual representation of these data to be confident that there are no hidden time bombs.

PRACTICES WE CAN'T EXPLAIN

Science has generally demanded that we understand phenomena in detail. If we can't explain something, it's in the realm of the occult. However, there are certain professional practices today that we can't explain. Acupuncture, for example, has been ignored by Western medical science because we do not have a scientific explanation for how it works. Yet there is no question that under appropriate circumstances acupuncture does work. In China many surgeons conduct major operations using acupuncture rather than anesthetics. In some cases the patient is alert while he is being cut open, but is free from pain.

Carl Sagan always commented that we should be highly skeptical about something we can't explain. He cautioned us that *extraordinary claims need extraordinary evidence.* Today we can establish extraordinary evidence for or against the various forms of alternative medicine. Computers can thoroughly and relentlessly analyze vast amounts of data about symptoms, treatments, and results.

It is becoming clear that in the future we will need to make use of things that we can't explain in detail. Computing itself, supposedly the most precise of engineering, is producing valuable results we can't understand. We can't follow the logic of alien-intelligence processes in detail.

The fact that science can't explain how something works doesn't mean that we shouldn't use it. We should, however, validate its usage with exceptional scientific thoroughness. We must fill data warehouses with examples of its use, where the data show in detail the circumstances and the results obtained. The results must be validated and any questionable results rejected.

Homeopathic medicine, like acupuncture, has been coming into use by a number of serious doctors, more so in Europe and Asia than in the United States. Research shows that in spite of the skepticism it certainly can work.[5] Homeopathy has sometimes been extremely effective in treating people with chronic diseases and has even corrected conditions that conventional medicine considered incurable.

AUTOMATING A BLACK ART

The problem with homeopathy is that it seems like a black art. There is no clear logical explanation of what medicine will be best for a particular patient and his particular condition. Black arts tend to attract snake-oil peddlers, and homeopathy is plagued with them.

But alien intelligence can sometimes turn a black art into a science.

To make a black art scientific we must collect vast amounts of data and use alien-intelligence techniques to relate complex cause and effect. When appropriate data definitions exist agents can relentlessly scour the world's Internet sites and bring data back to data warehouses. Alien-intelligence tools can then forage through the data looking for patterns. In homeopathic medicine they can identify what remedies work with what patterns of symptoms, and how they differ depending on characteristics of the individual. Neural networks provide ways to identify and classify such patterns.

Alien-intelligence tools often find patterns and correlations in the data that humans can't find. Sometimes these patterns seem counterintuitive to us, but if they are precise and relentlessly repeatable, we must take them seriously. This is how we convert a black art into rigorous methodology.

BEYOND DESCARTES

Descartes's *Discourse on Method* said that the key to thinking was to arrange one's thoughts in ordered sequences and to "follow obstinately such an order."[6] To computer pioneers this sounded like programming. Descartes was adopted as the patron philosopher of computing. This is ironic because computers give mankind the capability to move far beyond Descartes's methods.

Descartes analyzed the strengths and weaknesses of the human mind and wrote his *Rules for the Direction of Mind*.[7] He concluded that because we are capable of sequential steps in thought, problems must be broken into sequential steps so that we are capable of thinking about them. Our short-term memory is small. We can write down data or intermediate results, but we cannot hold too much in our head at one time, so scientific formulations must be compact as well as sequential. Descartes rejoiced in the fact that algebra is compact and sequential: "Whatever has the same order as things in mathematics is easily remembered. Other things are remembered badly and with difficulty."[8] Cartesian thinking had a vast impact on the development and teaching of science.

Throughout history data have usually been scarce and logic processes have been slow and sequential. Equations, classical mathematics, and classical scientific methods are ideal for a world of scarce data and sequential thought. Equations like Newton's Laws of Motion or Maxwell's Laws of Electromagnetism facilitated major leaps in human thinking. We are about to take another major leap.

Cartesian Method is based on the limitations of the human mind. A computer does not have those limitations. It can store vast quantities of bits and process them in ways that humans cannot. Computing—and, with it, science—is racing headlong in all manner of non-Cartesian directions.

THE POST-CARTESIAN REVOLUTION

For the first half century of computing, two dynamics have been playing out side by side. First, the mathematics of Descartes's world with its sequential processing of equations has been raised to phenomenal levels of performance. Second, totally different techniques have come into use that are dependent on high-speed computing. The techniques of alien intelligence are so foreign to traditional mathematicians that few paid attention to them. But these techniques open up study in many areas not accessible with traditional methods. They are in their infancy but have already produced some dramatic results. Today we are surrounded by important problems that cannot be dealt with using traditional mathematics because adequate sets of equations cannot be discovered.

Like the drunk looking for his keys under a lamppost because that is where the light is, we have tended to concentrate on those subjects where our mathematics works. Descartes advocated that in order to understand nature scientists should sequentialize it, artificially "assigning in thought a certain order *even to those objects which in their own nature do not stand in a relation of antecedence and consequences.*"[9] This was necessary because our thought processes are limited by our use of short-term memory. Now it is not necessary, and it has become clear that many of our most important problems cannot be tackled or thought about in sequential steps.

The Cartesian view of nature is something that we impose upon nature; it is not an inherent property of nature. A space alien might observe what is going on in a bank by examining the transmissions from security cameras, but this would not enable it to deduce the meaning and purpose of the bank. Like the bank camera, Cartesian thought has limitations.

Descartes's methods fit naturally with what humans are good at, but not with what computers are good at. The new computing techniques take us into powerful non-Cartesian realms. Alien intelligence sets the stage for the most significant changes in scientific thinking since the time of Descartes.

BEYOND COMMON SENSE

At the beginning of the twentieth century science painted a picture of the world that seemed to conform with common sense. We could *visualize* Newtonian mechanics, atoms behaving like billiard balls, electrons in orbits, and light refracted by lenses. Twentieth-century physicists shattered this commonsense view of the world.

> Computing—
> and, with it,
> science—is
> racing head-
> long in all
> manner of
> non-Cartesian
> directions.

Scientists found that a tiny particle behaves as both a particle and a wave. We like to think of a particle traveling with a single trajectory like a golf ball, but now it seemed to behave as both a particle and a wave at the same time. If this seemed to defy common sense, much worse was ahead. In Einstein's physics the particle changes its mass as it speeds up, until it approaches infinite mass at the speed of light. Mass and energy are interconvertible, and time and space vary with perspective.

If Einstein's world seemed an insult to common sense, physics was soon to become an insult to Einstein. Quantum mechanics, the foundation of much modern physics, is ruled by probability. Like a roulette wheel certain properties of fundamental particles are determined by chance, with an equal probability of alternate choices. Einstein said he could never accept that "God plays dice with the universe."

Even further from classical physics, a basic premise of today's quantum physics is that certain properties of fundamental particles are ambiguous until they are observed. A property has every possible value until a conscious observation causes it to select a value. The spin of the electron, for example, is ambiguous until a conscious observer observes it, directly or indirectly. There is an equal probability that it could select one spin or the opposite spin. This behavior, repeatedly demonstrated by experiments, has profound philosophical implications. It implies that our conscious observation of the world changes the world in subtle ways.

Even stranger, certain properties of subatomic particles are related, so if one property changes, it causes the other to change as well. This is referred to as *quantum entanglement*. Although the properties are related, they are undetermined until we consciously observe them, and when we observe one property and so make it unambiguous, the related properties must change correspondingly. Different particles can be quantum entangled; in other words, when a property of one particle changes, a related property of the other particle must change. These quantum-entangled particles could be far apart. They could be traveling across the universe in opposite directions at the speed of light.

This seemingly impossible behavior was predicted mathematically and has been demonstrated in multiple experiments. In one experiment an event causes two photons to travel in opposite directions at the speed of light. Because they originate from the same event they have certain properties in common, such as polarization. There is an equal probability that they could have positive or negative polarization, but it must be the same for both. However, they will not make a decision which polarization it is until they are observed. If one is observed and chooses positive polarization, then the other must adopt positive polarization *at the same instant*. They might be a long distance apart before they are observed—possibly light years apart. The experiment demonstrated that the photons do indeed adopt the same polarization at the same instant, even though they are so far apart that no signal could travel from one to the other fast enough to tell the other about its choice.

As physics moves further and further beyond common sense we might be tempted to regard it as an esoteric mind game, unrelated to reality. But, it is based on the reality of repeatable experiments that support mathematical theory. Experimental evidence has dragged physicists kicking and screaming into a world alien to their intuition.

Physics tells us that human common sense is a very narrow window into a complex world. As we explore the world beyond this window, it seems increasingly bizarre to us. We found words to describe the new laws of physics, at least in a limited way, but now some physics is so far beyond common sense that we cannot find words to describe it. Physicists communicate with abstruse mathematics. Now computation can take science where mathematics can't go.

We defined alien intelligence as processes where a human can neither follow the logic step-by-step nor come to the same result by other means. Computing is heading into the same territory as physics—beyond ordinary human logic or common sense.

For its first half century, computing has been used to augment the past. Now it is essential to break free from the past.

CHAPTER 5
The Jungle Fabric

I n the near future, complex microchips will disappear into the surroundings of our lives, no more visible or shocking than a thermostat. They will be in walls, furniture, appliances, cars, wallets, jewelry, and clothes. Electricity is ubiquitous. It is in the walls, in devices, in the car. Writing is ubiquitous. It is on restaurant menus, advertisements, everywhere. Ubiquitous computing will become similar—part of the environment, usually unnoticed.

As most computers disappear into the woodwork we will be largely unaware of what they are doing. They will seem no more extraordinary than the scores of electric motors that are hidden in the frame of your car.

Today most of these ubiquitous hidden chips are doing simplistic things, like controlling alarm systems or automatic sprinklers. Increasingly they will employ various types of computerized intelligence.[1] They will progress from merely detecting a burglar to helping the police convict the burglar, or from merely watering the flowerbed to using sensors in the soil to compute the proper mix of nutrients to put in the water in order to make the flowers look as beautiful as possible.

Chips with computers on them are becoming mass-produced, like newsprint. They are so cheap that they are sometimes referred to in the trade as "jelly beans." One industry spokesman calculated that a chip with an embedded processor costs less to manufacture than a ball bearing.[2] Soon such chips will have built-in alien intelligence.

A typical home today has a few dozen computers. There is a computer in each clock, in the oven, in the VCR, and in other machines. But these are stand-alone machines; in the era of ubiquitous computing many small computers will be *linked to networks*. Your digital weather instruments will check the weather forecasts. Your kitchen equipment will download recipes from the Internet. You will set the temperature of your house as you drive home. The electronic book that you read in bed will download music. Farmers' fields will have thousands of moisture sensors that transmit data to irrigation systems. Vehicle sensors will transmit to computers programmed to minimize traffic congestion.

Many microsystems will do their own thing. Your watch will use a wireless signal to set itself to the correct time when you travel. Your kids' toys will load themselves with software and behave as though they have a mind of their own. Sony's toy dog, Aibo, for example, learns about its surroundings and seems to have a strong-willed mind of its own, like a real dog. Security systems will take photographs of burglars and send them to the police. You won't have to call up an Internet server to check your e-mail; the mail will arrive automatically and be stored in your pocket machine, along with selected news items, jokes, and so on.

The cost of both computer power and computer memory has dropped by about a factor of ten every five years. Every three decades it becomes a million times cheaper. By 2010 it will have become a *trillion* times cheaper in the six decades since 1950. With microsystems of miniscule cost, computing can be built into every nook and cranny of society, much of it using alien intelligence.

The digital hearing aids that people now wear almost invisibly, molded to fit their ear canal, would have once needed two tons of air-conditioning equipment. Such hearing aids will in the future act as unseen, unheard communication devices or private hi-fi systems. Ubiquitous networked computing will pervade everything. Teenagers' wireless gadgets will find other teenagers with compatible interests.

Microsystems in your car will communicate with other vehicles to help prevent accidents. Your TV will learn what programs you like and help you find them. The groceries you need will be delivered so you don't waste time trudging around supermarkets. You will be able to have lush walls of hanging flowers that microcomputers water and fertilize in an optimal manner.

In the Hong Kong rush hour the jostling millions of travelers on the buses, trains, and ferries use smart cards with a tiny embedded radio antenna. The card, the size of a credit card, contains a purse of money. As you enter a bus the fare is deducted from the purse by a radio signal. You do not have to put the card in a machine. (The government can take money from your pocket without your even knowing.) Many microsystems will use such short-distance wireless communication, and, like the Hong Kong smart cards, will cost very little. Tiny network-connected microsystems will be everywhere, embedded in all manner of everyday artifacts.

The computers in walls and cars will react to our presence in a variety of ways. Urinals can flush automatically after we use them. Microwave sensors can detect our movement. Infrared sensors know where we are by the heat that we give off. Microphones can detect our sounds and possibly identify key words when we speak. As time goes by the invisible systems will become far more sensitive, understanding our movements and speech.

WEARABLE COMPUTERS

The ritual of exchanging business cards is a dreadful way to communicate data. The business card will become a relic of an inefficient age. Only people over thirty, who are not "with it," will use business cards. Radio-cufflinks will exchange data when you shake hands. Wireless systems are useful because they allow a large amount of data to be exchanged and they can automatically update personal computers.

In some security-conscious companies all employees wear an identification badge that transmits and receives data. It transmits its owner's identification number, opens secure doors, switches lights on, and allows employees to use key computer systems. Some badges communicate with other badges, silently exchanging information. Electronics can detect whether a person is wearing his own badge, and can locate any employee. Cows on large ranches have a small Global Positioning System device clipped to their ears so that they transmit their number and location.

> Chips with computers on them are becoming mass-produced. They are so cheap that they are sometimes referred to as "jelly beans."

Soon, wireless devices will be invisible parts of our clothing. We may wear them at cocktail parties because they communicate much that body language does not. The strangers-in-the-night of the Sinatra song will exchange more than glances.

It may become a ritual for teenagers to wear wireless devices to identify clique members or be a part of date-hunting rituals. They may be integrated with cellular phones. Your phone may be almost invisible—a ring on your finger linked by radio to an antenna in your pocket and an earpiece inside your ear canal.

Your hidden earpiece may let you know that a friend or a person of similar interests is approaching. It may tell you that a nearby shop carries a book that you want to examine. As you drive down the road a wireless device might tell you that a shop around the corner has antiques that you are interested in.

Tens of thousands of people die needlessly each year because nobody is around to notify an emergency medical service when they have a heart attack or are in a car accident. Wristwatch heart monitors like those now on the market can be designed to recognize unusual heartbeat patterns and radio a medical service if there is a risk. Cars of the future will transmit an SOS if a crash occurs, using information from a global positioning satellite to indicate the exact location.

Our wristwatch or earpiece computers will make us walking nodes of the Internet.

SECURE BUNKERS

USAA, one of the world's most profitable insurance companies, has a head office building in San Antonio so large that it has a scheduled bus service inside the building. USAA has an underground building with one of the world's most impressive assemblies of computing power. If the power fails, this vast array of machines runs nonstop from batteries for forty seconds while massive generators roar into action. The awesome computer center is designed to operate without human intervention for many days. It would survive the worst hurricane. If a fire starts, it will automatically douse the flames with fire-quenching halon gas. The person who showed me around the facility said it would likely survive nuclear attack because it was unlikely that there would be a direct hit!

The world we are building will have vast numbers of nonstop network servers ranging from tiny machines to giant computer centers like that of USAA. Many will be unmanned but will be able to indicate when preventive maintenance is needed. They will be fireproof, bombproof, burglarproof, earthquakeproof, and perhaps underground. Some of the biggest unmanned computer facilities are the telephone industry's switching centers. The Internet will have many millions of servers designed for nonstop operation. Some will be data warehouses; some Internet search engines. The public, even while asking for electronic commerce services and carrying out new Internet games, will usually be unaware of the massive bunkers of nonstop computer power that they are using, as awesome as the engine room of a battleship.

HIGHWAYS OF LIGHT

If the electronic jungle operated with the phone lines of today it would change the planet. But something much more dramatic is happening. The world is being wired with highways of light.

Until recently all telecommunications used electronics; it transmitted electrons. Now it can use light and transmit photons over optical fibers. Electrons travel much more slowly than photons, because they constantly bump into molecules like bumper cars at a fair. Photons travel at the speed of light.

Optical fibers make a difference in two ways. First, they allow a signal to go to the other side of the planet almost instantaneously. Second, optical fibers can transmit awesome quantities of bits. In ten-millionths of a second a thin hair of glass on the laboratory bench can transmit everything that Shakespeare wrote in his lifetime. To take advantage of this technology, scientists have enabled light to transmit end-to-end without converting into electrons, by replacing electronic amplifiers and multiplexors with optical amplifiers and multiplexors.

The electronic jungle with all of its Web sites and sensors will generate prodigious quantities of bits. But the inhabitants of the jungle will want to transmit not only these bits; they will also want to communicate with video. Fiber-optic technology enables the Internet to be fully integrated with digital large-screen television.

Imagine you are in a wonderful restaurant with old friends. The table setting and food are superb; the lighting is romantic. You choose the music. But there is a glass wall across the table. You can't hug the people on the other side of the glass, but you can communicate with them in most other ways. You are in Chicago and the people on the other half of the table are in Delhi. You have a great evening. We could build such restaurant booths today.

Computing has changed dramatically in the past few decades because the number of transistors on a chip has kept doubling relentlessly. It will change even more dramatically in the next few decades because the number of bits we will be able to transmit over fiber-optic highways will double every year or so.

THE FABRIC BECOMES INTELLIGENT

Cheap intelligent sensors will be integral to our world and will process what they sense in increasingly sophisticated ways. They may mimic the abilities of biological systems to learn from and adapt to their environment. Many machines will use intelligent sensors for specific purposes—for example, a robot lawn mower will sense where to cut the grass.

Most of today's microsensors are simple, like thermostats and motion detectors. In nature they are not simple. An insect eye processes the information it detects in complex ways and sends the results to the creature's brain. The chips hidden in our surroundings will progress from simple functions, like monitoring your heart rate, to complex functions, like monitoring the health of your heart. The economics of mass-producing chips are such that chips with simplistic functions cost almost the same as chips with alien intelligence. Increasingly the unnoticed sensors will have "brain" mechanisms in them to process the information they pick up. Nature's sensors send their signal a short distance; our sensors could send it to faraway computers or data warehouses.

> With microsystems of miniscule cost, computing can be built into every nook and cranny of society, much of it using alien intelligence.

Researchers who study nature's nervous systems are getting in bed with those who research electronic nervous systems. Designers of sensory systems are learning from neurobiologists who study nerve endings, eyes, neurons, synapses, and so on. In return, neurobiologists are gaining new insights from the experiments going on in the design of electronic sensors and "brain" mechanisms.

A CACOPHONY OF DATA

From the moment we're born our brain must learn to cope with the deluge of data assaulting our senses. Our eyes and ears learn to sift through the constant flood of data to produce representations of visible objects or words of a conversation.

Our senses continuously perform a heavy load of processing so that the information passed on to our conscious thought is miniscule compared to all the data that are sensed. Processing is done in the eye and in the ear before an encoded representation of the results is sent to a higher level. There the results from both eyes, and from both ears, are processed to extract stereo information.

Similarly in electronic systems, sensors need to sift through the flood of data and extract and pass on specialized information to higher-level computers. When the walls have eyes and ears, these do constant local processing so that predigested data are passed to high-level processors.

In electronic systems of the future, coordination between different senses will take place, where it is useful, before sensory information is relayed to the main computers. Silicon eyes sensitive to motion, as in the eye of a fish, will recognize a moving object directly without any computerized image processing. The information that is passed on to higher-level computers will be small compared to the data that are sensed.

THE HUMBLE FLEA

The humblest flea has much better senses than today's machines. This seems a little embarrassing. Furthermore, the flea learns about its environment and makes sense of it in a way that today's supercomputers cannot. While we might accept that we haven't made machines intelligent as humans are, it's sobering to reflect that nature's most wretched creatures outperform our machines.

Our body has many levels of real-time information processing between the input to our senses and the high-level thought processes of which we are consciously aware. Conscious thought is just the tip of a neural iceberg. Some of these levels are prewired at birth, but many others are learned from what we experience, especially in the first months of life. The term *neuromorphic* is used for electronic systems that have senses and adapt to their environment like living creatures. Caltech's Center for Neuromorphic Systems Engineering (CNSE) has set itself the goal of creating such systems.

Many smart sensors will need to learn from their environment and adapt to it. To achieve this they will incorporate neural networks like the eyes and ears of creatures. CNSE and many other research centers are experimenting with prototypes of neural networks for automatic learning.

Microsystems that *learn* will become an essential part of our environment. Their sensors will pass selected information to a midbrain (such as a security control panel); the midbrain will transmit it to higher-level computers (including data warehouses). As in our nervous system, there may be multiple layers of lower-level processing. The higher levels will also *learn*. We have an advantage over nature—the nervous system we can build is not confined to one creature or plant; it can span an entire city or virtual community.

SILICON EARS

Most computers respond to sound by using a microphone, digitizing its output, and processing the digital bits. This is crude and inefficient; it makes it extremely difficult to isolate separate sounds and identify their location. Silicon ears of the future will be much more like biological ears. Like our eyes, they will do substantial processing before they transmit information to higher-level computers. Our ear is a most intricate instrument.

Our ears and auditory systems evolved when we could grunt but not speak. The processing that takes place in our auditory system is intended to identify sounds and detect their location. Speech recognition came much later and uses a higher level of processing in the brain.

We can detect the location of sounds both in the horizontal and vertical planes. The primary way we locate sounds horizontally is the stereo effect of having slight differences in time between the sounds reaching our two ears. There is an average time delay of about 700 microseconds between a sound reaching the left ear and the right ear. Another way for us to locate sounds horizontally comes from the fact that the ear aimed toward a sound gets more high frequencies than the ear facing away from the sound. This is called the head-shadow cue.

Localization of sound on the vertical plane is less sensitive. It depends on there being a difference in time between sound going directly to the ear drum and sound that deflects off the lobes of the outer ear. This time difference averages about 70 microseconds. It depends upon the vertical angle from which the sound comes. When a horse sticks his ears up, he can locate sounds better.

Silicon ears do not have to be eight inches apart, as on our head. They could be on opposite sides of a building or a bus.

Our ears receive *sound* waves but feed *electrical* impulses to our brain. The conversion takes place in the *cochlea*, a small spiral structure that is filled with incompressible fluid. Pressure waves propagate down it like signals propagating down an electronic delay line. The fluid in the spiral is held by a membrane, and a large number of hair cells, called *cilia*, sense the rate at which this membrane vibrates. The tips of the cilia may move by an amount as tiny as a tenth of a nanometer (a millionth of the diameter of a hair on our head). If these hairs are ever dislodged by loud noises—in discos or with very loud machinery, for instance—they do not grow back. As the cilia move, they change the firing rate of neural cells to which they are attached. The neural cells send signals up the auditory nerve to the brain. To create chips that emulate functions of the ear, Carver Mead built an electronic version of the cochlea, designed to model the signal-processing capabilities of the human ear.

The processing done by the human auditory system is ideal as a front end to speech recognition. It helps separate the speech from the noise. When walls have ears, microsystems will process the sounds detected, much like the human ear, before passing the results to a higher-level computer. They could be programmed to detect the voice of the house owner, detect an intruder, or detect when certain key words are spoken. An intelligent cat-flap in a door could learn to detect the meow of the owner's cat and let it in, but not let in stray cats.

SILICON EYES

Many of today's systems have sensors that are clumsy and inefficient. A robot in science fiction films often has two eyes like video cameras on the front of its head. A bank or airport has little video cameras constantly observing. To enable machines to "see," the images from small video cameras are converted to a bit map, frame-by-frame, and processed. This is crude and expensive. Processing the image of a video camera is very complex, and requires massive computer power. Software is needed that can discover the boundaries of objects and their movements by correlating points among the images. Our eye does none of this, but instead senses the motion of objects directly by handling light variations as a continuous analog stream.

Much processing is done in our eye. Our retina uses an array of neurons lining the back of the eye to extract features from what the eye sees. It condenses a vast amount of raw data into information that it sends to higher levels of the brain.

Chips are now being built that work like the eye. They continuously register the rate at which the intensity of light changes, so that the motion of objects can be sensed. Such chips do not respond to absolute light intensities, but to ratios of light intensities. They have an array of photosensitive receptors each with its own processing elements. There is feedback to each photodetector so that that detector can sense motion. By replicating that simple circuit over the surface of the chip, an exceedingly small sensor can detect the movement of images. A second level of processing feeds information from one photodetector to its close neighbors. This enables the speed of motion to be detected. When the eye moves it can distinguish foreground objects from background objects. To carry out these functions with a dumb sensor like a video camera would require a supercomputer to do the processing. Instead we need cheap mass-produced chips with specialized intelligence.

Data can be represented in an *analog* or *digital* fashion. "Analog" refers to a continuously variable scale of values like an old-fashioned thermometer; "digital" refers to a discrete set of digits like those on the thermometers at the top of buildings. Our senses are analog, whereas today's computers represent data digitally, often with eight-bit bytes. It is being discovered that we can imitate nature better if we build sensors that are analog rather than digital.

The buzzing confusion of data that constantly assaults our senses would swamp any known digital system. There would be no time to swap the data out to disk. In each of our eyes the retina has a hundred million photocells and one million ganglion cells. Each ganglion cell uses the equivalent of a thousand instructions per second—the eye's ganglion cells together have the power of a large supercomputer.

As in nature, special-purpose systems are needed for specific sensory tasks. Today's digital computers are highly *generalized*. To create senses like those in nature, *specialized* devices are needed. Ubiquitous computing will often use tiny, mass-produced analog sensors as dedicated to a single purpose as the sensors that open automatic doors.

The vast number of sensors used by ubiquitous computing will need to operate with extremely low power. Biological nervous systems are a *billion* times more energy efficient than today's digital systems. By using analog chips, CNSE has built sensors thousands of times more energy efficient than equivalent digital systems. The computation that goes on in our ear is equivalent to 200 million floating-point operations per second. To do this digitally requires three digital microprocessors using about 90 watts of power. Our ear has been emulated on an analog chip with just 1 milliwatt of power.

DETECTING EMOTIONS

One intriguing use of this technology is software (or chips) that can recognize human emotions.

Microsystems can be designed to read our emotions by examining the parts of our face that are in motion. Raising eyebrows indicate surprise; a wrinkling brow indicates annoyance; stretching the mouth muscles indicates a smile. A computer program has demonstrated that it can identify human emotions correctly 98 percent of the time by examining only the parts of the face that are in motion.[3] Emotions have also been identified in other ways, such as by analyzing voice sounds.

A car could detect road rage in its driver. A PC could detect its user's frustration. A thermostat may not react to room temperature but to its owner's feeling of chill. Sensors in the walls and doorways will detect our presence and possibly anticipate our wishes. An electronic Jeeves would not hover around like an English butler but would be built into the walls, constantly aware of whether we are placid or frustrated or in need of something.

A key to success in electronic commerce will be the ability to detect customer reactions and respond to them. Electronic marketing will increasingly be concerned with learning about each individual and marketing to that individual. Marketing campaigns will be designed to present different messages to different people. Detecting emotions, even if done in crude ways, offers intriguing possibilities. In the future when you watch your TV, your TV will watch you. Advertisements will be designed so that they can be adapted to the reactions of the recipient. There may be many variants of each advertisement, and the appropriate one is selected for the viewer in question.

Hollywood.com enables you to find out what movies are playing within driving distance of where you live. You can read reviews or watch the trailer of any movie that is playing. For most movies there are multiple trailers. The trailer that plays in Manhattan is different from that in West Virginia. The trailer in a ski resort in Vermont might be different from that in the boondocks ten miles away. Even so, an elderly academic is often shown a trailer designed for screaming teenagers. If your PC has an electronic eye, it might register your reaction to trailers and send this in a brief signal to the studio's marketing computer. The marketing computer can then build up its knowledge of your tastes, just as Amazon.com knows the book-reading tastes of its individual customers. As the computer learns about you, it will guide you to those movies you would like and show you a version of the trailer specially selected to persuade you to go to the movie.

> In the future when you watch your TV, your TV will watch you. Advertisements will be designed so that they can be adapted to the reactions of the recipient.

If we have multiple versions of the trailer we can also have multiple versions of the movie. In digital movie theaters the movie will be transmitted to the theater. Theater chains may be encouraged to use equipment that watches or listens to the audience, and, without the audience knowing, records their emotions. Films may be reedited in response to the emotions of different audiences. In the

Gus Van Sant's shot-for-shot remake of Alfred Hitchcock's *Psycho* some audiences laughed at the buildup to the famous shower scene. *No one* laughed at Hitchcock's original. Electronic audience monitoring will lead to the playing of different versions in different theaters, perhaps even with different endings in some films. Films are now being shot for multiple edits so that the degree of violence, sex, and swearing can be adapted to different markets.

"Emotional engineering" of sensory chips will be an increasingly important commercial tool.

NEURAL NOSES

Chips have been built with a sense of smell; chemicals on the chip surface detect odors. A device called a *neural nose* also uses a neural network on the chip to help identify odors. Such devices can be autonomous and perform in real time.

A dog's nose is a million times more sensitive than a human nose. We can make neural noses that are also much more sensitive than human noses. Electronic noses may become a major aid to medical diagnosis. One neural nose used experimentally in Britain has already detected the onset of lung cancer from the smell of a patient's breath. A variety of devices can detect proteins emitted by precancerous tissues. If cancer is detected when it affects only a small number of cells, it can be cured; if it grows to the size of a tennis ball before it is detected, it will probably kill you.

The smart home of the future will check your health in many ways, with intelligent toilets, neural noses, stress detectors, heart monitors, and refrigerators that know how many cookies you eat. Such devices may transmit to your PC, which can give you health advice, or may send data about you to your doctor's computer, which accumulates the data and employs sophisticated computing to detect potential problems.

Chips with a sense of smell have important security applications—such as detecting explosives at airports. They could detect when a driver has been drinking or taking drugs. They can help enforce nonsmoking rules. Like the sniffer dogs used by customs authorities, they will be able to detect narcotics or biological substances that customs authorities want to keep out. They will be useful for inspecting food, for emission control, and for environmental protection.

The unseen electronic ecosystem will not only see and hear us; it will also smell us.

ALIEN SENSES

Even though we will have numerous devices with eyes and ears, that doesn't mean that the systems we build with them will be much like the creatures of nature. We can build things that don't exist in nature—intelligent buildings, remote-controlled weapons systems, air traffic control systems that allow higher plane densities, global surveillance systems, or medical monitoring systems that indicate that a faraway patient is likely to have a stroke and tell him to take his antistroke pill.

The ubiquitous microsystems of the future will often use noncreature-like senses—radar, sonar, CAT scanners, microscopic motion detectors, barometers, and nuclear particle beams that penetrate rock and buildings, GPS sensors that know their exact geographic position, microwaves, X rays, ultraviolet light... the entire electromagnetic spectrum.

> We will have alien intelligence with alien senses.

Senses different from nature may become more important than the senses of nature. But we have much to learn from nature in order to make these alien senses as effective as possible. As well as using fundamentally different types of sensors, artificial systems can transmit at the speed of light—a hundred million times the speed of our nervous system. A major difference between artificial systems and nature's systems will be the use of telecommunications. Artificial systems can have sensors on the other side of the planet.

Noncreature-like senses will use noncreature-like processing. Computing is lightning fast compared to nature and can use processes that are completely alien to nature. We will have alien intelligence with alien senses.

MACHINES SMALLER THAN ANTS

Chips are generally thought of as just manipulating bits, but some chips can do *physical* things.

Camcorders now have a chip that senses motion. Your hand shakes when holding a camcorder, but camcorders today can adjust the image electronically to compensate for the camera shake. A similar motion-detecting chip could be used in a bank pen to record the dynamic motion of the pen when signing a document. Forgers can copy a signature, but no forger can forge the dynamic motion of the pen when writing the signature.

The micromachine industry is building a vast array of motion detectors, vibration analyzers, pressure and temperature sensors, tiny devices for recording flow of liquids or gases, chemical vapor sensors, and moisture sensors. Tiny machines have been built with springs, levers, cams, and other mechanisms. These microdevices can be built to transmit data by radio.

Electric motors, one-tenth the diameter of a human hair, have run continuously for more than a year at 15,000 revolutions per minute. They have been powered by static electricity and by chemicals between electrodes. They have even been powered by blood sugar. Experiments have been done injecting microdevices into the bloodstream and putting them in pills for various medical purposes.

Tiny machines need tiny ball bearings. A spherical carbon molecule has been created. Named after Buckminster Fuller, they are called "Bucky balls," not because of his sex life, but because they have a lattice structure of hexagonal rings somewhat like the domes he built.

Microdevices are important in surgery. An optical fiber with tiny lenses can be inserted into the patient. The surgeon sees images on a large screen and may operate microdevices to crush a kidney stone or remove cancerous tissue. The surgeon may be far away from the operating room, linked across continents by fiber optics.

The Swiss Federal Institute of Technology has emphasized "nanorobots" that manipulate microparts with accuracy better than 10 nanometers. They are used for creating watch components and ultrafine jewelry, and for manipulating tiny flasks of substances in molecular biology work.

Micromachines and microsystems fit together well, and sometimes are on the same chip. A micromachine often needs electronic sensing and transmission capabilities. A microsensor might need to operate relays. Fabrication methods are improving for integrating micromachine actuators and sensors. Micromachines will use alien intelligence in diverse ways.

GLOBAL BRAIN

The cerebral cortex of your brain is heavily wrinkled and folded so that it fits neatly inside your skull. If stretched flat, it would be about a meter across. The signals in it travel over the nerve fibers—axons—at a relatively slow speed. Signals on a fiber-optic cable travel forty million times faster than signals on the brain's axons. Therefore, if your brain operated with fiber optics, it could be forty thousand kilometers across—the distance that signals travel when they go around the earth. A fiber-optic version of your brain could nearly cover the surface of the earth.

This coincidence of numbers conjures up science fiction–like images of the earth being wired like a giant brain. As the earth becomes increasingly wired, its interlinked computers will have a quantity of processing power enormously greater than that of your brain—eventually billions of times greater—and will have access to vastly more information than that in your brain.

When I describe this as a "coincidence of numbers," my friends say it does not sound like a coincidence. Some say it sounds like God's deliberate design. Others say our brain is nature's optimum size for creatures using a nervous system like ours, and the planet is the optimum size for brainlike behavior with a fiber-optic nervous system.

THE OPTIMUM SIZE FOR A PLANET

What is the fastest reaction time humans need from a computer?

This question was much debated in the 1970s when the early airline reservation systems and bank-teller systems were being designed, because it was expensive to engineer long-distance networks with very fast response times.

Behavioral psychologists experimented with the human effects of different response times. Airline agents, bank tellers, and their ilk, carrying on a fairly straightforward dialogue with a distant computer, needed a response in two or three seconds. But psychologists found that people doing creative or thought-intensive work at a computer needed response times of less than a second. Graphs showed the efficiency of work as response times varied, and the curves swung up to much higher efficiencies when response times were a third of a second.

Then the world began to get arcade games with computer users driving fast cars or flying jets on the screen. It became apparent that the game players needed *instant* reaction from the computer. So did fighter pilots in real jets. If you are in an aerial dogfight at twice the speed of sound and looking at your heads-up display, you want computers that respond *instantly*. The same is true in a growing diversity of virtual reality applications.

"Instantaneous" to the human operator means about 70 milliseconds. It takes 70 milliseconds for signals to get from your eyes to the appropriate part of your brain. Psychologists' experiments have demonstrated that our brain can't react to responses faster than that. This is referred to as a *twitch* reaction time.

So, suppose we asked: What would be the optimum size for our planet? We would like an instant (70 millisecond) transmission time to any location on the planet. The area reachable in 70 milliseconds has been referred to as the *twitch zone*. Electronic systems whose signals travel at 10,000 kilometers per second can cover a distance of 700 kilometers in 70 milliseconds. Because of its size, Britain could be a twitch zone; the United States could not.

> Can your corporation become a master of this new world, or are its embedded culture and its old-fashioned business model too difficult to convert?

A dramatic change occurred when fiber optics came into use, and signals were sent in the form of light rather than with the much slower electronic propagation. The speed of light is 300,000 kilometers per second, so a light signal travels 21,000 kilometers in 70 milliseconds. The circumference of the earth is 40,000 kilometers, so a signal can travel to the farthest part of the earth (half its circumference), by a slightly indirect route, in 70 milliseconds.

If we ask what size a planet must be to give the maximum living space with *twitch* reaction times, we must conclude that it would be the size of the planet Earth. No signal can travel faster than light. If the planet were larger than the Earth, *twitch* reaction times could not be worldwide.

It appears as though God made our planet the optimum size for cyberspace!

IMPLICATIONS

So here we are, sitting on a planet that is being wired for transmission of data at the speed of light. The Internet will be ubiquitous with intelligent sensors everywhere. A huge number of devices everywhere will be connected to the Internet, many of them connected by radio—the chips in the ceiling, the gadgets we carry, our televisions, the chips in our clothes, the chips in Federal Express packages, even chips clipped to the ears of cows.

As narrowly focused forms of machine intelligence race ahead of human intelligence, new forms of commerce will rage across the planet. They will pay for and take advantage of the new global fabric of computing.

We have an explosive mixture: cyberspace becoming ubiquitous and high bandwidth, e-business accounting for trillions of dollars a year, entrepreneurs everywhere struggling to invent the next fortune, and fast growth of a new type of computerized intelligence. A vital question for managers in traditional corporations is: Can your corporation become a master of this new world, or are its embedded culture and its old-fashioned business model too difficult to convert? Particularly important: Can you convert *fast enough*?

Many people express discomfort when I describe the world of ubiquitous chips—the walls have eyes and ears; alien senses are connected to alien intelligence; the chips are radio-linked to the global Web. I think that we will settle into such a world and accept it just as we accept living in a place like New York. What gives me more discomfort is that the rate of change will become so fast. Evolution has changed from nature's speed to civilization's speed, and now to Internet speed. Soon we'll have self-evolving technology linked to the fiber-optic network. We will reach a time when digital technology will evolve of its own accord with little need for human intervention. The amount of change that happened in nature in billions of years may happen in computer laboratories in months. We will barely have time to learn a job before it becomes obsolete.

How do we handle such a pace? How do you bring up your children to cope in such a world?

How will the relationship between humans and machines evolve as machines acquire their own advanced forms of nonhumanlike intelligence and improve it at an exponentially growing rate?

Even for the immediate future the answers to that are interesting and surprising. This is what we explore in the next section of the book.

PART II
Impact

CHAPTER 6
Winner Takes Most

Some years ago Bill Gates sat on the porch of my house in Bermuda, overlooking a private cove with a beach. He didn't seem to notice—or want to notice—the beach. Gates flew in economy class. He wore scruffy, cheap clothes. On the immigration form he described his occupation as "Programmer." He didn't want to go to a good restaurant. You have to eat, he said; it's a basic bodily function so let's get it over with as quickly as possible—like going to the men's room. He didn't want to spend money. But he was enjoying life. He sat up long into the night, excited like a child, nibbling junk food, his conversation endlessly fascinating.

Gates said he thought the old world was turning upside down. The law of diminishing returns didn't necessarily apply any more.

The law of diminishing returns is a mainstay of traditional economic theory. Companies that get ahead in a market, the theory says, eventually run into limitations that cause expansion to slow down. As size increases, limitations to growth increase. There are a limited number of customers who will ever prefer your product. As sales increase, the market becomes saturated. Access to raw materials might become more difficult. Paperwork and overheads increase. As a publisher expands, he goes from the cream of potential authors to progressively less appealing authors. Doubling the amount of fertilizer on a field doesn't double the crop yield. In growing a farming operation, a farmer has to expand onto less fertile land and so runs into limits.

Traditional economists describe diminishing returns as a natural law of economics that leads to stability. It leads to an acceptable level of pricing. Increased costs lead to lower profits. As prices and production reach equilibrium, competition levels out so that no one firm can make a killing.

In smokestack industries the law of diminishing returns continues to apply. But the cyberspace economy plays by different rules. In industries dominated by knowledge technologies, corporations that are ahead tend to get further ahead; corporations that are behind tend to slip further behind. Instead of success leading to diminishing returns, there is reinforcement of success, leading to increasing returns. Absence of success is also reinforced. A loser's reputation spreads, making it more difficult to succeed. The chain reactions caused by knowledge technologies enhance the chances of winners and make life more difficult for losers. Instead of *negative feedback* leading to stability, there is *positive feedback* leading to instability.

CHANGING THE RULES

Microsoft is ahead—far ahead—in the sale of operating systems. Because of its massive user base it can spend more money than its competition on enhancements or other software that links to its operating system. Thousands of software companies create software designed to work with Microsoft, and if, as a customer, you receive documents, spreadsheets, video, or graphic presentations, you want them to work easily with Microsoft Office. Success causes further success.

Positive feedback is a self-reinforcing cycle that can threaten to drive even apparently successful competitors to the wall. Netscape created the first Internet browser software and grew furiously. It went public when the company was only sixteen months old, with a valuation of $2 billion. Jim Clark, its cofounder, a former Stanford University professor, had shares worth $565 million at the end of the first day's trading. A few months later the market valuation of Netscape had tripled. But Microsoft saw Netscape cutting into its potential growth and launched an all-out battle to beat Netscape in a winner-takes-most game. (It could have done this without violating antitrust laws.)

In publishing, most books lose money, and the industry's profits come from its tiny minority of best-sellers. Except with established authors, it is very difficult to forecast what will become a best-seller. So computers constantly monitor the sales of each book. If a book begins to sell, it is given more shelf space and visibility. If it rises further, posters go up in the shops; money is spent on advertising and press coverage; efforts are made to get its author on talk shows.

Best-selling authors can make a fortune; most authors make peanuts. It's a winner-takes-most game. Much electronic commerce will follow a similar pattern. Confronted with the deluge of confusing data on the Internet, most electronic shoppers will go to brand names they know. Often they will make a favorite brand name an icon on their PC opening screen so that they can go to it with one mouse click. Making a brand name well known and building its reputation will be critical. The winning brands, like best-selling books, will capture most of the business.

A business question of growing importance will be: "In a winner-takes-most world, how do you become a winner?"

Knowledge technologies change the feedback loops in business. They often make events happen much faster. They link together events over large distances and in separate corporations. An event in one corporation can trigger an event in a different corporation at electronic speed. The company that plays it right is the company everyone flocks to.

> In a winner-takes-most world, how do you become a winner?

Through the 1970s almost no corporations grew to $100 million in revenue in their first ten years. In the 1980s the fastest growing corporations grew to a billion dollars in revenue in a decade. In the early 1990s McCaw Cellular Communications sold for $12.6 billion six years after start-up. In the late 1990s multiple internet companies reached market capitalizations of many billions of dollars two years after start-up. The masters of the electronic jungle become overnight billionaires.

A NEW TYPE OF LEADER

Bill Gates is the opposite of the IBM executives I worked with for a long time. IBM believed that general management ability was the key corporate talent. If you could manage a brewery, you could manage a software factory. Traditional leadership wisdom tells us that the best corporate leaders are generalists who hire experts and learn how to judge what they say.

Once, hours after midnight, Gates confessed to me that he had never wanted to be that kind of manager. You can hire those, he said. The best ones queue up to join Microsoft. Gates is something you couldn't hire. He is the computer industry's greatest guru. He knows everything important that is going on. He synthesizes everything in his head. He knows the tactics and strategies of all his competitors. He is the ultimate expert.

The quiet-spoken Gates looked anything but tough. He had a nervous habit of rocking back and forth in his chair endlessly as he talked. I remember looking at this rocking, nerdy, amiable, cheaply dressed, uncharismatic figure and reflecting how the power structure of the world was changing. This college drop-out had made himself richer than the oil sheiks, richer than history's warrior kings, and far richer than the head of IBM or General Motors. And this was only the beginning.

When India and Pakistan caused a furor by testing nuclear bombs, *Newsweek* reproduced a cartoon showing an aide saying to President Clinton, "More bad news, Mr. President—Bill Gates has the bomb."

INTEL: DOMINANCE THROUGH DESIGN

In the 1990s Intel has been one of the world's most profitable corporations. However, not long before, in 1986, it was heading for bankruptcy. Intel had been the preeminent memory chip manufacturer. It was said: "Memory chips are Intel; Intel is memory chips." The U.S. memory chip business had been very profitable, but in the early 1970s Japan's Ministry of International Trade and Industry (MITI) decided that Japan should dominate the chip business. By the early 1980s MITI's massively funded program started to succeed, and aggressive competition against Intel from Japan and South Korea made memory chip prices collapse.

Struggling to survive, Intel devised its brilliant "*Intel inside*" strategy and set out to dominate the processor chip at the heart of the personal computer. It evolved the 286 processor chip into the 386, 486, Pentium, and then Pentium Pro chips. In a brilliant campaign of managing relationships, Intel succeeded in getting their branding mark "*Intel inside*" on both personal computer advertisements and the machines themselves.

A memory chip has a simple structure that is easy to replicate, but the structure of advanced processor chips is exceedingly difficult to design and to copy. Intel spent a fortune on chip design and innovation to keep ahead of would-be clone-makers.

Once Intel dominated PC processor chips it was in a winner-takes-most position. It established a dominant position in a vast business ecosystem of hardware and software vendors and service firms, enabling some of these to establish profitable niches. It had to make sure that it used enough money and talent to keep ahead of would-be competition. Intel constantly redesigned its chips to make them faster than Intel clone-makers, and drove its prices down as production volume soared. In a gutsy roll of the dice it spent over a quarter of its revenue on design and fabrication facilities, a huge expenditure that enabled the company to maintain its controlling position in the PC industry.

The other independent memory chip manufacturers, Mostek, Unisem, and Advanced Memory Systems, all went out of business.

BOEING'S 777: DOMINANCE THROUGH CROSS-ENTERPRISE COOPERATION

When Boeing planned the 777 jetliner it drastically reinvented the process of designing and building aircraft. The 777 was one of the most complex machines ever built. Over four million parts from many hundreds of suppliers worldwide had to fit and work together with tight, electronic precision.

The 777 was the first commercial airliner to be designed and put into production by using three-dimensional design software rather than paper drawings. Boeing needed many partners, all of whom had to share Boeing's unique Computer-Aided Design (CAD) software. It was an extraordinary example of corporate cooperation. A global data network was established over which the partners could interchange designs. Every major part of the plane was modeled with the CAD software. These components were "assembled" in the software before they were built physically. Three-dimensional modeling enabled many design changes. Designers and potential customers could "walk through" the plane in virtual reality, check every aspect of it, and request modifications.

Because everybody used the same CAD software this gave Boeing more freedom in building an alliance of designers and manufacturers. Boeing scoured the world for the best capability. Many designs were done concurrently in different organizations, and the software ensured that they would work together. There were many *cross-enterprise teams* linking suppliers, consultants, and potential customers. By the time the components were ready to assemble *physically,* they had already been assembled in the software, and potential problems had been worked out. The software facilitated better design and greatly reduced the time and cost of development. Amazingly, the time from concept to customer delivery was three years, whereas with previous planes it had been more than six years.

Like Intel, Boeing used a level of computerized know-how in designing a complex product that no other airliner manufacturer could come close to. Its chief competitor McDonnell-Douglas, makers of the DC-10, gave up and merged with Boeing. There is no other manufacturer of jetliners in the United States. Boeing had achieved a spectacular winner-takes-most position. In Europe, Airbus used technology in a different way to achieve a dominant position. It focused on spectacular automation in manufacturing and achieved even higher profits than Boeing.

FAST DOMINANCE

When there is a positive feedback cycle of self-reinforcing success it's important to establish a winning position quickly. Amazon.com and many other dot-com companies set out to grow as large as possible as fast as possible, to achieve market dominance. They abandoned any thought of making a profit but achieved extraordinary valuations on the stock market. This has led some corporations to think in terms of what they can "give away" to achieve market dominance.

America Online built up a market lead by giving away free services. Sun Microsystems created JAVA, a new programming language that could become a language common to almost all Internet computers. Sun gave it away free, with massive publicity. It swept through the Internet community, quickly establishing itself as a de facto standard that other vendors had to support. Netscape gave away its Mosaic "browser" and for a brief period became the fastest growing start-up in history.

> The winner is not necessarily the company with the best product. It is the company with the best strategy.

Dominance in one market segment may be used to achieve fast growth in a different segment. Microsoft has used its massive user base in operating systems to sell other software that can be coupled to its operating system. It hoped to achieve dominance in Internet facilities by coupling them to Windows 98 and was charged with antitrust violations for pushing this strategy too far. It did not back off when challenged because it recognized, cynically, that the court case would be ponderously slow and by the time it reached its conclusion, Microsoft would have a major competitive advantage. Antitrust laws formulated in an earlier, simpler, age cannot cope sensibly with the issues raised by the global chain reactions of the e-jungle.

In a winner-takes-most world, the winner is not necessarily the company with the best product. It is the company with the best strategy.

VHS beat Betamax as a videotape format, and Betamax eventually disappeared. But Betamax was by far the superior product. In the early 1980s competition for personal-computer operating systems was between CP/M, DOS, UNIX, and Apple's Macintosh. Of these the Macintosh was much the most elegant and easy to use. DOS was crude, but it was owned by a master strategist, Bill Gates.

Bill Gates's start-up company, which was then tiny, had bought an operating system called QDOS (Quick and Dirty Operating System) for a mere $70,000. He quickly changed its name to DOS, and locked up a deal to supply it to IBM for their PC. DOS was a clunker, but it had IBM's customer base behind it, allowing Microsoft to spread its costs over a vast number of copies. Microsoft steadily made it difficult for those customers to switch.

METCALFE'S LAW

A telephone network with only one phone is of no value because there is nobody to call. With two phones it has some value. If it interconnects everyone in a corporation, it starts to be really useful. When it connects most people in society, it fundamentally changes society.

Bob Metcalfe, who invented the technology that became the basis of most local area networks, made a statement known as Metcalfe's Law: *The value of a network is roughly proportional to the square of the number of its users.* Metcalfe made this statement because the number of connections possible among N users is $N(N-1)/2$, approximately the square of the number of users. Not everybody will talk to everybody else, but size adds value in another way: When there are many users, high-capacity trunks are needed to carry the traffic. With high-capacity trunks each user can transmit a higher bit rate. The Internet evolved from being a typewriter-speed network to a network that can handle graphics, then voice, and then crude video. It will eventually evolve into a network that handles high-definition digital television.

Metcalfe's Law expresses the view that if the Internet doubles in size, it quadruples in value. It has roughly doubled in size *every year* for the past decade. Today's Internet connects a thousand times as many computers as the Internet ten years ago, and so in Metcalfe's estimate it is a million times more valuable.

The broad philosophy of Metcalfe's Law applies to Internet business. The more customers your Web site can link to, the more its potential value grows. The more the anticipated value grows, the greater the market cap. If the market cap is high (even if it's outrageous), there is more to spend on product improvement and business intelligence. In a business-to-business exchange, the greater the number of sellers registered the more it attracts buyers, and the greater the number of buyers registered the more it attracts sellers. The rough equivalent of Metcalfe's Law applies. The more users a Web site has, the greater the money that can be spent on getting more users. The value of a computer system increases with each service it provides. You may have difficulty setting up the first service; the second comes easier. The greater the number of customers, the greater the budget for expanding the number of services.

Rather than having diminishing returns, technology feeds on itself, making it possible to build better technology. There is a positive feedback loop of spiraling improvement.

VERY FAST GROWTH

In 1992 the United States owned the cellular phone business. It had pioneered the technology and spent a fortune on research.

But, suddenly, a Finnish company called Nokia that had made forest products for 130 years decided to make cellular phones. American executives laughed at the very idea.

Nokia was in deep financial trouble, and it had a new, untested chief executive in thirty-eight-year-old Jorma Ollila. Ollila decided to build his mobile phone division like a virtual company. He out-sourced much of the design, chip production, component produc-tion, and sales.

Nokia advertised its small phone as "the world's most portable phone." It swept the world. Nokia quickly became the number one company in digital cellular phones. In 1993, after only two years, Nokia's digital cellular operation had revenues of $2.25 bil-lion and a 20 percent profit on its phone manufacturing.[1] Almost overnight, the forest products company became the world's twelfth largest telecommunications manufacturer.

Ericsson was just across the water from Nokia, in Stockholm. Amazingly, Ericsson's board had passed a resolution that the company would not go into the cellular phone business. Seeing Nokia's success, the board reversed that decision. Nokia and Ericsson set out to estab-lish a global standard, GSM (Global Standard for Mobile telephony). With that standard, their pocket phones could be carried worldwide. Their phones worked in the remotest parts of China. But their phones didn't work in the United States (except for a few cities). Nevertheless, like Microsoft, the two Scandinavian cellular phone makers set out to own the standard and saturate the market.

Nokia demonstrated that when technology makes possible a new winner-takes-most game, speed is much more important than size. By creating a virtual operation, a small player can move with lightning speed. It can grow or change direction very fast com-pared to an old corporation with fixed assets, permanent employ-ees, and an embedded culture.

A corporation may try to sustain high margins by making itself unique. It may be unique because of special skills or art, as with a fashion designer, top architect, or movie director, or because of the way it looks after its customers. It may be unique because of an unbeatable mix of competencies. Sometimes patents protect uniqueness, as in the pharmaceutical industry, but increasingly uniqueness comes from creating a special role in a corporate ecosystem.

In a winner-takes-most world, industries with many small players will tend to coalesce until there are a small number of global giants. The world telecommunications industry is struggling to evolve from national carriers to global carriers, and from circuit-switched telephone technology to a technology that integrates voice, video, and the Internet. It will become dominated by a handful of worldwide giants with massive fiber-optic highways vying to become the winner in a world where future Internet generations fuse with digital television. A similar dynamic is happening in banking, insurance, computing, pharmaceuticals, entertainment, and aerospace. It will happen in other industries because they are evolving into a game dominated by knowledge technology.

THE NEXT INSANELY GREAT IDEA

New ideas sweep through the electronic jungle like a forest fire, with new runaway businesses coming from unexpected sources. Two people in a garage created Apple. Steve Jobs talks about the search for the next "insanely great idea."

The next insanely great idea often comes from a small company that thinks differently. Packet switching technology represents the future of telecommunications, but it did not come from the giant telecommunications industry; it came from university professors and small-time entrepreneurs. WebTV did not come from the TV industry. The personal computer didn't originate in IBM or Digital.

In London, a small company, WIN (Worldwide Insurance Network), set out to change the insurance industry radically by creating a computer network that would enable insurance brokers to interchange deals. It strove to gain fast and widespread industry support by creating partnerships with four large insurance brokers selected because they were similar in culture and goals. It outsourced its application and technology development and had British Telecom do its network management. Because of these relationships WIN could operate as a global company with only thirty employees. WIN invented the game but let other people do the work.

John Sortino was an eccentric character who sold teddy bears from a street cart in Vermont. Nothing could have been further from the high-tech world. But Sortino invented "Bear-grams."

> In many industries there will be a battle between traditional companies and companies that master the technologies that enable them to "skim the cream."

The public could dial an 800 number on Mother's Day, or any other day, and send a greeting message that had a teddy bear packaged with it. Sales suddenly soared. A computerized system was set up to market directly to the people who had sent Bear-grams, most of whom had never seen the bears. Sortino established a Web page that explained why big folks needed teddy bears. The computer indicated that the things the bears customers wanted were quite different from what Sortino expected. He changed his design accordingly and set up a large bear factory. The Vermont Teddy Bear Company went public and had a frenzied first day of trading.

When a small corporation is in an exploding winner-takes-most market, it may not be able to grow fast enough with its own resources. Virtual operations can allow the corporation to keep up by using resources in other organizations. A virtual company is often one with exceptional ideas or an exceptional understanding of what is happening, but it can use other people's money and effort.

Knowledge technologies make it possible for nimble newcomers to erode the old power structure. The giant telephone companies were challenged by new kids on the block brimming with new ideas. Doug Terman, a thriller writer in a Vermont cottage, operates a basement full of electronics allowing foreign subscribers to make cheap international calls.

Some knowledge-based corporations are constantly seeking the next product or service to which a winner-takes-most dynamic could apply—the next Web fad, a chip that can detect gene sequences, the Viagra pill, third-generation cellular technology, a computerized process for designing state-of-the-art products, the next pocket electronics device, casinos on the Internet, an alien-intelligence system that generates brilliant sales leads. To be well positioned to find a winner, you have to have a thorough understanding of new directions in the technology. The key often lies in a technology most people are not as yet aware of.

RUINOUSLY INTENSE COMPETITION

When there were four gas stations at the same crossroads, they used to have price wars. They drove each other's prices down but served only a limited number of customers. Sooner or later some of the gas stations went out of business; sometimes *all but one* went out of business. Cyberspace will tend to put global competitors on the same virtual crossroads. It will often create ruinously aggressive price wars, in which nobody can make an acceptable profit.

In the world of cyberspace certain types of competition will become ruinously intense. For example, if you are buying Solti's last recording of Beethoven's Ninth, you might use a software "agent" that searches the Internet to find the lowest price for that disk. When people who buy goods use computers to search for the lowest price, vendors' profit margins will be cut to the bone. Often the lowest price will be from cheap-labor countries.

In the early 1990s U.S. airlines went through a period of intense competition triggered by deregulation and electronic booking systems, and they piled up losses of $13 billion—equal approximately to all the profits in the history of American aviation. "Open skies" policies for international airlines, combined with electronic booking, will be a disaster for many taxpayer-supported national carriers.

Many high-margin products are being reinvented as commodity products. The computer business, for example, evolved quickly from very-high-margin mainframes to cutthroat competition in PCs. Customers wanted open systems with plug-in components. I used to pay $400 for eyeglasses (which I lose regularly), but now I pay $10 at Walgreen and find them more than satisfactory. Commodity products can be easily copied. Copycat products are made in vast quantities in cheap-labor countries, and such competition has wiped out whole industries in the West.

The United States, more than any other country, is the land of television; the first competing networks spread there, and the TV industry took off with feverish enthusiasm. Yet America lost all its TV-set manufacturing to foreigners, at first to Japan. Then Japan was hit by the same problem; Japan now imports nearly three times as many TV sets as it exports. No videotape machine of any type is made in the United States, although video recording was largely invented in America.

The technologies and business interactions of the e-jungle will greatly increase this ruinously intense competition At the same time that winners make fortunes in a winner-takes-most world, many ordinary businesses will be wiped out by new competition.

CREAM SKIMMING

The manager of a local bank confided to me that he would like to get rid of 80 percent of his customers. The computer, he said, made it clear that the profits came from a small number of customers, whom it identified. Customers who exclusively use ATMs or electronic banking facilities are highly profitable; customers with small accounts who wander into the bank in person are mostly unprofitable. He could make more money by closing unprofitable accounts and the resources that support them, and focusing on the most profitable accounts.

A variant of this is true in many businesses: 80 percent of the value comes from 20 percent of the effort. The use of automation often produces an even more skewed distribution: 80 percent of the value comes from 10 percent of the effort, and sometimes from less than 5 percent.

> Many businesses are far too small to dream of being a winner in the new economy. So they need to ask: Can we be one of the partners on a winning team?

A danger of computerized commerce is that computers can identify the highly profitable 10 percent. New corporations will want to skim the cream of established corporations. For many corporations one of the most dangerous aspects of the technology revolution is that new companies can attack the high-profit part of their business, leaving them with the low-profit or loss-making part. Computerized cream skimming will be a highly profitable game. In many industries there will be a battle between traditional companies and companies that master the technologies that enable them to skim the cream.

Ohio's second largest bank, Hamilton Bancshares of Columbus, found, like most banks, that most of its profits came from frequent users of ATMs. So it replaced many of its branches with inexpensive *unmanned* branches. These used enhanced ATM-style machines that provided twenty-four hour video access to personnel at a central location. Customers could, by video, set up an account, ask for loans, or do other banking functions that needed human interaction. This worked well; there was no need for most people to go near the bank. Virgin, in Britain, did something similar. They set up banks with no outlets and only telephone service. With such virtual banking, a relatively small bank could have branches *worldwide,* focusing on only the most profitable cream of the banking business.

With the right software, telephone calls can be made over the Internet. Because Internet pricing is independent of distance, Net users can make long-distance telephone calls at a tiny fraction of their normal cost. This is bad news for traditional telephone companies that make a fat profit on long-distance calls but almost no profit on local calls. The charge for international calls is sometimes *one hundred times the actual cost* of those calls. Telephone regulations in many countries provide that local telephone service be partially subsidized by lucrative long-distance fees.

There are no regulations that can prevent cream skimming in insurance, publishing, travel agencies, banks, distribution companies, and so on. For some old and profitable companies the main effect of electronic commerce will be the loss of their profits.

AVOIDING RUINOUS COMPETITION

With wonderful cynicism Bill Gates says that we should rejoice at the impact of network computing because it produces "friction-free capitalism"—commerce so smoothly oiled that it approaches perfect competition.[2] But nothing could be less friction-free than Gates's breed of capitalism.

Many new technologies will devastate existing businesses. Once-profitable products will become low-profit commodities. When profits turn to losses, corporations cut employees and slash expenses. This temporarily restores profit, but morale sinks, the infrastructure is damaged, it becomes more difficult to move into new areas, and unless a different strategy is put into place, the brutal effects of ruinous competition will return.

The way to avoid such profit destruction is to learn how to play a dominant role in a business ecosystem.

Many businesses are far too small to dream of being a winner in a winner-takes-most game. Such businesses need to ask: Can we be one of the partners on a winning team?

Boeing needed hundreds of partners in order to build the 777. Being a respected partner of Boeing meant that you were on the winner-takes-most team. Boeing made it clear that there was a price of entry. Its partners had to learn the new process for developing the plane using the sophisticated CAD tools linked to Boeing's global network. In Boeing's new ecosystem, corporations that were bitter competitors cooperated, and all companies that were part of the ecosystem were strengthened by it.

JUNGLE MASTERS

The big winners will increasingly be those who work out how they can play a controlling or dominant role in the ecosystems they are part of.

The fastest growing companies will be those that understand the ecosystems they operate in and discover how to dominate them, as Intel, Microsoft, Boeing, America Online, and many others have done (while avoiding antitrust violations). Winners nurture relationships with the other members of their business ecosystem.

Microsoft, while less than a tenth the size of IBM, led and shaped the behavior of many hundreds of associated companies. So did Benetton when it was less than a tenth of the size of the clothing giants, and so did Rupert Murdoch when his operation was much smaller than Time Warner's.

The best strategic managers think not just about products and competition within their industry, but about how they might play a profitable long-lasting role in a cross-industry ecosystem. This will become increasingly important as the alien-intelligence jungle intensifies. When an executive thinks in terms of ecosystems rather than one industry, he can play a grander game, often with higher growth rates and higher return on investment.

Bill Gates is so successful because he thinks in terms of how Microsoft can dominate an ecosystem. Bill Gates is determined to be master of the jungle.

Gates always asks, "What standards does the ecosystem need, and how can Microsoft establish and own those standards?" Where other ecosystem players, like Intel, cannot be dislodged, Gates cooperates with them and helps them, working out how he can share in their success. Sometimes he cooperates with them until he has obtained all the benefits possible and then moves into competition with them, as he did with IBM. PC ecosystems are littered with ex-Microsoft partners where only Microsoft acquired a long-term benefit. Gates is a dangerous bedfellow.

CHAPTER 7
Masters of Alien Intelligence

The marriage of the Internet and computerized intelligence is ushering in a new era of business—but it will be a winner-takes-most world. In this world some individuals will make great fortunes—the individuals who master the complexity or invent corporations that take advantage of it.

As the industrial economy gives way to the intelligent-Web economy, individuals who become masters of the new techniques will have numerous opportunities to get rich. The stars of the alien-intelligence jungle will earn vast sums.

Mankind faces a rising tide of complexity with computers becoming more powerful and widespread. As alien intelligence evolves, this tide will rise faster. Wireless networks and microsystems ensure that the tide will flood into every nook and cranny of society. As software becomes more capable, much professional work becomes more intellect-intensive. The difference in capability between people who master some aspect of the complexity and people who don't will become much greater.

There will be great rewards for great results.

The computer acts as an intellect amplifier. Just as a person in a giant excavator can move hillsides, so a person with the right software can use logic of immense intricacy or can scour the world for information. Alien-intelligence techniques take the individual into new intellectual realms. Putting the most valuable techniques to use will require a level of human expertise beyond that in many corporations. We see highly skilled specialists, such as bond traders, inventors, production planners, movie special effects staff, and experts on electronic commerce, refining their knowledge of how to use these techniques.

The right software tools allow one individual to do work that previously needed a substantial staff. A one-person architect with a digital camera and a Macintosh does more creative house designs than those of a large architect firm. An individual working at home with a computer can edit television better than the staffs in multimillion-dollar analog-tape editing suites of the big studios. For some subjects the Internet offers better research facilities than great libraries. Elaborate computerized tools exist for most types of knowledge work, and individuals who master these tools command high fees. Some are skilled at data mining and can work on any data warehouse. Some use new alien-intelligence tools such as neural networks.

The world has many thousands of professional money managers. Only a few of those are the top stars—the Kasparovs of investing. In a fiber-networked world they have access to vast amounts of information and new intelligence for processing this information. As we will see in the next chapter, some have "black boxes" to automate key decisions in money management.

The most powerful uses of computers, along with the professions they are applied to, take a long time to learn and demand much skill. Relatively few individuals master them. Many areas of knowledge work will operate with a star system in which a small number of individuals become stars of their profession and command incomes much higher than the crowd. The film actors in most demand have huge salaries, but the vast mass of actors earn little. The same is true with writers, investment managers, bond traders, derivative designers, and chief executives. It will become true in all those professions where the star performer can bring in far more money than the average performer can. This will include fashion designers, chip builders, programmers, entrepreneurs, and experts in many fields.

The cyberspace economy has brought great inequalities of income; these inequalities will deepen as the masters of alien intelligence apply their know-how to big-money applications.

In the 1990s the standard deviation of incomes (the difference between low and high incomes) became much larger. A top chip designer, software architect, or movie animator made less than $100,000 in 1990; now the top ones earn over $500,000. The top money managers now earn fortunes because they get results. George Soros, for instance, makes more money than all 170,000 employees of McDonald's combined. Entrepreneurs who take a hot company public pocket millions of dollars, sometimes hundreds of millions. The key employees in such companies also become wealthy because they demand a piece of the action. Few top executives in 1990 earned more than a million dollars; the top ones now earn many millions, often with stock options.

This trend toward large incomes exists because individuals can achieve large results. The trend will increase because the Internet and computerized tools will enable the most skilled (or lucky) individuals to achieve even larger results.

AMPLIFIERS

In the intelligent-Web world, each enterprise needs to ask what it should be brilliant at and what it should outsource. Each individual needs to ask what he or she should be brilliant at and how he or she should market that skill. This encourages the growth of business ecosystems where companies of different types cooperate in intricate ways, and each asks how it can achieve a secure or high-profit role in its ecosystem. The ecosystems are increasingly international, allowing corporations and individuals to choose where they want to live and work.

Network technology amplifies the capability of start-up corporations. Web-based start-up corporations grow much faster than they possibly could have ten years ago.

Cyberspace is full of David-and-Goliath battles where David wins. The David is fast, fluid, and original, whereas the Goliath is bureaucratic, arthritic, and encumbered with the baggage of the past. An amazing number of large corporations seem trapped in an old world, unable to adapt themselves to the new e-commerce inventions. A David can use the new principles from the beginning, recognizing that its lumbering competition is not using those principles. A small corporation can have many partnerships using Web interaction. It can outsource its bread-and-butter activities so that it focuses on what makes it unique. It can use faraway partners to sell its products. Traditional capital-intensive advertising favors the large corporation, whereas cybermarketing techniques can favor the small corporation. A new company that positions itself right can take off spectacularly.

GREAT REWARDS FOR GREAT VALUE

The typical graduate of the industrial era tried to find a large corporation to work for, often seeking stable lifelong employment. The typical graduate of the cyberspace era will realize that there is no such thing as lifelong employment stability, and that much higher rewards come from being in charge of his or her own career with the ability to grow by changing who he or she works for. Rather than working for the giants of the past, he or she is better off working for the Web-centric companies of the future that grow fast and offer a piece of the action.

Many young people, trying to plan their careers, are uncertain about the cyberspace era and the turbulence it will bring. They no longer have the safety of planning a cradle-to-grave career with an IBM. Instead they need to be masters of their own destiny, recognizing that the future economy will provide great rewards for work that adds great value. You should ask, "What work would I enjoy? What could I be brilliant at? In what work can the star performer achieve financial consequences far higher than the average performer? Could I become a star performer?" The masters of cyberspace will select types of work that permit mobility. They will become very skillful at something that generates high value and is globally marketable.

> The great inequalities of income will only deepen as the masters of alien intelligence apply their know-how to big-money applications.

For every billion-dollar story like eBay or Yahoo!, there are many thousands of small successes and, of course, many failures. Many Net entrepreneurs work from home. One entrepreneur dreamed up a service for allowing a person to order flowers with his or her PC. The site showed pictures of flower arrangements, and when a person placed an order, the entrepreneur's computer relayed it automatically to an international florist network and billed the person's credit card. The company, PC Flowers, never dealt with a customer by phone, but it grew quickly to $10 million a year. There are endless opportunities like this.

The young person thinking about his future should think about how he will use money if he makes it. One might categorize people as having three types of goals in life. The people in the first category spend their life seeking happiness. Somehow this group rarely seems to succeed; happiness proves to be remarkably elusive. In the second category are people who build or create things, often with great originality. This group seems to be the happiest of the three because much of the joy of life comes from building or creating things. The third category consists of people who spend their life trying to make money. This group sometimes finds happiness because in order to make money they end up building or creating things. The happiness comes from the accomplishments more than from the money. For many people reflecting on their career in the cyberspace era, an achievable goal could be to make enough money to accomplish something really worthwhile. Today there are astonishing opportunities for new forms of creativity.

ONE MAN AND HIS DOG

At a time when it became fashionable to say that "smokestack industries" ought to migrate to the third world because they need masses of low-skill labor, Gordon Forward created Chaparral Steel in Texas— and Chaparral grew rapidly into one of the world's most innovative and successful steel companies. Today, when asked what the steel mill of the future will be like, Chaparral's chief operating officer, Dave Fournie, smiles and says it will be operated by one man and his dog: the man will watch the computers and the dog will prevent him from touching them! Similarly, in the latest passenger jets the pilot rarely touches the controls. Crashes are very rare, and those that do occur are most often caused by "pilot error," so there is an argument that he should *never* touch the controls except in catastrophic emergencies. A human is more likely to do something wrong than the computer.

Hands-off operation will apply to more and more of mankind's work. For many specialized activities computer capability will far exceed our own. If corporate profits depended on playing chess well, it would be folly to let humans do that; computers play better. Most business operations are much easier to automate than chess but are still done manually. But humans are reluctant to take their hands off the controls. In fact, in most business operations people carry out activities that would be better automated.

Business is steadily progressing toward high levels of automation—if not quite Dave Fournie's one-man-and-his-dog operation. Smokestack industries are turning into knowledge industries, and knowledge industries are increasingly computerized.

INVESTMENT

If the stars of this new world want to be wealthy, they need to ask not only how they will make money but also how they can keep it.

For most wealthy people the best way to invest money in the cyberspace era will not be to select good stocks but to select good money managers. The best money managers are much more skilled than individuals at picking the right investments and getting the timing right. They use computers in highly elaborate ways. There are tens of thousands of money managers, but fewer than fifty are the top stars with repeatable performance. Banks and large institutions usually have a poor track record at investing compared with the stars with sophisticated techniques for focusing on specific types of investments. The most savvy investor tracks down the investment stars; the least savvy investor does what his bank tells him to do.

As home Internet trading of stocks and commodities becomes widespread, replacing other forms of gambling as the common man's dream route to untold wealth, it seems likely that many home traders will simply buy the stocks that are rising fast, hoping to get out before they go down again. The professional trader uses elaborate knowledge and sophisticated computing to beat the odds. The home trader then has the chips stacked against him, just as he does in Las Vegas, but he will gamble anyway and tell dramatic tales about the times when he won.

The amateur traders will be a source of income for the master traders.

THE ALIEN-INTELLIGENCE ECONOMY

Peter Drucker points out that a new form of capitalist society has evolved which he calls "post-capitalist."[1] The resources of capitalism described by classical economists are capital, equipment, labor, land, and natural resources. Today the most important resource is none of these. It is *knowledge.* Value is created by applying knowledge to work. This may be human knowledge, but increasingly it will be computerized knowledge.

An era in which the key economic resource is *knowledge* is startlingly different from an era with traditional economic resources for two reasons.

First, most knowledge is endlessly replicable. It can be duplicated on computer disks, transmitted worldwide in a fraction of a second to machines anywhere. Customs officials have no idea that the most valuable economic resource has just flitted past them.

Second, knowledge can be amplified. With so much knowledge residing in complex software, computers can constantly add to the accumulated knowledge. Alien-intelligence techniques breed knowledge, or extract knowledge from the dumb data that our machines collect constantly.

Computerized knowledge translates into wealth in many different ways. It enables the design of better goods. It helps find customers, worldwide. It lowers inventory costs and enables more efficient production. It creates digital goods that can be distributed and replicated at very low cost, with no physical inventory. It accelerates automation so that we will eventually have almost fully automated factories, mines, hydroponics farms, and other enterprises, producing the world's goods at very low cost.

We are heading toward a totally different type of economy. The term *"information economy"* is repeatedly used, but this does not fully describe what is happening. Information becomes valuable when it is connected to intelligence, either human or machine. As we have stressed, machine intelligence will grow at a furious rate, but it will be mainly *alien* intelligence, not human-like artificial intelligence. What is evolving is an *"intelligent-Web economy,"* with corporations designed for increasingly automated, increasingly intelligent, worldwide interaction with interlaced virtual operations. Such corporations will increasingly be *non-national,* with capital, management, talent, and resources coming from around the planet.

> An economy in which most of the wealth is based on replicable knowledge and computer intelligence can grow much faster than an economy based on flesh and steel.

An economy in which most of the wealth is based on replicable knowledge and computer intelligence can grow at a much faster rate than an economy based on flesh and steel. This is not simply a speeding up of the old economic environment; it is a fundamentally new kind of economic environment.

As the intelligent-Web economy becomes advanced, it will have global enterprises interacting across the planet, each creaturelike with its own nervous system and built-in intelligence. In industries where automation brings economies of scale, numerous mergers and takeovers will result in giant worldwide enterprises.

> The combination of the Web, alien intelligence, and new ways of running business is an explosive mixture.

We have seen the early stages of this massive consolidation in industries such as finance, automobiles, and telecommunications. While giants consolidate, numerous small companies are inventing new ways to achieve excellence in a selected niche, some hoping to grow large, some hoping to be taken over in a winner-takes-most world. The fast evolution of these interacting creaturelike enterprises will be driven by the immense profit potentials of electronic commerce.

We are at the beginning of the era when software (as well as hardware) is able to learn and change its own behavior automatically. We have genetic algorithms breeding better processes and exchanging those processes with other computers on the Internet. We know that alien-intelligence techniques can help design things that humans cannot design. We will use them to create products of extreme complexity, as with today's processor chips. We know that when software has the ability to improve itself, it will do so at electronic speed. When computers scattered across the planet do this, and there are means for exchanging software, we will have a spectacular chain reaction.

Danny Hillis, who created the ultra-parallel Connection Machine, has spent much of his life thinking about such software. He comments: "We're heading towards something which is going to happen very soon—in our lifetimes—and which is fundamentally different from anything that's happened in human history before.... We're close to the singularity."[2]

The chain reaction of automated generation and replication of new knowledge will develop rather like that which has occurred in the foreign exchange markets, where the *daily* volume of currency exchange trades became larger than the entire reserves of the trading countries. The new knowledge is new wealth, so economic growth will tend to follow the accelerating upward curve of the chain reaction, rather than the slow and steady growth of the factory era.

NEW INDUSTRIES

The combination of cyberspace and alien intelligence will breed massive new industries. Later in the book we will see how a Japanese research lab developed a machine for breeding "neural" modules that can be assembled into "brain" mechanisms, which in turn can be assembled into higher brain mechanisms. Eventually "brain-building" machines around the planet will breed such mechanisms at a furious rate.

At first clever humans will wrestle with the problem of breeding neural modules that are useful. These modules will be interlinked into "brains." Components of brains will be catalogued and standardized like other engineering components, but unlike physical components they can be transmitted over the Internet and replicated endlessly.

Techniques will be developed for assembling such capabilities from libraries of neural modules. Brain-breeding will become a vital technique in machine design, robotics, biotechnology, quantum chemistry, production engineering, electronic commerce, filmmaking, and many other disciplines. However impressive today's brain-breeding, it is a baby's first steps.

Hugo de Garis, the father of the brain-breeding techniques, describes a new profession that will come into existence—engineers trained to grow and evolve "brain" mechanisms. Once this is an accepted part of industry it will rapidly become much more sophisticated. It will be one of the computer industry's chain reactions, awesome in its potential. De Garis believes that it will grow into a trillion-dollar global industry.

To be effective, robots need far more intelligence than they have today. They also need far more computer power than today, but this will happen fairly quickly because computer power is rapidly dropping in cost, and techniques like those de Garis is developing can make alien intelligence much more capable. Robots will not be automated versions of English butlers. They will not be anything like the robots that clomp around in movies. They may be invisible security guards, tiny mechanisms for assembling Swiss watches, and automated production lines that keep running when the lights are out. New industries will produce increasingly sophisticated goods with decreasing numbers of people.

Robots will be physical manifestations of alien intelligence. They will be a key component of the translation of knowledge into wealth—a major part of the alien-intelligence economy.

THE NEW WINNERS

Knowledge technology has changed economics, bringing winners in a winner-takes-most environment.

The reasons for winner-takes-most segments of the economy are as follows:

■ *Extreme complexity:* We are in a steadily rising tide of complexity. Alien intelligence makes the complexity much deeper. Individuals, like George Soros, or corporations, like Cisco, can become the ongoing master of an act so complex that competition cannot catch up for many years.

■ *Extreme cost of entry, low cost of production:* A knowledge-based product can be extremely expensive to develop but once developed is extremely inexpensive to mass-produce, as we've seen with such products as software, processor chips, DVDs, and Viagra pills.

■ *Worldwide access:* A knowledge-based service may be extremely difficult to create, but once it exists can be accessed worldwide on the Internet.

■ *Virtual operations:* Computer networks enable corporations to pool their competencies. The combination (a virtual company) can be so skilled—consider, for example, Boeing's consortium for building their 777 jet—that other corporations cannot achieve the same results.

■ *Owning the standards:* An industry dominated by knowledge technology must have de facto standards. When a corporation (like Microsoft or Intel) manages to establish and effectively own those standards, it can be in a winner-takes-most position.

■ *Compatibility needs:* Customers need compatibility of products to achieve worthwhile results. For example, users of Microsoft's Office 2000 want people they communicate with also to have Office 2000. A winner-takes-most company can enhance its products to make sure that competing products are not compatible.

WHO WILL THE WINNERS BE?

How does a company become great in the new world of cyberspace? Some authorities will advocate grand-scale strategic planning.

Boldly go where no corporation has gone before. Plan predator value streams and world-beating projects like Visa's fiber-optic network. Shoot for the moon with big hairy audacious goals. Think big because technology makes grand schemes possible.

Other authorities will say there is no roadmap for cyberspace so you have to feel your way. There are too many surprises in store for long-range planning to work. Trial and error is essential. It is an age of great creativity so stimulate unplanned experimentation everywhere. Build a mutation machine. The winners will be the masters of high-speed evolution, ready to capitalize quickly on the unexpected. The losers will be those trapped in rigid structures.

> **Robots using alien intelligence will be a key component of the translation of knowledge into wealth.**

In reality, the two viewpoints need not be mutually exclusive. There will be successes, like 3M, based on constant unplanned innovation. There will also be grand cliff-hanger stories of heroic leaders who bet their company on a great project, the future equivalents of IBM's 360 or Boeing's 747. A visitor to Boeing, worried about Chairman William Allen's bet-the-company commitment to the 747, asked him, "What would you do if the first airplane crashed on take-off?" After a long pause Allen replied, "I'd rather talk about something pleasant—like a nuclear war."[3]

Projects of Wagnerian grandness used to be appropriate for only a few corporations like Boeing and IBM, but today grand-scale projects can be tackled by connecting together core competencies in different corporations. Relatively small corporations may have large ambitions, which they fulfill by assembling the right group of partners, as Nokia did when it moved into the cellular phone business.

Reinventing killer value streams often requires quantum-leap change, not evolutionary change. But corporate quantum leaps introduce a deluge of new problems, so those involved should expect trouble and be prepared to deal with it. All the employees involved with a new value stream should be busy inventing as many improvements as they can think of. Many changes will be tried but only the best accepted. Still, the more new ideas tried, the greater the probability that some will hit the jackpot.

Of course, corporate success will not hinge solely on what amounts to corporate bungee jumps. Grand quantum leaps and intelligent but fast evolution should coexist like the yin and yang of Chinese dualistic philosophy. Technological change will lash about in an ever more frenzied way—and its pace will continue to accelerate—so the search for valuable evolution will be an increasingly intense competitive force.

The company with the most new ideas has a good chance of winning if those ideas are constantly tested, refined, and linked to good marketing—and if the poor ideas are dropped quickly.

LEADERSHIP

When the business world is changing this fast, it is dangerous for corporations to be set in their ways. Today many corporations with great names are missing the boat with e-commerce.

The combination of e-commerce, alien intelligence, and the new ways of running business is an explosive mixture.

In the mid-1990s Microsoft management was complacent about the Internet, in the way that many corporations today are complacent about e-commerce. Some of Microsoft's youngest employees were the most influential in causing management to take the Internet more seriously. They had come out of universities where the Internet was widely used, so they said, "You guys just don't get it. You've got to try this."[4] They succeeded in getting their message across to Bill Gates. Gates led an astonishingly fast, expensive change in direction. Few corporations could succeed in making such an all-embracing transformation so quickly. Microsoft has a culture of making employees send e-mail, sometimes disrespectful e-mail, and making heroes out of a small number of employees whose outspoken criticisms trigger valuable change.

It is certain that many corporations will fail to take appropriate action as the tsunami of e-commerce heads in their direction.

Most institutions designed before the age of cyberspace need to be radically reinvented. Some are no longer relevant. However, it is difficult to reengineer corporations with a deeply established culture. Mike Hammer, the high priest of business reengineering, estimated that roughly 70 percent of attempts to reengineer business have been abandoned before completion.[5] Of those completed many were judged as "producing mediocre, marginal, or failed results."[6]

A vital question for all top executives is: Should management attempt the traumatic reengineering of an old organization or build new units that embrace the new principles?

Building fundamentally new units is usually easier, more exciting, and more successful. Many executives say, "Let's swing the old corporation around slowly and cautiously," but newcomers are heading into their territory like speed boats racing around a big liner. They can skim off the most profitable part of the business. This is an age in which aggressive new corporations can easily outmaneuver old ones.

NETIZENS

A rapidly growing number of knowledge workers work for themselves or set up their own company. They realize that they can make more money on their own than by working for someone else.

As high-paid work becomes knowledge work, a person's ability to make money will increasingly transcend national and geographic boundaries. Writers, designers, investors, lawyers, programmers, and the innumerable types of "symbolic analysts" can be anywhere on the planet with adequate Net connections. Movie stars, performing artists, lecturers, and so on can live where they want and travel to the many countries where they work.

Enthusiasts of cyberspace often refer to themselves as "netizens" — citizens of "The Net" as opposed to citizens of any nation. Often they have not thought about the implications of being a citizen of cyberspace.

In an economy based on electronic commerce, the boundaries drawn on maps become increasingly irrelevant. Cyberspace makes distance disappear. Star performers, whether in cyberspace or not, become citizens of the planet rather than citizens of one nation. Increasing numbers of individuals are becoming *world citizens.* This is already proving beneficial. Best to move directly into what we know the positive effects have *already* been.

Bermuda has a hospital that seems much more pleasant to be in than most hospitals. The staff is unusually caring and kind. One might worry about the quality of medical diagnosis and action, but the Bermuda hospital is thoroughly wired into the Massachusetts General Hospital in Boston, one of the world's most respected hospitals. Doctors in Bermuda can consult specialists in Boston to examine medical cultures, X-ray images, electrocardiograms. There is also online guidance from Boston when certain operations are performed in Bermuda. Medical care will increasingly need kind and caring nurses and paramedics *locally*, linked to first-rate diagnosis and advice *wherever on the planet that might be.*

Many of mankind's activities will be redesigned after thinking out *what should be done locally and what should be remote.*

The Department of Defense has developed surgical procedures where the surgeon is remote from the patient. Statistics show that most soldiers who die in battle die because they did not get to the hospital quickly enough. It makes sense to have armor-plated medical trucks near the battlefield linked by satellites to surgeons far from the war zone.

REDISTRIBUTION OF WEALTH

Most governments in the industrial era have had a policy of redistribution of income. High earners pay large taxes, and the money is used to benefit low earners and the unemployed. Because there are few high earners and many low earners, politicians can gain votes by making promises to the low earners that the high earners have to pay for. Different social systems have all tried to "level the playing field," though they differ in how much they think it should be leveled or how many promises politicians can get away with.

As the industrial era gives way to the cyberspace era the difference between high earners and low earners is becoming much greater. The cyberspace stars of the future will earn far more than those of today. Indeed there is a danger that a rising percentage of the public will be unemployable except in menial tasks. Social philosophers will say there is a greater need for income redistribution and for social services. Politicians will have an even higher incentive to make promises that the rich pay for.

But the intelligent-Web economy brings a fundamental change: most knowledge work can be performed anywhere with the aid of computer networks. Most high earners can be highly mobile. They can work anywhere they choose because most knowledge work transcends national and geographical boundaries. They can earn and invest money anywhere in cyberspace. They can move, if they choose, from a high-tax to a low-tax jurisdiction.

The cyberspace corporation will increasingly tend to be stateless. Its directors, investors, and customers can be from anywhere on the planet. Its private capital can come from anywhere; its public capital is traded on global stock markets. Non-national corporations can set up subsidiaries for specific purposes in any jurisdiction they choose. Many big corporations, for example, insure themselves with a "captive" insurance company that they control, established in a low-tax jurisdiction. Similarly, they can set up e-commerce servers, subsidiaries, or financial gateways wherever taxes are low. The basic business calculations of many start-up corporations will relate to what subsidiaries they should have and where they should be located. Just as there are computer programs for finding you cheap airfares, so there will be programs for determining in what tax juris-dictions companies should base their e-commerce operations.

> The well-designed Web-centric corpo-ration is likely to change virtually every aspect of employment.

As business moves into cyber-space, nations with excessive taxes will find both corporations and individuals relocating elsewhere. As this happens, the tax base will be eroded. The high-tax nation will try to pay for its promises by raising taxes still further, which will increase the exodus of the tax-producing stars. It will be a vicious circle that seriously erodes governments' ability to redistribute income on a large scale.

The Bank of England, the "Grand Old Lady of Threadneedle Street," waves the Union Jack. Like other central banks it is a vestige of earlier nationalism. Part of its function has been to support sterling. As we will see in Chapter 8, nationalistic support of exchange rates does not normally work today because of the power of hedge funds and other investors to speculate against it. Collectively, hedge funds can bring $1 trillion in assets to bear on the market and can move with computerized speed.

Nevertheless, most governments are not yet prepared to leave the shaping of exchange rates to market forces. Almost universally they have used national funds to intervene in markets to try to control currencies. But today's foreign exchange market obeys laws of its own, as does everything else in the alien-intelligence jungle. The foreign exchange market cares little about economic and political issues. Central banks are clearly no longer capable of exercising control over foreign exchange. Experts have said that they should abandon their futile, costly, and often counterproductive attempts to support national currencies. They should be autonomous institutions actively investing their reserves, with scientific risk management, not playing a grander but delusionary role of protecting a national currency.

One of the characteristics of the alien-intelligence economy is that individuals with computerized tools can smoke out delusionary exchange rates, excessive broken commissions, and prices that are out of line.

In numerous ways there will be a *separation of state and economy*.[7]

FROM KAFKA TO CYBERCORP

The new digital corporation is the culmination of the twentieth-century journey from treating employees as dumb slaves who must be made to obey orders, to challenging every employee to use his wits in devising new ways to add value.

The century started with Kafkaesque bureaucracy and contempt for employees, with Frederick Taylor timing every motion of workers with a stopwatch. By the end of the century the entire corporation was being designed so that it could climb the steepest learning curves, with everybody challenged to strive for their full potential.

In the past what was good for the corporation was often bad for the individual. Corporations created soul-destroying jobs. The best corporations today are creating a work environment where difficult challenges energize and excite people. They are reinventing work so that what is good for the corporation is good for the individual. They aim for the highest of Maslow's hierarchy of human needs so that everybody tries to achieve his full potential. Most boring jobs can be abolished.

Humans no longer need to act like robots on a relentlessly moving production line. Robotlike jobs can be done by robots. Bookkeepers no longer add up columns of figures. Staffs of many types, working with new tools, are expected to make better and larger-scale decisions. Designers have tools of great power that enable them to be more creative.

The dehumanizing jobs of an earlier age are gone, but as automation and alien intelligence become more powerful, many people are expected to move into jobs requiring more training and higher skills. In highly automated corporations the revenue generated per person is often several times higher than in corporations with little automation. Automated corporations demand greater skill for greater pay.

Unlike Adam Smith's revolution, the wealth of nations is maximized by maximizing the value added by everybody.

In cyberspace there are few secrets. Information passes around the world at electronic speed. When one corporation produces a good idea, others can copy it quickly, and increasingly those others are in distant countries. While many organizations ignore anything "not invented here," the Japanese in the 1970s and 1980s systematically trolled the world for ideas they could adopt and gurus they could brainsuck. Today much of the trolling can be done on the Net. Generally, whatever strategic advantage a corporation gains from technology is short-lived because other corporations copy that technology.

When he was head of planning for Shell, Arie de Geus expressed the view that the only *sustainable* competitive advantage would become *the ability to learn faster than one's competition.*[8]

Competition can quickly replicate a new thrust, and the time needed for replication is getting shorter. In the 1970s and 1980s cheap-labor countries often copied products and found alternatives to patents. The best of the developing world had a high growth rate. Today the developing world is having more difficulty competing with the first world because the first world is on a much steeper learning curve.

The great rate of change means that much work will be *learning-intensive*. If an employee spends ten years without learning, he probably loses the ability to do learning-intensive work. The corporation with its eye on the future keeps its employees constantly learning. All employees should be encouraged to think creatively about how their procedures can be improved.

In the most learning-intense corporations the proportion of the time employees spend on learning is steadily rising. IBM in its great days spent almost 2 percent of its gross revenue on internal education and customer education. Motorola requires many of its employees to spend a total of one month per year on training. At Chaparral Steel, at any given time 85 percent of its personnel are in part-time training courses and all personnel take an educational sabbatical during which they visit customers' plants, other steel companies, or universities. The corporation of the future will allow employees to work at any time of the night or day. Staff that are part of intense person–machine partnerships will have attractive offices with protection from interruptions. Some corporations are providing them with free gourmet meals, masseuses, and exercise rooms.

The well-designed Web-centric corporation is likely to change virtually every aspect of employment—compensation, appraisal, rewards, measurements, motivation, education, teams, management, unions.

A major concern in this alien-intelligence economy will be the growing gulf between those who are technology-capable and those who are not. The masters of alien intelligence will earn fortunes and move, if they wish, to low-tax jurisdictions. At the opposite end will be those stuck with low-paying work, often in high-tax jurisdictions. It is essential that society should grow human potential as fast as it possibly can, trying to keep up with the racing technology. Fortunately, there are superb new technologies for education—the DVD, interactive video, chatterbots, the Internet, digital satellites, and intelligent machines. Today's corporation should be designed to take its people up the fastest learning curves practical.

CHAPTER 8
The Root of All Evil

T he masters of alien intelligence can make money in many knowledge-intensive disciplines. Perhaps not surprisingly, a field to which the new tools have been intensely applied is investing. Any technique that improves investment performance is worth detailed development.

NO CARDBOARD BOX

You probably wouldn't think of keeping large amounts of money in a cardboard box under your bed, but large numbers of ordinary brokers and banks around the world do something not much better. They keep your uninvested funds in cash (accumulating a small amount of interest).

The dollar was worth 360 yen in the 1970s; it steadily fell to 90 yen in the 1990s. A person holding dollars would have been much better off if he had converted his dollars to yen. He would be *much* better off if his uninvested money were controlled by a computer that did a reasonably decent job of continuously moving it to the best currencies. Better still the *entire portfolio* should be hedged against currency fluctuations.

You need a black box, not a cardboard box.

Investors use the term "black box" to refer to software that takes information about the market and makes investment decisions *automatically*. If the black box is online linked to currency-trading systems, it can switch currencies automatically. The ultimate goal is to produce a black box for trading that achieves better results than the best human traders. We have shown how computers and the Internet create a deluge of information. Various alien-intelligence techniques are fair game in trying to extract insight from these data that can be used for improving investments.

THE EXPLOSION IN CURRENCY TRADING

The story of how computers have changed foreign exchange dealing is extraordinary. It is typical of the chain reactions brought by network-based computing.

In the old days, long, long ago, when chips had only a few thousand transistors, currencies had fixed exchange rates. The fixed-exchange-rate system collapsed in the Nixon era when banks adopted floating exchange rates. The idea of computerized trading of currencies took a while to catch on. When it finally came into accepted use, huge amounts of money began to flow through computer networks.

Foreign exchange trading soon became global. Half of all transactions are with parties in a different country. The global trading day moves in a virtually unbroken twenty-four–hour cycle around the world, from Hong Kong to Tokyo to Sydney, across the United States, across Europe, across the Middle East, and back to Hong Kong.

By 1995 the *daily* total of currency exchange trades was larger than the entire reserves of the trading countries. The reserves of all 140 countries belonging to the International Monetary Fund total about $1 trillion. Currency trades amount to about $1.7 trillion *a day*. On some days the volume is twice that amount. The daily dollar value of all transactions in the currency trading market is seventy-five times larger than that of all transactions on the New York and London stock exchanges combined.

Computer networks globalized trading, brought almost instantaneous exchange, and increased complexity of such financial instruments as derivatives.

As the market spread across the globe, trading became increasingly pressurized and volatile. Fortunes could be made and lost very rapidly. Banks and traditional trading organizations faced tough new competition and declining margins. Insurance companies, pension funds, entrepreneurs, and corporate treasuries entered the market directly, both to trade for profit and to hedge their commercial investments. Meanwhile, hedge funds such as George Soros's Quantum Fund and Tiger Management were able to focus massive sums of money on particular points in the market.

STORMY WEATHER

As the computerized deluge of money surged back and forth around the planet, exchange rates became unpredictable. Trading became massive, volatile, and fiercely competitive. Like the weather, trading would be calm for a time, but then storms would break out.

The growing use of computer networks made the storms worse. Designers of computerized financial instruments concocted ways to achieve leverage, obtaining big results with a relatively small amount of capital. But the more the leverage, the greater the risk. Global use of hedge funds and derivatives severely worsened the volatility of an already volatile market. Financial storms of unprecedented intensity blew up with astonishing suddenness. One swept through Europe in September 1992. Sweden raised interest rates to 500 percent trying to defend the krona, but the defense failed. Sweden lost $26 billion in six days. Norway lost 46 percent of its reserves in two days and gave up. Finland lost *all* of its reserves. The speculators, most of them not in Europe, made great fortunes.

> Alien-intelligence tools can be set to detect highly sophisticated patterns in the markets that humans cannot detect.

Business executives were like farmers, praying for good weather; a bad change in interest rates could wipe out profits. Like farmers they needed protection from price changes, so *derivatives* based on currencies were invented.

A derivative is a financial instrument expressing a valuation formula involving the future value of one or more items such as a stock, bond, currency value, or interest rate. There are numerous formulas and so there are many different types of derivatives. The derivatives market is double the value of all U.S. stocks, estimated at $60 trillion.

The complexity and proliferation of derivatives is a commentary on our times. Complexity expands to make use of the available computer power. Mathematics Ph.D.'s flocked to Wall Street to design increasingly abstruse financial instruments. Computers can be designed to provide protection from volatility, but they can make financial volatility much worse.

In late 1997 funds flooded out of third world countries, leaving economies crippled, until a worldwide panic set in. Stock markets crashed as news commentators talked about the possibility of a global depression. A hedge fund, Long-Term Capital Management, lost so much money that it could have wrecked major banks, forcing the U.S. Federal Reserve Board to organize a bailout.

With financial weather like this, good predictions about foreign exchange prices could be worth a fortune. A number of firms searched for computerized techniques that might enable them to predict price movements. Even if they nudged the probability of being correct by only a minor amount, that could translate into big money. The realization that exchange-rate forecasting might be possible lured brilliant mathematicians from fields like nuclear physics (and weather forecasting).

Currency prices often seem to be unrelated to economic fundamentals. So what drives them? Can they be predicted? Can a highly leveraged investor cause financial storms to happen so as to profit from them?

The "efficient market" theory holds that present prices are based on complete information about the past, and so information about the past is of no use in predicting future prices. But when computers analyzed price movements in detail it became clear that there were certain *patterns*. Alien-intelligence tools can be set to detect these patterns. If an investment firm could understand the patterns better than its competition, it could use computerized trading in a dramatic way.

BLACK BOXES

A number of firms have operated proprietary black boxes for trading. Some have given good results for a time but then slipped as trading patterns changed. A few have operated successfully for many years. The best black boxes are closely guarded trade secrets that produce excellent results for selected investors. They demonstrate that we must take black-box trading seriously. The future of finance will be a battle of black boxes.

There are many ways for software builders to skin the black-box cat. The creator might make money by *using* the software or *selling* the software. Some owners of today's black-box software operate private investment funds and keep the workings of their black box strictly secret. Some sell a small number of proprietary copies of the black box at a high price. In the future we will probably see black boxes for investment on sale to the mass public. Suppose that the latest Microsoft offering allowed you to invest money with somewhat greater returns than you could achieve from banks or fixed-interest investments; how many copies would Microsoft sell?

Electronic trading, automated exchanges, derivatives, and hedge funds have all changed investment patterns; mass use of competing black boxes will bring even greater changes. It is interesting to explore what these changes might be.

VOLATILITY

When fixed interest rates gave way to foreign exchange markets, transactions flooded in staggering volumes through the computer networks, and exchange rates grew more and more unpredictable. Computerization brought fierce competition with phenomenal profit opportunities. It also brought extreme volatility and enormous risks. In 1991 Allied Lyons, the food and drinks group, lost £150 million in currency speculation. In 1994 the Japanese oil company Kashima Oil admitted losses on dollar derivative deals of $1.5 billion. Because of the extreme volatility of exchange rates, risks reached levels that would previously have been unimaginable and intolerable. The market could make massive moves with vicious speed. There was little advance warning of these moves. The weather was calm before the sudden onset of extreme storms.

The emergence of electronic information sources, such as Reuters and Bloomberg, meant that news could be instantly disseminated around the globe. The competitive advantage of early access to information disappeared. Many economists expected that the lower inflation achieved in much of the developed world in recent years would bring lower volatility in the foreign exchange market, but, in fact, volatility increased because computerized trading with leveraged instruments reached massive volumes. Technology presented huge opportunities to foreign exchange investors but increased volatility greatly. Increased speculative gains brought with them, as always, increased risks.

In March and April 1995, the dollar was tumbling and the European System was coming apart at the seams. On several days the daily range of the dollar/deutsche mark spot price rose to five times its average. Spreads on deutsche mark/lira options increased from around 0.5 percent in late 1994 to as high as 10 percent at their worst in March 1995. There was little advance warning of these sharp moves. Trading was light in the days leading up to the onset of extreme volatility. Such sudden storms are scary, but the suddenness of their arrival presents massive opportunities to traders who are appropriately computerized.

DERIVATIVES

With growing volatility came the need for greater protection from risk. Derivatives provide that protection by offering elaborate ways to hedge against different types of future events. Computers made the design of derivatives practical. They started with relatively simple *futures* (contracts for future delivery at a specified price) and *options* (contracts where the party had the option at a future time to buy or sell at a prearranged price). They steadily evolved toward more complex contracts designed to achieve prescribed levels of growth or risk.

Quantitative analysts (called "quants") designed abstruse mathematical formulas to specify elaborate systems of side bets to cover endless possibilities. Derivatives can be highly leveraged. The money paid for an option is usually only a small fraction of the amount covered by the deal. They became steadily more exotic and were given exotic names. Their designers used supercomputers to create derivatives for different purposes and model how they would behave in different circumstances. Computer networks allowed these complex instruments to spread at an amazing rate.

PROCTER AND GAMBLING

Some businessmen need to worry about possible future losses due to factors over which they have no control. A winery, for example, is vulnerable to crop failures and hail storms. People whose financial survival is vulnerable will pay more than the odds to avoid that vulnerability. A computer can detect when they are paying more than the odds and can bet against them. If it spreads its bets, the computer will win.

Commodities dealers with computers can make money in the long run because many farmers sell futures at a lower price than what the goods will probably sell for, in order to have guaranteed income.

Currency fluctuations affect most people who do business internationally. Laker Airlines, for example, a highly popular upstart in transatlantic travel in the 1980s, ordered a fleet of DC-10s to keep up with its soaring growth. Its revenue came mainly in British pounds, but the company paid for the jets in dollars. The exchange value of the pound sank until Laker could not pay off its dollar obligations, and the airline was forced into bankruptcy. Other companies have been knocked out of business when oil prices went through the roof or prices of memory chips shot up. Savings and loan associations went under when interest rates rose while fixed-rate mortgage loans did not. Storms of unexpected volatility have left many carcasses on the corporate landscape.

Derivatives were originally intended as protection from risk. But soon they began to be used in ways that greatly increase risk. They can be designed to allow a business gambler to take highly leveraged bets. Nick Leeson of Barings Bank used derivatives to make bets so large that they brought down the whole bank.

In 1993 Procter and Gamble's corporate treasurer nearly wrecked the venerable corporation. For four years short-term interest rates had declined steadily from about 10 percent to less than 3 percent. When such a trend happens, it is likely that rates will adjust upward. But P&G used a derivative effectively betting that interest rates would *not* go up. Four months later they *did* go up. Like a gambler covering a bad loss, P&G bet again that interest rates would fall. Once again they went up, from 3 ¼ percent to 6 ½ percent. The loss was potentially catastrophic for P&G.

> In the age of the Internet, investors working on laptop computers have tackled some of the most venerable financial institutions.

Good use of derivatives controls the downside; bad use of derivatives bets the farm. The upside of P&G's bet was low. The downside was a loss of hundreds of millions. Security law is supposed to protect widows and orphans. Nobel Laureate Merton Miller joked that Procter was the widow and Gamble the orphan.

The problem with computerized complexity is that top management can be "widows and orphans."

BETTING AGAINST THE BANK OF ENGLAND

The Bank of England was once the grandest of central banks. This all-powerful institution spent taxpayers' money when necessary to support the British currency.

In the age of the Internet, investors with laptop computers, sitting in some far-off country, could outrage the Grand Old Lady of Threadneedle Street by speculating against it. In September 1992 some investors did just that, borrowing to the hilt on the Internet to do so. In just a few days George Soros earned a reputation that would stick as "the man who broke the Bank of England."

In the three months from June to September 1992, the Bank of England used around $40 billion *a month* trying to defend sterling. Sweden, as noted, tried to defend its currency by temporarily raising its interest rates to 500 percent. Soros and others believed that such exchange rates were undefendable. During a few days in September 1992, sterling lost 15 percent of its value. George Soros's Quantum hedge fund made a $1 billion profit in those few days.

Similarly, in a single day, July 30, 1993, the Bank of France used FF300 billion of its reserves in an unsuccessful attempt to keep the franc within European Monetary System limits.

In March 1995 the dollar dropped below 95 yen, and the world's central banks mounted a desperate intervention to stem the dollar's fall. Once again this gave traders an opportunity to speculate against the central banks. But this time the central banks joined together to defend themselves. There was a shootout worthy of the old cowboy films. The U.S. Federal Reserve, the Bank of Japan, the German Bundesbank, and fifteen other European central banks joined forces with a massively funded effort. Still, speculators used derivatives to obtain the highest possible leverage. The dollar stubbornly fell a further 10 percent. The central banks lost.

By using the leverage of derivatives, the world's hedge funds can collectively muster a trillion dollars to speculate where their computers tell them they can win. During the 1998 crisis many voices clamored for laws to restrict the activities of U.S. hedge funds, but Federal Reserve Chairman Alan Greenspan commented, "Any direct regulation restricting the flexibility of hedge funds will induce the more flexible funds to emigrate from under our jurisdiction."[1] Welcome to cyberspace!

DETECTABLE PATTERNS

Alien intelligence can detect highly sophisticated patterns that humans cannot detect.

For decades some financial analysts have drawn charts of price movements in an attempt to find patterns. Analysts try to detect when prices are breaking out of a range that is drawn on the chart. This is called "technical analysis" or "chartism." It didn't work very well.

These analysts usually studied charts that showed only end-of-day closing prices. Unlike humans, computers can work with a deluge of data. They see tick-by-tick details of every change in quoted price, and of every trade, its volume and price. Quoted prices of major currencies can change twenty times a minute, or more. The U.S. dollar/deutsche mark rate, for example, changes *18,000* times in a typical day.

Such a body of data made it possible to test hypotheses about price movements and experiment with proposed techniques for automated trading. Investment tools were programmed, run against historical data, and modified until they produced the best results achievable.

In 1986 Richard Olsen, a Swiss whose father was a banker and whose mother was a professor, started a company in Zurich, Olsen and Associates, with the goal of predicting the future prices of financial instruments using only information from past prices. He recruited the brightest young Ph.D. physicists and statisticians he could find, from CERN and other top research centers.

Olsen tells his team that the science of financial markets is more intellectually fascinating than particle physics. This new science, he says, is in the position today that quantum mechanics was in the 1920s before it wreaked havoc in physics. The understanding of foreign exchange markets is condensing into reliable theory, made practical by computers, which will wreak havoc in the financial world.

Olsen's Zurich team couldn't be less like a Swiss bank. He and his people wear jeans, not ties, and indulge in intense intellectual arguments. Olsen gives them massive computer power, detailed data warehouses, and infectious enthusiasm. His team is convinced that it is involved in an area of science that is about to explode. Olsen likes to say that events affecting the market are like stones dropped into a lake. His company is not interested in trying to predict the stone's fall, but thinks that it can predict the pattern of waves that spreads from it.

After many years of research, Olsen and Associates claims to be predicting the general direction of currency markets 60 to 65 percent of the time for short-term (three-month) predictions and 70 to 75 percent of the time for longer-term predictions.[2] These figures are significantly better than those of the highly paid floor traders.

DRUNKEN SAILORS

The efficient market theory says that the price of a stock or currency always reflects all knowable information; no additional information can be gleaned by studying price history. It is impossible to use past prices to predict future prices. Prices stagger like a drunken sailor—no matter where he's staggered in the past, there is an equal chance that his next step will be in any direction. Currency trading seemed particularly difficult to predict.

Computer analyses of price movements seemed to verify this, so the "random walk" theory of price movements became part of Wall Street folklore. However, analyses from the past were based on coarse-grained data such as daily closings. The more powerful computers of the 1990s were able to analyze fine-grained data—every single price tick. This more detailed analysis showed that the walk was not quite random. A computer can detect certain deviations from the perfect market. Today's detailed analysis shows that under certain circumstances we can estimate the probability of when the drunk will drift.

Furthermore, once the drunk starts to stagger rapidly he will do so for some time. Once a period of volatility starts, it tends to last longer than expected. This is contrary to the efficient market theory, which says that volatility is no more predictable than anything else.

The recognition of subtle patterns has a substantial effect on intra-day trading (that is, the buying and selling of a currency within one day), which constitutes 90 percent of the volume of foreign exchange trading. Long-term patterns cannot be recognized without detailed historical data that span many years, perhaps decades.

Some early efforts at computerized pattern recognition worked well for a time and then went to pieces. Credit Suisse ran an automated system for currency trading that used alien-intelligence (neural-network) techniques to recognize trading patterns. For five years it did well but then for two years it performed poorly and was switched off. The software had detected a pattern that held for a time but

> Trend-monitoring black boxes generally do best in times of chaos. Multiple black boxes may cause chaos and at the same time benefit from that chaos.

changed unexpectedly when macroeconomic conditions changed. Such a system needs to be run against decades of historical data that show every trade and price movement, but those data were not collected until relatively recently.

Relentless monitoring is needed to warn of any changes in fundamentals that could invalidate black-box behavior.

AUTOMATIC TRADING

Most older traders and money managers heap scorn on the notion of computers making trades automatically. Investing, they insist, needs human intelligence and intuition. There is no way that you could trust a computer to manage your money.

Many black boxes for investment have been programmed by academics or by researchers in big financial institutions. Most are used for intellectual research, testing investment theories. Many academic black boxes have proven disastrous in the heat of battle, while a few trade-secret ones have had great results. Firms with successful black boxes don't talk about them because they don't want competition. But many of the black boxes that have had success in practice are designed to work with a skilled trader: alien intelligence is combined with human intelligence.

When a firm discovers a technique that enables it to forecast price patterns, those patterns will disappear if many other firms use the same technique. But if the firm keeps its forecasts and methods secret, it can control how much is invested and can avoid pushing the market so hard that the patterns vanish. Firms that publicize their techniques are probably suspect; firms with successful techniques keep them secret to gain a market edge. The Prediction Company in Santa Fe, New Mexico, believes that more and more traders will use machine-based forecasting tools but says that secrecy is the key to success.[3]

Because of this secrecy, articles in the financial press often fail to mention the most successful uses of investment black boxes. Probably several dozen firms are managing more than $100 million in assets with black boxes; a few are in the region of $1 billion in assets.

A company called Trendstat Currency Management (TCM) offers a currency hedge program. If you have a large stock portfolio valued in dollars and the dollar goes down against other currencies, you can be protected from the decline. Trendstat makes trades automatically with its own black box.

Many automatic trading systems use neural networks (see Chapter 14) to compare price movements with historical patterns.

The Trendstat black box is different; it is merely concerned with trends. Whenever the box detects a trade, it analyzes that trade and decides whether the action indicates a trend in price movement. The black box is concerned with second-by-second directions of currency movements. It is completely unconcerned with economic fundamentals or political motivations for supporting currencies. It merely participates in what its algorithms say appear to be significant trading trends. It doesn't know the reason for the trend.

To be successful this trend-following black box must distinguish between significant trends and noise fluctuations. It has a sophisticated filter for attempting to separate the trend from the noise. The noise varies depending on circumstances, and so the filter is dynamic, changing its characteristics as appropriate.

Trendstat's black box demonstrates consistent performance in both bull and bear stock markets, and when the bond market is rising or falling. The black box does best when there is major activity in the currency markets and many trades are happening. It does least well when there is stability and few trades are happening. It makes money in times of turbulence. Trendstat investors pray for chaos.

The two main executives of Trendstat explained their program to me. I was intrigued to know how they could be managing moment-by-moment currency trading with no pagers or cellular phones. They said that no action of theirs would improve the performance of their black box. If the markets reacted violently to any news, the black box would act in response to currency movements. And it would act very quickly. The computer would have taken action if it needed to, automatically, before the people at Trendstat could have done it. Human intervention in the process would normally produce worse results than allowing the black box to work automatically.

Like any black box, Trendstat's software has had good years and bad years. From its inception in April 1991 to 1998 it provided average annual net returns of about 17 percent on assets traded. Many investors found 17 percent a decent rate of return, especially because it could be liquidated immediately at any time. But its performance fell in 1998 because the patterns changed. The year 1998 broke the rules in most investments. The designers, of course, are working to detect the patterns that caused the bad performance in 1998 so that the tool can avoid such drop-offs in the future. Mature black boxes need to be tested against many years of experience.

Many customers of Trendstat have major investments that are linked to the dollar. They want to create a hedge in case the dollar falls. The black box provides an appropriate hedge because its performance is noncorrelated with stock and bond performance (the correlation is only 0.0025).

> Like online stock trading, user-friendly financial exchange trading will become a feverish form of home gambling.

Suppose that a customer has $100 million invested in a stock and bond portfolio. That customer has in effect taken a $100 million bet on the U.S. dollar. If the dollar falls, the purchasing power of the portfolio falls against a basket of other world currencies. That customer might use a $100 million Trendstat hedge against the dollar. This would require $5 million (or less) actual dollars because Trendstat can obtain a coverage of twenty times (or more) the amount invested, secured by the Trendstat account. This leverage is acceptable because Trendstat trades only the major stable currencies, and the currency exchange market is one of the most liquid markets in the world. If the dollar falls, Trendstat's currency exchange helps the client preserve the portfolio's global purchasing power.

The higher the leverage, of course, the higher the risk. After the crash of 1929 laws were introduced in an attempt to limit excessive stock market risk. With today's computerized instruments, such as derivatives and hedge funds, risk can be hidden and is extremely difficult to regulate. The public doesn't necessarily know when they are investing in funds with excessive risk. Many of the world's prestigious banks and funds were caught by surprise by the catastrophic crash of Long-Term Capital Management in 1998.

BLACK-BOX PROLIFERATION

The Trendstat example is of interest because, while most money managers dismiss black boxes, the Trendstat black box has done much better than most money managers.

If it becomes accepted that black-box software can trade in the vast currency exchange market better than most human traders, then there will be a wild proliferation of black boxes. It seems inevitable that this will happen. Some authorities think it may be decades away; some think it will happen when today's computer-happy youth rise to power.

Different black boxes are likely to use fundamentally different techniques. There is no relationship between the black-box mechanisms of Olsen and Associates in Zurich and those of Trendstat, for example. When multiple black boxes compete there will probably be black boxes for selecting black boxes.

The spread of computer networks with *manual* trading fundamentally changed the behavior of currency markets, making them behave in ways that usually did not reflect underlying economic fundamentals. It made them highly volatile and subject to sudden extreme movements. Computer networks with automated trading, which, like Trendstat, gives instant reactions to currency movements regardless of their underlying cause, would likely produce far more volatility, with extremes that would be even more sudden and unpredictable. Computers around the world could all decide in unison to dump a certain currency, for example.

Trend-monitoring black boxes generally do best in times of chaos. Multiple black boxes may *cause* chaos and at the same time benefit from that chaos.

It has been suggested that new laws be introduced into currency trading to damp down the volatility. In reality it would be difficult to find legal mechanisms that would work and not cause other forms of speculation.

Where restrictive laws are passed, computerized trading will simply go "offshore."

DOWNSIZING THE TRADERS

Many computer applications that once needed large mainframes can now be done with personal computers. Electronic fund transfers used to take place solely among banks with big computers. With the spread of electronic cash it can take place in the home.

Like online stock trading, user-friendly financial exchange trading will become a feverish form of home gambling.

> Where restrictive laws are passed, computerized trading will simply go "offshore."

There will be a massive market for software for home investors. Black boxes for currency trading can run on home PCs. There is nothing inherent in the Trendstat black box that would preclude it from being rewritten to run on home computers. An online service could constantly adjust the rules it uses to respond to changing economic conditions. New services will be designed to allow individuals to obtain leverage so that their port-folio can be hedged. When trading and black boxes proliferate to this extent, the returns will be more ordinary. It is the players who do something *out of the ordinary* that obtain out-of-the-ordinary returns.

When many individuals use software for currency trading, this will further increase volatility. The herds of the electronic jungle will all panic together. Millions of black boxes will exhibit a herd instinct, all taking the same action and perhaps reacting to that action very fast. It will be even more difficult for central banks to support their currencies or control crises. Truly savvy investors may have a way of anticipating the crises and placing large bets, as Soros did in betting against central banks.

Proprietary alien-intelligence software using neural networks may alert its owners to the imminence of wild swings before they occur.

AMATEUR HOUR

The best traders are very professional and use highly elaborate com-puterized tools. The owners of the best proprietary black-box tools claim (rightly or wrongly) that they are outperforming the best human traders. Hedge funds can increase their leverage by trading much more than the cash a customer puts in. When Soros bets on currencies, for example, the bet is sometimes leveraged as much as twelve times the cash invested. Some Trendstat investors use twenty times the cash invested. This is less risky than it might sound because the investment is in stable currencies. The dollar may lose 2 percent against the deutsche mark, but it doesn't lose much of its domestic purchasing power.

The great Grand Master Kasparov was beaten by a chess-playing machine. And as machines become far more powerful, in the long run humans don't stand a chance against chess machines. Similarly, in the long run humans don't stand a chance against currency-trading black boxes. Ten years ago we would have said, "Chess machines need to get much better." They did. Today we might say, "Black boxes need to get much better." They will.

Computerized currency trading is largely unaffected by downturns in the stock or bond markets. The stockbroker tells you about his successes but not about his bad times. Averaging over the good times and bad times, hedge funds using leverage, with the best automation, are doing better than most stockbrokers.

Given the performance of foreign exchange traders, the last thing to do with spare cash is to keep it in one currency or to let banks or brokers invest cash in their traditional way. Some brokers ask their customers what currency they want to keep spare cash in. They lament that exchange rates have become so irrational that it is difficult to predict which currency is best. Most never raise the issue.

Active trading with alien intelligence has reduced the High Street broker and bank to amateur hour. And most do not even know it.

BIG GAMES

In fifteen years currency exchange trading grew from almost zero to over a trillion dollars *a day*. The notional value of derivatives grew to over $60 trillion. This may oil the gears of commerce somewhat, but otherwise it is a zero-sum game. What one investor gains, another loses.

When traders like Soros, or speculators sitting at home in tax havens, make vast fortunes in foreign exchange trading, other people somewhere lose the equivalent amount of money. Similarly with derivatives, when one institution wins, others lose.

This is a game played on a grand scale. In financial terms it is much larger than the wars mankind has waged. The winners are those who invent and master new techniques. To stay ahead they must improve their techniques before they become widely copied. They tune their black boxes or sharpen their processes of computer-aided speculation, often with devilish complexity.

When a foreign exchange black box ramps up profits, it is sucking money from less capable investors. The main losers are ultimately the mass public. They follow the amateur advice given by their local banker and their money passes in ever increasing volumes to the computer-savvy investors. Money now flows worldwide over computer networks from ordinary savers to people who know how to play the new games. It is rather like a worldwide taxation system—taxation by Soros.

As always in history, the barons extract money from the peasants. It is less painful for the peasants if they don't know it is happening.

CHAPTER 9
The Doctors' Dilemma

The practice of medicine is a natural territory for alien intelligence because it involves exceedingly complex bodies of knowledge. Health care could be greatly enhanced by appropriate use of knowledge technologies. It seems a sad indictment that the best user of knowledge technologies is the financial community while the worst is the medical community.

We rarely ask questions today about the value to society of intellectual effort—society's return on intellectual investment. An enormous amount of intellectual effort has gone into computerized financial activities. The overall value to society of the explosion in foreign exchange trading is close to zero because it is a zero-sum game. What one investor gains another loses.

If the same intellectual expenditure were put into applying knowledge technologies to education or medicine, it would not be a zero-sum game. Spectacular advances in health care are within our reach from appropriate use of computerized knowledge. The costs involved are probably much less than those of the schemes the first lady wanted to achieve at the start of the Clinton administration. For the past thirty years medical costs in the United States have been growing exponentially, and the cost of computers has been dropping exponentially. It makes sense to apply computers to medicine.

We can now look back on giant government bureaucracies, frenzied Wall Street activities, spectacular weapons laboratories, and lament the appalling waste of talent. We should ask where this talent could best be used to improve the condition of mankind. If we don't constantly ask this top-level question, the chain reactions of cyberspace will lead to explosions of complexity and a stressed-out Prozac-plus society far removed from what we would have described as quality of life.

Mankind could grade its activities in terms of society's return on intellectual investment. Some intellectual effort improves quality of life; much does not.

DETECTABLE PATTERNS

Alien-intelligence techniques enable us to detect patterns in large masses of data. This can enable market traders to make more money. It can help Wal-Mart position products in its stores. It can also help us find means of both preventing illness and designing better treatments. Health care patterns are more complex than Wall Street's patterns, but there could be more success in using them because they do not have the random-walk nature of the financial markets.

If people's health were quoted on the stock market and you could invest in it, shorting when necessary, it would be easier to make money than investing in companies.

In the last chapter we explained how computerized pattern recognition helps analysts and traders detect patterns in financial data. This has direct application to medicine. The handwritten chart that the nurse updates is crude and of limited value. If a computer had access to a large amount of relevant medical data, it could detect patterns that humans cannot detect—perhaps in time to prevent serious medical incidents.

Computer-aided understanding of health care patterns will slowly condense into reliable theory that will have a major effect on preventing serious illness.

ALIEN THOUGHT

The recognition of intricate patterns of clues is critical to improving health care. Some patterns can be observed with human senses. A doctor gets important clues from looking at your eyes, smelling your breath, or listening with a stethoscope. Many of the most important patterns, however, can't be observed with human senses.

Much of the knowledge that should be used to make key medical decisions can't be conveyed effectively in writing.

> Our grand Cartesian legacy limits what medical practice achieves (as it does in all complex fields).

Documents have difficulty conveying subtle visual patterns. Nor can such patterns be described with mathematics or Cartesian logic. We are now finding that patterns more subtle than visual patterns are critical for diagnosis but even more difficult to describe. They are in the realm of cyberthought and alien intelligence.

We commented that classical scientific methods are ideal for a world of scarce data and sequential thought. But we are now racing into a time when we are deluged with data and processing can take place on ultra-fast parallel computers. We are surrounded by vitally important problems that cannot be dealt with using Cartesian thought. Kant argued that the Cartesian view of nature is something that we impose upon nature, not an inherent property of nature. It enables us to think sequential thoughts with compact formulation, but many aspects of nature are not visible using such methods.

Our grand Cartesian legacy limits what medical practice achieves (as it does in all complex fields).

A challenge of our time is learning how to tackle these subjects with alien intelligence. We need to capture vast amounts of data, design systems such that the data are well defined and compatible, and put the new computing techniques to work to monitor the data and forage for new insights.

COMPUTER-AIDED DIAGNOSIS

The health care world is full of stories of misdiagnoses. Robert Brook, a health professor at UCLA, states, "Nearly a third of the things we do to patients are not needed and a third of the things they need they don't get."[1] A major focus of knowledge technologies needs to be to improve the diagnostic process and link it to the right care plan.

Medicine is so complex that no doctor can always have the knowledge to make correct diagnoses. A computer can enormously enhance the doctor's capability. It can simplify and codify the diagnostic process and provide a means to capture the outcome.

A doctor making a diagnosis relies on many types of clues. He looks for physical signs—the appearance of the eyes, the tongue, and nonverbal signals of distress. He asks about past medical history, family history, and recent exposures to disease. He can request various tests, some performed by himself, some requiring laboratory analysis, some needing a visit to a hospital.

A diagnostic algorithm is a computerized method of determining whether a patient has the characteristics of a given condition. The algorithm may start with a set of symptoms that might be caused by many possible conditions. It will guide the doctor as to which further questions to ask and tests to carry out in order to eliminate some of the conditions. The computer has the goal of successively narrowing the range of possibilities.

The doctor is fully in charge of the diagnosis and can override challenges by the computer. Diagnostic algorithms serve as

> Computers will help us understand health care patterns and ultimately prevent many serious illnesses.

an aide-mémoire to doctors, prompting them to seek out the right diagnostic evidence. There is a danger in trying to reduce to a standard procedure something as complex as an individual's health. Some patients tell the doctor what they think he wants to hear. It is the doctor's responsibility to guard against false conclusions. The computer acts as a friendly colleague to the doctor as he reaches his own conclusions, but it has an enormous amount of knowledge—far more than the unaided doctor.

Having arrived at a diagnosis, the computer will *suggest* an appropriate care plan. The doctor may accept this, or choose a different care plan if he judges that the computer's suggestion is not the best for the patient. Responsibility for assigning a patient to a care plan must always rest with the doctor. The computer can't force the outcome, but it can leave an audit trail.

Most doctors are familiar with only a very small percentage of the many thousands of drugs on the market. A computer can advise a doctor about all the drugs that might be considered for a particular situation. It may suggest a first-choice drug and allow the physician to browse through other possibilities. It will indicate the current best prescribing practices, experiences with possible side effects, and any conflicts with other medication the patient may be taking. The doctor might be prescribing one drug, and the computer will point out competing drugs at a third of the price.

It is essential that we replace the fat folders of patient records with indecipherable doctors' note with precise computer-meaningful data.

A problem in applying computing to the doctor's work is that most doctors don't want to fiddle with computers while interacting with patients. They are concerned that they may lose the human touch that is so important, and pay more attention to the machine than the patient. Some doctors like handheld devices that accept handwriting, such as the Palm Pilot. Some doctors make manual notes and have a clerical assistant transcribe those into computerized charts and patient records. The computer should check that what is transcribed seems to be correct, because there are countless examples of assistants' misinterpreting doctors' handwritten scrawls. Computers can also allow doctors to give patients a printout of treatments and perhaps details of where to find further information on the Web.

To achieve good-quality care the doctor needs a total picture of the patient, often with input from many sources. Computerized records make possible cooperation between multiple doctors and care providers who have worked with the same patient. It seems outrageous that doctors without computerized records sometimes kill patients by prescribing, in an emergency, drugs to which patients are severely allergic. This has happened, for example, with heart-attack victims being given a beta-blocker, when a record in some paper folder says that this must never be done. The verdict never says, "Cause of death: failure to use data on patient's record."

While the old-time doctor had a personal relationship with his patient that enabled him to understand the subtleties of the patient's condition, today's physician often falls between two stools. He has no deep relationship with the patient and no ability to harness the new power of computers. Some HMOs (Health Maintenance Organizations) aim to change this. The medical director of United Health Care comments that if he had appropriate electronic records he would start paying doctors based on their performance.[2]

COST CONTROL

The costs of health care have been rising alarmingly. Cost control has been a major focus of health care management, but, in spite of that, health care spending as a percentage of GDP is greater than it has ever been in almost all developed countries.

Cutting costs is a tricky business. It can lead to highly publicized stories of damage done to individual patients. Reducing costs in the short term can sometimes increase costs in the long run. For example, squeezing what is spent on drugs in the short term can exacerbate problems in the long term; speeding patients through the hospital can lead to marked increases in costly readmissions. Some actions that are extremely simple can have a big effect on costs. For instance, telling patients above a certain age to take an aspirin a day lowers the number of heart attacks and strokes.

Managed health care has been associated, especially in the United States, with pressure to control costs. That concept is now coming under fire for three reasons:

- The payer is actually paying more.
- The patient often feels shortchanged. There are many stories about not being able to get needed care.
- Most doctors find the reimbursement environment the most unfavorable they have experienced.

In many cases what is being discredited is not managed care, but managed cost. Many attempts to cut costs have in fact cut quality.

This doesn't work in the long run. Large corporations that assume responsibility for the health care of their employees often comment that quality health care is ultimately the least expensive. As General Motors' director of health care says, "Improved care gives us the best cost at the end of the day."[3]

Improving the quality of health care requires measuring the outcomes and comparing them with objectives. Standards can then be defined, validated, and implemented. The U.S. Healthcare Finance Administration (HCFA) has indicated that the definition and measurement of health care outcomes require the *integration of clinical and financial data*. Achieving such integration is necessary for the improvement of managed health care, whether seen from the micro level—the doctor's desk—or the macro level—the state population or the customers of a large HMO. By using knowledge technologies intelligently, we can reach this goal.

THE GREAT CHALLENGE: PREVENTIVE MEDICINE

A spectacular goal in health care is now in our sights—to change medicine so that it is focused on *preventing* illness rather than curing illness.

The one thing—perhaps the only thing—that can bring down medical costs is to move to an era of preventive medicine. Preventive medicine ranges from simple measures like immunization to high-tech electronics that can detect the likelihood of a stroke before it happens. Spending money to prevent serious illness is much less expensive than coping with the damage after it has happened.

We commented earlier that HNC sells software that identifies bankruptcies before they happen. HNC works with a consortium of corporations to collect data about situations that have led to bankruptcy, and then uses alien-intelligence techniques to identify the telltale patterns that warn of impending bankruptcies. Neural networks (see Chapter 14) can be trained to recognize telltale patterns that humans cannot recognize, and the more the software does that the better it becomes at it. Just as we can flag bankruptcies before they happen, so can we flag people who are likely to develop serious illnesses before the sicknesses occur. Indeed, computers have already been developed that learn to give early warning that a medical crisis is imminent.[4] We need to build up large amounts of information in data warehouses so that computers have as much raw material to chew on as possible. Computers generally need data that are much cleaner and more precise than the data available today.

A jetliner has built-in preventive medicine. When the 777 jetliner first flew, Boeing stated that it was the most complex machine ever built. It has over four million parts from many hundreds of suppliers, and all the parts have to work together in the most intricate way.

> Classical scientific methods are ideal for a world of scarce data and sequential thought. But we are now deluged with data, which ultrafast computers can process.

The plane constantly monitors all of its systems and has subtle ways to detect that something might go wrong before it happens. It usually takes corrective action automatically.

Well, our body is much more complex than a jetliner. The body couldn't possibly work without automatic means of detecting and correcting problems. Components of the body such as the liver have their own means of self-repair. The body as a whole has an immune system. If our body's immune system is working well, health care is inexpensive. If it breaks down, this can be very expensive, as we have seen with the AIDS crisis.

The most important part of preventive medicine is to harness the body's own natural defenses.

Our body has an amazing set of mechanisms to combat invading infections. We can design medical remedies to harness and work with the body's own defenses, or remedies that work independently of it. Many of today's drugs ignore the body's defenses. Antibiotics, for example, attack bacteria directly. Both types of remedies are needed, but future medicine will harness the body's own preventive mechanisms much better than it does today. Knowledge technology will eventually help us to predict disease and work with the body to take preventive measures.

HEALTH CARE WAREHOUSES

To put computers to good use we must have good data. A problem with today's medicine is that most available records are a mess. Due to an absence of standards, data in different places are represented in incompatible ways. In order to achieve the benefits that alien intelligence now offers, we must clean up the records. This is not particularly expensive for a new system. The difficulty is in cleaning up old systems and achieving agreement and standardization among the different players.

I tried to examine my own medical records, kept in a folder in my doctor's office. They were hopelessly incomplete. Hospital records were missing, as were X rays, results from visits to other doctors, and details of serious medical events that happened elsewhere. My doctor's records were handwritten and almost impossible to read. Nothing was computerized.

Most patient records give incomplete case histories; parts of them are often illegible or damaged. Vital data get lost. Critical data cannot be analyzed. The records are often not available in emergencies, or for multisite care. Patient records need to be compatible with other records—those of the doctors, clinics, hospitals, pharmaceutical companies, HMOs, and insurance companies. Unfortunately, the same data are represented in incompatible ways. A data item in one computer is represented differently from the same data item in a different system.

Problems like these have been corrected in other industries. But it takes discipline. The need for clean-up in health care is critical today because the new computer techniques present such a great opportunity for radical health care improvement.

Wal-Mart's data warehouse for optimizing the delivery and positioning of goods on supermarket shelves has over twenty trillion bytes of data. Wal-Mart needs details of every customer purchase. Black boxes for foreign exchange trading need tick-by-tick details of every change in quoted price, and every trade, its volume and price.

Such bodies of data make it possible to test hypotheses and experiment with proposed techniques. Investment tools are programmed, run against historical data, and modified until they produce the best results achievable. To be as effective as possible medicine needs to be based on similar techniques—vast amounts of collected data, alien-intelligence techniques to recognize patterns and correlations in these data, constant measurement of the care process, and, based on this, constant computerized refinement of the process.

Alien intelligence can monitor our health, detect problems before they become difficult to correct, learn the most effective ways to deal with problems, and relentlessly refine these processes through experience with millions of patients.

Computer-aided health care starts with computerized records—accurate, complete, and compatible. As in other fields, vast amounts of data will be accumulated in data warehouses, and computers can derive valuable conclusions by searching the data and looking for patterns. But they can do this only if the data are consistent and compatible.

Today health care has four collections of data—those of the four players that interact with the patient:

- Medical records of the individual.
- Records of the doctor, clinic, and hospital.
- Records of solution providers—for instance, HMOs.
- Records of insurance companies.[5]

These records, if compatible, form a valuable body of information. The four types of players need sophisticated software that shares common data. Unfortunately, today their data are usually incompatible because they have been designed in different organi-zations at different times to different or nonexistent standards.

As in many other organizations data have to be made consistent before computerized tools can extract value from them.

HMO DATA

Where health care is handled by one party such as a large HMO, it can establish consistent data representation within its domain. Aiming to deliver better care, the HMO Kaiser Permanente is spending about $1 billion on a national clinical-information system that will keep records in a standard format. Over a five-year period it is creating a nervous system for its nine million members, linking ten thousand doctors and other care providers. Kaiser can impose the standards for data that are essential for computer-aided health care because it has exclusive control over nearly all of its doctors, hospitals, pharmacies, and laboratories.

HMOs cover nearly seventy million Americans. Their competition for patients is growing fiercer, and increasingly the public wants quality care, not simply lowest-cost care. As Kaiser brings its new system into operation, smaller HMOs will feel the need to follow suit. To do so they will have to form agreements about data standards. The advantages but high costs of such systems will force mergers and consolidation in the health care industry.

Security and privacy are major concerns in health care. Many people worry about their medical records being easily accessible. They worry that they might be turned down for a job, or even by a would-be spouse, or that their insurance rates will be too high. Privacy has been used as an argument for not creating the data standards that can help to bring preventive medicine.

Data in computers can be made extremely secure with tight encryption and positive identification of who accesses data. Kaiser Permanente has built a high level of security into its system, with passwords and sophisticated audit trails of who uses the data. Data used for research purposes or data-mining applications are aggregated, and personal identifiers are stripped off. Kaiser employees are fired if they breach security, even casually.

PATIENT-FOCUSED HEALTH CARE

Just as industry has become increasingly customer focused, so is health care, rather late, shifting to patient-focused care. The patient is becoming more and more a direct customer, and doctors, dentists, and HMOs must compete for that business. This shift implies a change in the balance of power in health care. The "patient" will increasingly be seen as a client. Most of the time this client will be healthy, not sick, and *prevention* of illness should be a priority. More and more health care services will be integrated with related services, such as insurance, pensions, and housing that incorporates health care facilities.

When people become sick, they need to understand their condition, its management and treatments, and how best to respond to various symptoms. They need to know what to do to get better. If you get kidney stones, you suddenly want to learn about them so that you can avoid a repeat performance. When doctors started to have their records computerized, many patients wanted to have a printed copy so that they could study it, take it home, and file it.

As computers assume a more prominent role in health care, it makes sense for patients to have access to their own *computerized* records. If charts for disease management are used the patient should be able to access his chart with his PC. The chart may be linked to details about medication, explanation of measurements, diet recommendations, and comments on how to help combat the disease.

> We need to capture vast amounts of data and to put the new computing techniques to work monitoring the data and foraging for new insights.

An individual's medical records, like his financial records, contain much sensitive and personal information. The individual ought to *own his own records,* and they should be kept strictly private. You might employ a third party—for example, your doctor's clinic—to maintain the data and keep them strictly private. You wouldn't dream of letting your financial records be scattered among different organizations in a way that prevented you from using the information, yet that is the situation with most people's medical records.

Medical records should be computerized and transmittable over the Internet when needed. They can fit on a card in your wallet; records that contain X rays and photographs can fit on a computer disk. If you are in a car crash or collapse in the street, the computer in the ambulance could examine your wallet-card and transmit its contents to the destination clinic. That might save your life. By 2010 it will be possible to have your entire DNA code stored on a wallet-card.

BENEFITS OF INTEGRATED DATA

Cleaning up computerized health care data has great benefits to various parties:

■ *Benefits to the patient:* The patient will have better information about his or her condition, how to treat it, and how to live in a way that will encourage long-term health. The patient can be given optimal care plans based on computer analysis of large numbers of results. Access to correct and complete medical records is vital in an emergency and in some cases may save the patient's life. When a person's medical records are on his PC, they can be linked to medical tutorials, so that the patient can understand his and his family's conditions better. A computer can guide him in how to avoid sickness rather than solely in how to cure it.

■ *Benefits to the doctor:* The doctor will have more complete and accurate records about his patients. The computer will offer the doctor guidance on diagnosis, prevention of illness, treatment options, the best protocols and codes of practice, drugs and their correct use, and overall disease management strategies. It will provide a doctor–machine partnership in which alien intelligence backs up the human intelligence of the doctor.

■ *Benefits to the HMO or solutions provider:* Good data create the means to offer innovative care packages based on outcomes known to arise from particular treatments. Machines will constantly learn about how to improve the best practices. The HMO can then assess the economic impact of generic treatment strategies, advise practitioners about the current best practice, and record the outcomes.

■ *Benefits to the insurance company:* An insurer makes more profit if the people it has insured stay healthier. A mechanism that captures health care costs and quality indicators will help spread the best medical practices. Moreover, the tools will enable the insurer to enhance the processing and audit of claims. There can be far more effective risk management, leading to higher profits.

■ *Benefits to pharmaceutical companies:* Health care data warehouses will be able to provide a mass of anonymous data about the outcomes and side effects of drug usage with specific diseases. Data from diverse areas can then be absorbed, analyzed, and compared, and can provide therapeutic and economic evidence of the value of new medicines.

■ *Benefits to government:* The integrated capturing of health care information for entire communities will enhance the ability to recognize infectious diseases and stop their spread at an early stage. Continuous monitoring of diseases and their treatment can lead to improved disease management. Medical data warehouses will enable government to improve its resource planning and management, against a background of better understanding of health care patterns and trends.

Good computerized tools exist for each of these groups, but the tools need good data. To have good data the health industry has to get its act together.

The radical improvement in health care that computers make possible is generally beyond the capability of one organization. So partnerships and alliances need to be forged, with integrated systems. Once such partnerships are well established the solutions they create will become the basis of de facto standards, which in turn will find their way into laws or legally enforceable codes of good practice.

In 1996 Congress passed its Health Care Portability and Accountability Act. This act requires the creation of common data models to spur computerized improvement in health care. Laws and standards such as these lay a foundation for widespread use of knowledge technology that will improve both the quality and cost of health care. There are also standards for electronic interchange of health care information.

Changing medical data from a chaotic mess to integrated databases will make possible alien-intelligence techniques for continuous improvement of diagnosis and treatment. It is high time the improvement was made.

REAL-TIME CONTROL IN MEDICINE

If something is going wrong with one's body, it is desirable to catch it at the earliest possible stage. If caught early, the problem is usually easy to fix; if it is not caught and becomes chronic, it may be very difficult to fix. The same is true in corporations or other complex organisms. Usually when a corporation gets into serious trouble, it is because a problem was not detected and dealt with quickly, and was allowed to fester. Real-time control is needed to detect problems as soon as they appear and to deal with them.

Real-time control starts with the ability to monitor and detect if anything is going wrong. Most of the time our body does this— we get a headache, temperature, or generally feel ill. But our body does not detect some illnesses. We may have a cancer growing without knowing it, or conditions developing that could lead to a stroke or heart attack.

A person is more likely to stay healthy if he has regular check-ups. Still, doctor visits are expensive, and infrequent, so a person should monitor his own and his family's health. You watch your weight if you have a bathroom scale. Many health-monitoring instruments are becoming inexpensive. Net-order services sell cheap gadgets for taking medical measurements such as blood pressure. Heart monitors, worn on the wrist, can help a person improve the strength of his heart, for example by weekly hill walks. Soon home analysis of electrocardiogram signals will be inexpensive. Some drugstores offer inexpensive services for testing blood, stool, and cholesterol levels. It will always be cheaper to catch problems when they are easy to fix than to let them become chronic.

With some types of sickness you need to have tests conducted regularly by a clinic. But many tests that have been done in a clinic can now be done at home, thanks to advancing automation. Some people in Japan have an "intelligent" toilet that weighs them, takes their temperature, and does some types of urine or stool analysis. People with potential problems may have electronic monitors attached to their bodies—for example, heart monitors or blood chemical sensors. Neural nose technology can smell your breath and detect early-warning signals of problems. In short, home health monitoring will be a mix of automatic tests and self-administered tests.

THE PC DOCTOR

A major change in health care will come when individuals use their personal computer to checking their health constantly.

All health-monitoring devices, from bathroom scales to wearable heart monitors, can have a wireless link to your personal computer, which may be designed to do certain tests itself. It might take the temperature of your hand on the keyboard or have a digital camera chip that examines your eyes. It might have a neural nose that smells your breath. Software will steadily accumulate data about your body and its health, and give advice when needed. Preventive medicine is much cheaper than curative medicine. When you have a PC that monitors your health and keeps your medical records, you are more likely to be aware of anything that needs attention.

"Microsoft Doctor" might have larger sales than Microsoft Office.

The measurements collected at home may be automatically transmitted to a clinic, and results from clinics transmitted to your PC. Results from doctors should be integrated with measurements made at home. Your PC can have its own data warehouse containing all medical information about you and your family. A pocket Jaz disk, which holds two billion bytes, would suffice for this. PC versions of alien-intelligence software can be constantly learning about its owner and looking for early-warning signs of medical conditions that need attention.

> A spectacular goal is now in our sights—to focus medicine on *preventing* rather than curing illness.

It would be a valuable public service to make free software for home medical diagnosis available. Some governments may decide to provide such facilities; if not, it could make sense for insurance companies or HMOs to provide them. Commonly used diagnostics could reside on the home PC, with less-frequently used ones accessible on the Internet. Such software might take the form of expert systems that have been approved by medical authorities. It would tell its user when home treatment of the illness is appropriate and when it is desirable to visit a doctor or clinic.

Many drug companies could benefit from providing components of medical diagnosis for free. It should be made law that pharmaceuticals come with a Web address at which the user can find detailed advice and tutorials. The Web site may link to sophisticated computer processes for diagnosis. The drug company, in turn, would use the Web site to obtain valuable information about the product use.

Widespread use of home diagnosis and treatment of straight-forward illnesses will reduce the costs of health care in two ways. First, it will eliminate many expensive visits to the doctor. Second, it will help people identify problems at an early stage, before they get out of control and become expensive.

EMPOWERING THE CITIZEN

A major factor in lowering the cost of health care will be getting individuals to take more action themselves. As we shift more toward patient-driven health care, the individual will take actions that were previously the responsibility of doctors. The individual should be given the capability to do diagnosis wherever possible.

As technology has progressed, it has enabled the individual to have his own music, films, transport, and so forth. He should also have his own medical technology.

People no longer need priests to read the Holy Book to them; they can read themselves. As priests, professors, and professionals become less shrouded with an aura that protects them from being challenged, the public begins to question what they say. As we learn to probe professionals we find that many have feet of clay. The dignified banker is incompetent at investing our money. The doctor makes as many wrong diagnoses as right ones. The lawyer is outrageously inflating his own fees.

> "Microsoft Doctor" might have larger sales than Microsoft Office.

With this new iconoclasm comes individual responsibility. The individual will be able to take charge of his own destiny. I have observed that people with heart monitors become serious about keeping their heart well exercised.

Societies with socialist leanings have thought of health as being a responsibility of government. This has not worked well. If we think that our health is in the lap of the gods of government, we don't take care of it as we should. The individual must take responsibility.

As the tools for personal health care become widespread and sophisticated, it is necessary to connect education and health. Do-it-yourself diagnostic software might often recommend changes in lifestyle or diet to its user that could help keep him healthier. The individual needs to be taught that how well he or she deals with health care has a major effect on life and longevity.

A problem with patient-driven health care is that only some people have computers; only some use the Internet; only some have the intelligence or responsibility to take charge of their own health care. Today most individuals spend more money maintaining their car than maintaining their health. Can the pregnant woman smoking a cigarette in front of a poster that says "Smoking damages your unborn baby" be made to be responsible about health care?

Are we moving to a society with better health for the intelligent than the unintelligent? Or better health for the computer-capable? This question applies to many other aspects of life in the cyberspace era. Technology-capable people can invest money better, find better jobs, and find information when they need it. Perhaps the most dangerous consequence of the alien-intelligence revolution will be that it widens the chasm between the haves and the have-nots.

LIFE EXPECTANCY

Life expectancy has gone up ten years since I was at college. It can certainly go up more. Japanese males live substantially longer than American males, in spite of the fact that many smoke like chimneys and have lives of substantial stress. Probably the major reason relates to nutrition. The individual can raise his probability of a long life by eating better, avoiding saturated fat, controlling cholesterol, not smoking, avoiding stress where possible, being careful how he drives, and exercising regularly. Better health care can help to avoid life-terminating accidents, such as fatal heart attacks and strokes. It can help to detect cancer at the earliest stage, when it can be treated fairly easily. Future medicine should constantly monitor to detect problems and then deal with those problems before they become expensive or dangerous. Responsible patient-driven health care can lead to longer life.

> As technology has progressed, it has enabled the individual to have his own music, films, transport, and so forth. He should also have his own medical technology.

In many ways a healthy immune system is better than a good doctor. Taking medicine that makes the immune system do its work as effectively as possible is generally better than indiscriminately using drugs to try to correct problems. Whereas the immune system is immensely subtle, many drugs are crude and have serious side effects. Casual and excessive use of antibiotics has encouraged viruses to mutate into resistant strains.

When darkness falls, our penal gland secretes melatonin, which is part of the immune system's process for cleaning house. Unfortunately, the designer of the penal gland didn't expect us to live over sixty, for the melatonin production dries up around that age. For people over sixty, taking melatonin at bedtime is an example of how we can give the immune system a helping hand. Specialists in homeopathic medicine believe that there are multiple ways to help the immune system do its subtle work.

The above techniques are not particularly dramatic, but, used collectively, they may enable many people to live to be 100. A more dramatic attack on aging will come from our understanding of the human genome. Certain genes appear to cause aging, and it could be possible to turn them off. Like the penal gland they have been designed to support a shorter life expectancy than we now aspire to. Researchers in this area are saying that in two or three decades we may be able push life expectancy to 110.

If we turn off the aging genes, we will still have brain-cell death; some people will have Alzheimer's and other problems. By messing about with nature we will keep many individuals alive in a frail and demented state. This will raise serious ethical problems; if we prolong life artificially should the individual be able to pull the plug? Longevity will increasingly become a matter of choice.

WARNING LIGHTS

If you have a medical problem, it makes itself apparent by means of the symptoms you have. You may go to the doctor and tell him you have a headache, fever, and extreme drowsiness. He gives you some medicine that cures these symptoms and you are pleased. But the symptoms are different from the underlying problem. If all the doctor has done is suppress the symptoms, the underlying problem is still there and your sickness will probably return.

Using a painkiller doesn't correct the cause of the pain. Fixing the symptoms without dealing with the underlying cause is rather like fixing a car with a flashing emergency oil light by unplugging the light. It removes the source of irritation but might cause the real problem to become worse. Symptoms are a signal that something else is wrong, and treating the symptoms doesn't necessarily change that "something else."

The symptoms are not merely a signal, like the flashing light on the car. They are usually part of nature's technique for trying to correct the situation—the body's adaptive responses trying to fight a problem.

The body creates inflammation as an attempt to wall off, heat up, and burn out infective agents or foreign matter.[6] A cough is a protective mechanism for clearing breathing passages. Diarrhea is a defensive effort of the body to remove pathogens or irritants more quickly from the colon.[7] Discharges are the body's way of ridding itself of mucus, dead bacteria, viruses, and cells. The body creates a fever when it has bacterial or viral infection because the fever makes it more able to produce interferon (an antiviral substance), and it also increases white blood cell mobility and activity, which are factors instrumental in fighting infection.[8]

Some problems return again and again in spite of the doctor's treatment. Often a problem seems to disappear after treatment, only to return in a different form because the cause of the problem wasn't addressed. It is important to recognize that symptoms are efforts of the body to defend itself. Because a fever is an adaptive defense of the body, it is not a good idea to suppress it with aspirin. When doctors prescribe a drug to control or suppress *symptoms* rather than deal with the underlying cause, they may actually *inhibit* the body's own defense and immune processes.

THE IMMUNE SYSTEM

Our immune system is a highly intricate facility that protects us from infectious organisms. It uses multiple components, including antigens, antibodies, and various types of white blood cells such as B and T lymphocytes. The interaction of these components protects our body from organisms that invade it.

Until we get old, disease is most commonly caused by the invasion of an outside agent—microorganisms such as bacteria, viruses and fungi, and larger organisms such as ticks and worms. Today we are more often invaded by substances that are not naturally occurring, such as cigarette smoke, alcohol, radiation, pollution, and food additives. While our immune system is astonishingly effective in dealing with naturally occurring invasion, it is not as good at coping with non-natural invasion, such as the side effects of the drugs we take.

Just as human intelligence is immensely subtle and complex compared to machine intelligence, so our immune system is immensely subtle and complex compared to artificial medical remedies. Many of the drugs in use today are powerful but about as subtle as a terrorist bomb.

Our immune system has two remarkable properties: it attacks *specific* invaders and it *remembers* them. When an antigen invades our body, our immune system produces a *specific* antibody or *specific* cells for attacking the invader. Because they are specific the antibody or the cells will neutralize

> The most important part of preventive medicine is the harnessing of the body's own natural defenses.

only the invader in question. Once challenged by an antigen, such as the measles virus, our body "remembers" it for years—often for life. The child who has an attack of measles becomes immune for life. If the child is exposed to this specific antigen at a later date, the immune system recognizes it, attacks, and prevents a reinfection.

These two characteristics of the immune system, protection from *specific* invaders and *memory* of those invaders at a later time, serve as the basis for immunization. Inoculating children with a biotic agent alerts their immune system to that agent should it invade the body at a later date. Poliomyelitis, for example, once dreaded as a cause of paralysis and death, has been effectively abolished with the polio vaccine.

The two characteristics are also the basis of homeopathy, a potentially powerful form of "alternate medicine" that is not part of accepted medical practice yet, but which knowledge technology could help to make scientific.

HOMEOPATHY

Various forms of "alternative" medicine are not a normal part of today's medical practice. Some of these are pure quackery, but some can be demonstrated to be effective even though we do not know how they work. Homeopathic medicine has demonstrated some powerful results. In the *Encyclopedia Britannica*'s CD-ROM, I could find the term "homeopathic" only under the subject "occult," and this is close to the attitude of the established medical profession toward homeopathy. Nevertheless, homeopathic medicine has been coming into use by a number of serious doctors, and some respectable authorities believe that it may become the primary form of future medicine because it works by harnessing and strengthening our own immune system.[9] It should be of interest in an era of escalating medical costs because if it works it could lower the cost of health care. And research shows that in spite of skepticism, it certainly does work.[10]

Homeopathic medicines are made from plants and other natural substances that produce pathological effects similar to diseases. The operating premise is that a medicine that *produces* a set of symptoms in a healthy person will *cure* the same set of symptoms, presumably by causing the body's immune system to go to work. When this happens one dose can be effective for a long time. Homeopathic medicines are prepared by a process of repeated dilution so that they are taken in extremely small quantities. In these minute quantities they are capable of stimulating the body's own defense system. Because our body is designed to fight most illnesses in complex ways, it is important to intervene as little as possible. The aim is to prime the immune system so that it either prevents the pathogen from establishing itself or else mobilizes the protective mechanisms to destroy the infection.

Our body is subtle and intelligent in the way it fights disease. The ability of the immune system to attack specific antigens and remember them, often for life, is amazing. Because of the remarkable memory of our immune system, homeopathy has been effective with illnesses that return time and time again. Homeopathy has sometimes been extremely effective with people who have chronic diseases. Sometimes it has corrected conditions that conventional medicine considered incurable.

When the body's own defenses can be harnessed, they can be very powerful. Most traditional medication ignores the intelligence of the body. An antibiotic, for example, attacks a virus directly without using the body's immune system. Some antibiotics cause serious side effects. Homeopathic practitioners believe that it is usually much more effective to choose a remedy that can strengthen the body's ability to heal itself.

Different individuals experience sickness in different ways. Sick individuals have their own idiosyncratic physical, emotional, and mental symptom patterns. They are not identical in the treatments they need. Treating flu in one person is different from treating a similar flu in a different person. The homeopathic doctor would not prescribe one medicine for a headache and another for an upset stomach; he would try to find a single medicine appropriate for that particular individual that covered the entire set of symptoms.

He is matching not single symptoms but the whole pattern of symptoms—the gestalt. A patient who complains of headaches may also have depression, stomach ailments, low energy, and other problems. Often these problems stem from the same root cause, and if that cause is dealt with, all of the symptoms will fade away.

AUTOMATING A BLACK ART

Homeopathy seems like a black art, but as we commented earlier, alien intelligence can sometimes turn a black art into a science. To make homeopathy scientific we must collect vast amounts of data and use alien-intelligence techniques to relate complex cause and effect. Neural networks provide ways to identify and classify patterns of symptoms and associate them with homeopathic medicines that cure them. Such tools need consistently to correlate the symptoms, the characteristics of patients, and the results produced.

INTO UNKNOWN TERRITORY

Homeopathy is not the only form of medicine that could benefit from the rigorous analysis and codification made possible by alien intelligence. Some ancient forms of medicine—including traditional Chinese medicine—worked amazingly well but were completely undocumented. The techniques were passed by apprenticeship from generation to generation and took half a lifetime to learn. Today's Chinese drugstore is full of strange ancient remedies prescribed by hands-on physicians who are sensitive to holistic patterns of symptoms. The remedies are often remarkably successful. They are also inexpensive.

Computers will find patterns and correlations in the data that humans can't find. If they are precise and repeatable, we must take them seriously. If homeopathy is as valuable as its proponents say it is, then we must convert it into a precise discipline where computers can predict the results. We then need computerized guidance for the practitioner. Our new tools should be able to take homeopathy from the realm of witch doctors into the realm of measured predictable science.

A hundred years ago the steam-engine industry ridiculed the coming of electric motors. How could anything as flaky as electric current drive great factories and their machinery! The emotional hostility of the health industry to homeopathic medicine seems somewhat similar. It often stems from vested interests. The drug industry is huge and uses aggressive sales techniques. Homeopathic practitioners note that many of today's drugs are crude instruments with damaging side effects. If homeopathic medicine became widespread, the sales of traditional drugs would plummet. If there were ways to keep people healthier, the revenues of many clinics would plunge. There would be less need to use expensive equipment, so equipment manufacturers would lose sales. But if it were scientifically proven that homeopathy could improve health while lowering health care costs, the benefit to society would be great. It seems likely that this can be achieved and homeopathy will become very important. We should be exploring it with the rigor of computers.

If Western medicine is dominated by what the HMOs practice today, it is fortunate that China and the East will explore other avenues.

Alien-intelligence techniques are finding patterns and correlations in complex data that humans can't find. Where alternate forms of medicine appear to be valuable, like homeopathy or Chinese medicine, we are challenged to use our new methods to determine if they are valid, and to establish techniques that are precise and repeatable. We now have the tools to convert medical practices from black arts into precise disciplines where computers can predict the results and give computerized guidance to the practitioner. Some authorities believe that medical practices that trigger the human immune system into effective action will dominate twenty-first-century medicine.

As we employ alien intelligence to develop new medical practices, we will sometimes be able to cure, or better, prevent illnesses without fully explaining how the practice works. In other disciplines also, like computerized hydroponic flower-growing, we'll use techniques that work without necessarily understanding how they work. Such will be the nature of alien intelligence as it matures.

CHAPTER 10
Reinventing the Corporation

This is an age of drastic reinvention of business. One can look at certain periods and admire turbulent reinventions of science—the coming of the steam engine, or the motorcar, or biotechnology. Today the big-money change is coming from the reinvention of business. Businesspeople are confronted with a plethora of new mechanisms, some difficult to understand, many hard to cope with because they cut across the culture, politics, and traditional wisdom of a well-established corporation. The sweeping innovations in business are made possible by technology, but are created by businesspeople dreaming up new ways of doing business, rather than by an inventor in a laboratory or an engineer at a drawing board.

In the face of exploding e-commerce, particularly as cyberspace becomes ubiquitous, and of rapidly developing alien intelligence, managers in traditional corporations must ask themselves: Can our corporation keep up and get ahead in this new world, or is its embedded culture and old-fashioned business model too difficult to convert? Perhaps most important: Can we convert *fast enough*?

New technologies bring change, and change brings disequilibrium. Today's seemingly severe disequilibrium will probably become even more severe. Disequilibrium creates conditions in which fast-growth companies take control and slow-moving, traditional ones lose the game. It is not a time for the cautious. The fast drivers who understand the new rules can make a fortune. In the words of Gary Hamel, distinguished research fellow at Harvard Business School, in this environment you are either drivers, passengers, or roadkill.[1]

Business has become like the Wild West, with corporate battles everywhere. Some grand old corporations are crumbling while the Wall Street valuation of many newcomers seems beyond all reason. There's a new megarich class, scruffily dressed but far richer than the oil sheiks or maharajas.

Whereas scientific and engineering inventions can often be patented, business inventions generally can't. As soon as they are seen to be effective, they are likely to be copied at high speed. So the new ideas of e-business spread like a brush fire. Because a corporation with a great new business invention can't protect itself with patents, it needs to pick up the ball like a rugby star and move at maximum speed.

We have reached an age where the businessperson who hides from technology is an endangered species. Managers, entrepreneurs, and people concerned about their children's future ought to think about the consequences of the extraordinary changes we describe. By the time these changes have run their course they will have radically changed the entire planet.

THE KNOWLEDGE ECONOMY

Francis Bacon said, "Knowledge is power"; today's executive should say, "Knowledge is money."

New knowledge can translate directly into money. It enables more profitable decisions to be made. It translates into better investments, good marketing, automated production, low inventories, worldwide sales, satisfied customers, better health care, and good design. The goods and services that constitute the economy have growing value as built-in chips and know-how increase their knowledge content. Corporations beat their competition when they are better at idea generation. As knowledge flows over networks, it enables events to happen more efficiently, saving intermediate steps. Knowledge, constantly renewed and enhanced, is the primary source of competitive advantage, so corporations must be designed to expand the knowledge of all employees.

The knowledge corporation should be designed to climb the fastest learning curves that are practical. The more we enhance the way employees use knowledge, the more they contribute to corporate profits. Human expertise can be greatly amplified with knowledge technology. The corporation needs a knowledge infrastructure to capture and create knowledge, store it, improve it, clarify it, disseminate it to all employees, and put it to use as automatically as possible.

Unlike physical goods, knowledge can be multiplied. It can be taught to vast numbers of people and spread with the use of software and chips. Computerized intelligence can create new knowledge. Knowledge in one place can be spread to millions of places on the Internet. The knowledge economy has skills, rules, and software that can rapidly capture, generate, and distribute new knowledge.

The knowledge-based economy will grow very differently from the traditional economy. The traditional economy is tied to the slow and steady building of factories and growth of physical facilities. The new economic growth follows the accelerating upward curve of knowledge creation. The extreme stock market capitalizations reflect this much faster type of growth.

The transition to the knowledge economy has as yet barely moved out of first gear. As the knowledge economy accelerates, there will much more money to be made than in the economies of the twentieth century because the knowledge economy by its very nature can grow faster. Physical industry is severely limited in its speed of growth; knowledge-based industry can grow faster because computerized knowledge can improve rapidly. Much knowledge is in the form of bits, and bits can be moved and multiplied very fast. The cost of storing and processing bits is relentlessly plunging downward, and fiber optics move bits around the planet at the speed of light. Where alien-intelligence techniques help to evolve and breed knowledge, it will grow at great speed.

It is often almost impossible to calculate the value of knowledge in a fast-growth company, so we should expect the knowledge economy often to have unrealistic valuations. The combination of the alien-intelligence jungle and electronic herd behavior will produce extreme fluctuations. An ongoing characteristic of the knowledge economy will probably be wild turbulence in stock prices. The most skilled investors with advanced computer tools can make money in times of turbulence.

BEYOND *DR. STRANGELOVE*

Do you remember the days when there were movies like *Dr. Strangelove* and *Fail Safe*? In those days nuclear bombers took twelve hours to reach the USSR, or vice versa. The United States built the SAGE defense system to warn President Kennedy if Soviet bombers were on their way.

Ten years later ICBMs could make the trip in twenty-five minutes, so NATO built the BMEWS system, with radars on many mountain tops designed to detect Soviet ICBMs and funnel this information to a science fiction–like computer center deep in the rock of Colorado's

Cheyenne Mountain. It would take half of the twenty-five minutes to confirm that the Soviets had really launched an attack (and that it was not a computer error); then in just a few frenzied minutes nuclear bombers would take off, ICBMs would be activated, and President Nixon could decide to launch a counterattack.

Then we got nuclear submarines like *Red October*. That class of Soviet "boomer" carried twenty missiles, each with ten independently targeted warheads, so it could vaporize two hundred cities with a much shorter flight time than ICBMs making the long journey halfway around the planet. There would barely be time to wake up President Reagan.

In the 1980s the game speeded up even more. Cruise missiles and stealth planes were designed to carry a nuclear warhead immensely more powerful than the Hiroshima bomb, and small missiles could be hidden undetected in, for example, a cargo ship approaching the coast near Washington, D.C. There was massive publicity for "Star Wars" (the Strategic Defense Initiative) but no publicity at all for nuclear command-and-control systems designed to be set to "Launch On Warning," meaning that at the very highest level of alert, nuclear retaliation could happen *automatically* with preprogrammed missiles. Both the United States and the Soviet Union implemented automatic Launch On Warning, because if they were attacked there would be no time for their leaders to press "the button."

> In the words of Gary Hamel, in this new environment you are either drivers, passengers, or roadkill.

The two sides had built a computerized nuclear creature. It was chained up with superb security. It had many safety catches that could be successively released as a crisis grew (DEFCON 5,

DEFCON 4, DEFCON 3…). At the highest level of alert the computers might warn the head of state that the safest option was a pre-emptive nuclear strike—use them or lose them. Fortunately no crisis reached the alert level of the Cuban missile crisis (DEFCON 2) before the USSR collapsed and the superpowers were able to back away from their confrontation and rethink.

What happened in this scary and misunderstood segment of history illustrates the inexorable logic of the computer age. Computers become steadily more powerful and become linked to a nervous system whose senses are constantly alert. As computers become more and more intelligent and as complexity increases and reaction times decrease, we ultimately have alien-intelligence systems confronting one another in real time.

In the computer age, the leisurely pace of *Dr. Strangelove* changes to automated Launch On Warning.

The consequence of computerized capitalism is that the battle between the competing corporations becomes ever faster until business reaction times are like those of gunfighters. Because they're so fast, they must be automated. Corporations are linked in real time to multiple players in their ecosystem. Prices change dynamically and instantly. There's a shifting web of virtual operations. The electronic jungle has electronic herds that can charge when their Bloomberg or other screens tell them to.

The methods that have served business well for many decades are being replaced with radically different methods appropriate for the alien-intelligence jungle.

THE CREATURE-LIKE ENTERPRISE

The future corporation must be designed to thrive in this jungle. It needs senses, conditioned reflexes, and a nervous system. A creature in nature's jungle, stalking its prey, is constantly alert to both prey and predators. The corporation monitors its environment in real time and can make immediate adjustments. It has a clearly defined goal, but its tactic for achieving that goal may switch instantly.

Today's electronics enable a corporation to react to events at great speed. Like nature's creatures the new corporation should have conditioned reflexes. Much decision making can be automated, which leads to much faster reaction times. Decisions needing human attention can be automatically routed to the right person.

Alien intelligence enables very complex decisions to be made automatically. It facilitates computerized learning to improve processes continuously or to get detailed information about each customer's wishes. Vast amounts of

> Using alien intelligence to forage for insight in vast warehouses of data will play a key role in ensuring the corporation's survival.

data can be automatically collected and digested, as in Wal-Mart's data warehouse of twenty trillion bytes. Using alien intelligence to forage for insight in vast warehouses of data will play a key role in ensuring the corporation's survival.

The corporation should have three types of nervous systems: *external* use of the World Wide Web linking it to potential customers, suppliers, and the public at large; an *internal* network that is private and secure (referred to as an "intranet"); and a private network linked to many trading partners (referred to as an "extranet"). It may use a variety of virtual private networks, like those handling funds transfer, travel bookings, stock market trading, goods distribution, and specialized research. Many virtual private networks will be derived from the Internet, making all manner of valuable information usable, at first by humans and then by machines.

THE CYBERNETIC ORGANISM

In the year that the Kinsey Report on sexual behavior was first published, another book rivaled its success. *Cybernetics* was about organisms, not orgasms. Most of the public could barely comprehend the book, but its title caught on in the popular press, and it went through four printings in its first six months.[2] The book compared behavior in creatures with behavior in machines. Author Norbert Weiner, a wonderfully eccentric MIT professor, showed, with much mathematics, how electronic or mechanical devices could have control mechanisms like those of biological creatures.

During World War II, Weiner worked on servomechanisms that could steer ships and weapons. After the war he steadily extended his work to more complex situations, using the flexibility of, first, electronic circuits and then, later, computers. Together Weiner and his assistant—a neurologist—applied the theories of servomechanisms to experiments with animals. They could predict the behavior of muscles under different loads. Weiner's ideas caught the attention of the mass media when he generalized them into a universal principle: lifelike self-control could be done with electronic circuits.

> The businessperson who hides from technology is an endangered species.

Weiner defined *cybernetics* as "the science of control and communication in the animal and the machine." Today we should extend that to "control and communication in the corporation." The modern enterprise can be thought of as an organism, rather like a biological organism, except that it consists of people and electronics organized to achieve certain goals. It has a nervous system going to every employee's desk. A corporation, like an animal, is exceedingly complex and cannot be described with simple equations. The mechanisms for corporate control and communications are changing greatly as we race into the era of fiber optics and alien intelligence. Corporations now emerging have a vast web of electronic links to other corporations. They will have virtual operations worldwide and will be designed to adapt rapidly to changing environments. They will learn and evolve constantly at all levels.

The new corporation has been referred to variously as "Virtual Corporation," "Adaptive Corporation," and "Learning Enterprise," but such terms describe only one aspect of the human–electronic organism that is now evolving. We need a word that encompasses all of them. We will use the term *cybercorp*—short for *cybernetic corporation*.[3]

CYBERCORP ['sī-ber-kŏrp] noun

[From Greek *kubernētēs*, governor, from *kubernan*, to govern.]

A corporation designed using the principles of cybernetics. A corporation optimized for the age of cyberspace. A cybernetic corporation with senses constantly alert, capable of reacting in real time to changes in its environment, competition, and customer needs, with virtual operations or agile linkages of competencies in different organizations when necessary. A corporation that can harness the power of alien intelligence. A corporation designed for fast change, which can learn, evolve, and transform itself rapidly.

The word *cybernetics* derives from the Greek word for "steersman," which was also used in ancient Greece to denote a governor of a country. The Latin version of the word *kubernetes* means *governor.* The famous physicist André-Marie Ampère described cybernetics as the science of governance.

The prefix *cyber* became popular when hackers started to discover that roaming the planet on computer networks was very different from roaming physically. The traditional sense of geographic space was replaced by *cyberspace.* The cyberspace explorer can find himself in a world in many ways richer and more complex than his physical world. The modern enterprise exists in cyberspace (whether or not it takes advantage of it). Managers, executives, change agents, and creative people everywhere need to ask what their corporation should look like if it takes maximum advantage of cyberspace, cybernetics, and alien intelligence. For many in traditional corporations the answers are startling.

Unlike an animal the cybercorp is not confined in one small skin; it can be worldwide. Computers in New Zealand can decide to make a financial trade in Chicago and move the money to the Cayman Islands in a fraction of a second. If bad weather closes Newark Airport, computers can reschedule the operations of flights, crews, and maintenance worldwide to minimize the disruption in service and maximize the airlines' profits. An order placed in Spain with an order-entry computer in France triggers manufacturing planning software in New York to schedule production in Dallas, which requires chips from Japan to be built into circuit boards in Singapore, with final assembly in the robotic factory in Dallas and computer-controlled shipment from a warehouse in Milan.

The future corporation will bear no resemblance to traditional corporations, so the transition to a cybercorp is a strategic issue, not a tactical one.

If reengineering a business takes years and has a high probability of failure, it is more prudent to start new corporations where the culture of digital business is there from the beginning. The new corporations, unlike the typical pre-Internet corporation, are *designed to evolve constantly and rapidly.*

ELECTRONIC REACTION TIMES

One of the key characteristics of the electronic jungle is that *things happen fast.* An event in one location is immediately felt in other locations. Corporations trigger action in other corporations at electronic speed.

Worldwide events affect computerized stock markets immediately. Electronic herds can stampede with startling suddenness. An event anywhere causes reactions to flash instantly through global computer networks. Because of computers, corporations can design new products and bring them to market quickly with automated production lines, minimizing the time between a customer's ordering a product and the product being delivered. Some products are delivered within hours of being ordered. Funds move between banks on opposite sides of the earth in seconds. Switched video links reduce executive travel and expand the ability to help customers.

The windows of opportunity in business become very short when corporations are linked electronically. Price advantages have to be used quickly. In computerized auctions and exchanges, prices are scanned worldwide and change electronically. To minimize inventory-holding costs with "just-in-time" inventory control, suppliers have to deliver exactly when computers tell them to. A salesman can use a computer to generate a sales proposal while he is with the customer. Networks connecting manufacturers to suppliers facilitate quality control on the supplier's premises and ensure just-in-time delivery. We now have just-in-time manufacturing, just-in-time education— just-in-time everything. Customers wanting a mortgage, insurance, credit, financial quotation, or other such information once had to wait for weeks; now these services can be provided in minutes. We can provide instant gratification for most things that can be gratified.

Speed is the deciding factor in many competitive situations: in satisfying new customer demands, in getting products to market, in making product improvements, and in responding to fashion trends.

It is desirable to minimize the time from having the *concept* of a new product or service to having *cash* flowing from its sale. An important characteristic of digital business is the minimization of *concept-to-cash* time. The car industry, for example, used to take six or seven years to go from the concept of a new car to the first customer delivery; it battled to drive that figure down to five years by the end of the 1980s, to three years by the mid-1990s, and then in some cases to less than two years. In the future, customers will be able to design their own car, within the constraints of a model range, and have it delivered quickly.

When the world changes with Internet speed, *strategic* decisions need to be made fast and implemented fast. Rupert Murdoch has repeatedly beaten other tycoons in the news and entertainment business because he moves faster. Murdoch's president of telecom and television, Preston Padden, says: "We have no five-year plan. We have no strategic planning group. It's really a sort of personal business being executed on a scale you don't normally see."[4] Murdoch doesn't need to call a committee or do battle with a contentious board as at Time Warner. He makes sure he is in control so that he can act on good ideas fast. If a jungle animal sensing a new predator had to convene a committee before it could act, it wouldn't survive long.

SENSES AND CONSTANT MONITORING

Corporations in the electronic jungle, like creatures in nature's jungles, need to be constantly alert, always monitoring what is important and able to make adjustments. Airlines continuously monitor bookings and adjust the prices at which seats are offered. Supermarkets continuously monitor sales and take action to increase the sales of slow-moving items and replenish fast-moving items, and react to the balance between physical shopping and electronic shopping.

The corporate creature needs senses. In the past, humans have provided most of the senses; in the future most of them will be automatic. Information from bar codes read at supermarket check-out counters can provide immediate information to remote systems for planning purchasing, restocking, distribution, pricing, and advertising. Many industries use handheld computers with sensors and radio transmission. Global Positioning Satellite (GPS) electronics enable computers to be aware of the position of cars, trucks, containers, and so forth, accurate to a hundred feet or less.

When Federal Express picks up a package, the courier uses a handheld menu-driven computer called a Supertracker to scan the smart bar code on the package. He keys in information such as the type of service and destination zip code. The Supertracker knows the time and date, which route it is on, its own zip code, and who the courier is. When the courier returns to his van he places the Supertracker in a port in the van computer, which radios details to the dispatch center. FedEx knows

> The future corporation will bear no resemblance to traditional corporations, so the transition to a cybercorp is a strategic issue, not a tactical one.

the whereabouts of the package at all times as it moves through the system, and ensures that no packages are delayed.

The cybercorp needs sensors that tell it immediately when public buying habits shift. When credit cards are used, customer information can be linked to sales information. Smart cards can be used for a diversity of purposes. A mass of information can be collected from the Internet.

It is inexpensive to make chips that send radio signals, like car keys that unlock your car door with a radio signal. Vending machines, for example, should send radio signals to their supplier whenever items are bought. This gives the supplier immediate information about what is selling. Soft-drink machines can transmit real-time data about the changing mix of drinks sold in a summer heat wave, and this should feed directly into production scheduling. Devices like cars and computers can send a radio signal when they are stolen. Chips can be designed so that their memory can be interrogated or updated by radio. Chips will be so cheap that they can be in items like clothes or food packages to indicate where and when the item was made, when it arrived in which store, when it was sold, who purchased it, and for how much.

Sensors with built-in neural networks will become a major segment of the electronics industry.

B2C AND B2B

Three terms have come into use to describe Web-based business: B2C, meaning business-to-consumer; B2B, meaning business-to-business; and C2C, meaning consumer-to-consumer.

C2C refers to e-mail and the ability of the public to create bulletin boards, chatrooms, auctions, or political forums. One company that made big money in C2C operations was eBay, an online auction house that quickly built up to more than 2.5 million auctions a day.

The first wave of e-business was B2C; it was highly visible because it affected mass-market consumers. Amazon.com sold books, music, and video on the Web; e*Trade.com enabled people to play the stock market without stock brokers; eToys.com persuaded kids that it had a direct line to Santa Claus, who, of course, used e-mail at the North Pole. Millions of people started to "surf" the Internet using search engines and portals like those of Yahoo!

and services like America Online. The stock price of such companies went through the roof.

The media concentrated heavily on B2C uses of the Web, and "www" addresses appeared on products and advertisements everywhere. But behind the scenes a second wave was starting, which was B2B. This was to become immensely larger in financial volume. IBM CEO Lou Gerstner described the B2C companies that the press has written so much about as "mere fireflies before the storm." He added, "The storm that's arriving—the real disturbance in the force—is when the thousands and thousands of institutions that exist today seize the power of this global computing and communications infrastructure and use it to transform themselves. That's the real revolution."[5]

In 1995 B2B transactions were almost zero; in 1998 they reached $43 billion. By 2003, according to Forrester Research, they will reach $1.3 trillion in the United States alone, with the rest of the world catching up fast and then surpassing the U.S. volume. Annual U.S. business-to-consumer sales will grow to more than $100 billion by 2003.[6] These figures, assembled with thorough research, are so large that they indicate that great upheavals will occur; great fortunes will be made or lost.

THE E-BUSINESS REVOLUTION

The e-business revolution is occurring in three stages.

The first stage came with the highly publicized rise in business-to-consumer commerce. Companies now interact with customers on the Web.

The next stage establishes business-to-business linkages online, though the changes essentially update business-as-usual procedures for the e-business climate. Goods are bought and sold on the Web, so the slow cycle of paper purchase orders, delivery notices, invoices, and payments is replaced with fast online interaction. Inventories are linked to online ordering. E-mail spreads information in corporations. An increasing number of operations are outsourced with online linkages to trading partners.

In the third stage, a more radical reinvention occurs. A corporation may become part of a broad-ranging ecosystem involving the electronic linkage of diverse enterprises. Dynamic pricing may be used. B2B exchanges (described in the next chapter) link corporations together in new ways. The corporation may be restructured to capture global markets and take advantage of global resources. The Internet captures an ocean of available information in massive data warehouses. Advanced computerized intelligence extracts business insights from data far too voluminous for human processing. There are complex interlinkages among corporations with numerous mergers and takeovers. The distinction between different industries becomes blurred as corporations invent cross-industry relationships and often prey on each other's territory.

Aggressive corporations try to leapfrog the progression and go straight to this third stage of radical reinvention. David-and-Goliath battles occur between newcomers who want to change the world and large traditional enterprises. Many traditional corporations have great difficulty transforming themselves, so David wins.

By the time this third stage is mature, the world will have changed in dramatic ways.

THE GREAT DIVIDE

The Web is forcing prices down. Global, real-time price wars ensure that companies can no longer charge exorbitant prices if a competitor offers the same product for substantially less. For cars, chips, appliances, oil—almost any product—when you add up what could be produced if all the world's production facilities were operating at capacity, that number far exceeds the world's expected consumption. The Web is bringing these production facilities into direct competition with one another. Companies have to lower their prices in order to keep their facilities operating closer to capacity.

The Internet brings global competition to knowledge-based products as well as factory-built products. Most new software tools are easy to imitate and can be built where labor costs are low, such as India or China. In Russia skilled programmers earn peanuts; so do well-educated research scientists and aerospace engineers. Because the Web has made outsourcing standard operating practice, internal suppliers of a part or service are in competition with external suppliers. Many companies are finding that the external suppliers are cheaper. It is easier to get tough with an external supplier than with an internal supplier.

The Web and the new business inventions we describe are setting the stage for brutally intense competition that drives down the prices and profits. Skilled global fulfillment organizations are working out how to deliver to shopping chains the goods they want at lower prices by using global manufacturing. Often they can turn expensive goods into low-priced commodities.

This brutally intense competition exists at the same time that we are seeing winners make fortunes in a winner-takes-most world. Some corporations will be very high flyers; some will be wiped out by the new competition. This is the great divide in the new world of the cybercorp. The same set of technologies that creates spectacular winners on one side of the divide also creates losers on the other side. Many businesspeople will find themselves on the wrong side of this divide. Those on the right side will often make vast fortunes.

To be on the right side of this great divide, a corporation needs to race as fast as it can for a position of dominance. When there is a fast feedback cycle of self-reinforcing success it's critical to establish a winning position quickly. Today's technologies make it possible for nimble newcomers to do that, though the competition will become furious.

The most successful Web start-ups understood the need to achieve market dominance. Amazon.com and e*Trade.com started with afterburners on, determined to grow as large as possible as quickly as possible. They were prepared to be unprofitable for a long time in order to grow furiously and reach an unassailable position. They realized that the world was changing and that eventually there would be a small number of global e-business players with great financial and social power. The stock market also perceived this and rewarded the most aggressive new e-businesses with sky-high valuations.

Building an e-business fortress requires a gamble on a grand scale. The most aggressive dot-com companies drive for dominance at all costs. For a time the losses must be huge as the company strives to be a winner-takes-most brand. Only the most gutsy, single-minded, dictatorial executive can pull off a gamble of such magnitude. The CEO who says "I want the board to tell me what to do" is dead. Like a high roller at a casino, the successful e-business leader doesn't want nervous shareholders telling him to be cautious. He wants to slam his foot on the accelerator as hard as it can go. "Maximum speed. Damn the torpedoes." If he crashes in flames, he can try another venture; he has plenty of ideas.

Managers everywhere need to understand this great divide. They must ask under what circumstances the new inventions make possible self-feeding tornadoes, and when they lead to situations that drastically drive down margins.

Knowledge industries (which will be most industries) are characterized by positive-feedback loops. Success breeds success. The *perception* of success breeds success. Companies with inadequate strategies learn the hard way that corporations that are behind tend to slip further behind.

Unfortunately, most managers still think in terms of the old paradigms of business. They are concerned with product-to-product competition within their own industry, which can lead to computer-aided price wars. The technology-aided price wars of electronic business, as well as the cream-skimming techniques we saw in Chapter 6, will leave many traditional operators devastated. When profits turn to losses, corporations often react by downsizing—laying off employees and slashing expenses. Although this temporarily restores profits, in the long term the corporation is damaged. Unless the company addresses the cause of its inability to compete and institutes an entirely new corporate strategy, it will again wither under the competition.

In the face of this competition, many businesses will be left on the wrong side of the divide if they try to go it alone. They will not be among the winners. Instead, such businesses, particularly those too small to enter the winner's circle, must adopt a new strategy to determine how they can join forces with a winning team.

High-performance teams should be designed to pay attention constantly to customers, to determine how to delight them. Companies often have to think in terms of providing a solution to a customer problem, not just selling a product. Complex solutions often require a diversity of skills from different organizations, but the customer wants to deal with *one* organization. Therefore, that organization uses *virtual* linkages, which is how smaller companies remain viable—by becoming partners with a successful organization.

CYBERCORP ECOSYSTEMS

Today's economy is a little like the early days of the universe after the big bang, before the galaxies started to congeal. There will be numerous mergers and takeovers forming global corporations that can benefit from economies of scale in the digital economy. Much rethinking will happen about what virtual corporations make sense and what the digital galaxy will eventually look like.

As electronic-jungle businesses evolve and become more complex, a major key to business success will be inventing, developing, and nurturing business relationships. To avoid being forced into low-margin situations, corporations need to search for win-win associations in which different contributors intricately cooperate. The allies need to understand the ecosystems they play in, form alliances with a shared vision, and then pay close (human) attention to the alliance. There are many types of alliance that avoid antitrust implications.

Many corporations will go under because of the intensity of electronic-aided competition, but others will use the new mechanisms to dominate global ecosystems. The fastest growth rates will be much faster than in previous corporate history.

> Speed is the deciding factor in many competitive situations: satisfying new customer demands, getting products to market, and responding to fashion trends.

Most managers think about competing products within one industry, but the cyberspace economy is more complex than that. Corporations will be interleaved in complex cross-industry relationships. Intricate ecosystems will form, and companies will battle for dominance within these ecosystems. As commerce becomes computerized globally, traditional product-to-product competition will drive down prices and profits. The key to sustaining profits will be understanding the new ecosystems and how to carve out key roles within those ecosystems.

Unlike biological ecosystems, a business ecosystem has an intelligently planned purpose and vision for the future. Each member must examine what role it wants to play within that vision and to what extent it can influence or manipulate the overall ecosystem. Some corporations maneuver themselves into a dominant role in their ecosystems. Managers everywhere need to understand the ecosystems they play in, the jostling for position within these ecosystems, and how the ecosystems of the electronic jungle evolve.

Intel spent a fortune on chip design and innovation to make itself unique and to keep ahead of would-be clone-makers. Intel and Microsoft struggled to create de facto standards for the PC industry. A galaxy of hardware vendors, software vendors, service firms, and consultants evolved to play in the ecosystem dominated by Intel and Microsoft. Some of them established profitable niches.

The big winners, remember, will work out how to control the ecosystems they are part of. Microsoft, while less than a tenth the size of IBM, led and shaped the behavior of many hundreds of associated companies, as did Benetton when less than a tenth the size of the clothing giants, and Rupert Murdoch when his operation was much smaller than Time Warner.

When an executive thinks in terms of ecosystems rather than one industry, he can often play a grander game with higher return on investment.

EXTREME RATE OF CHANGE

The new high-tech entrepreneurs thrive on change, training themselves to search constantly for new ideas. With some, the grander and more outrageous the idea the better. Ideas sweep through Web-based ecosystems, changing from concept to implemented reality faster than anyone expects.

To advance successfully through the radical third stage of the e-business revolution, a corporation needs to be extremely light on its feet. It needs to be able to innovate quickly. To avoid being taken by surprise it must constantly try to predict the next waves of change—both technical and business change. It needs good early-warning radars. Many of the new-economy companies believe that they have to "morph" their business plan every few months in order to ride the waves of change. This level of flexibility is not possible in companies controlled by pre-Internet structures.

In some cases change is so fast that there's no time for a detailed business plan. When Jim Clark raised the capital for Healtheon and MyCFO, intending to build multibillion-dollar companies, he was asked for a business plan and said, "There's no business plan."[7] The game was changing too fast to have time for a traditional venture-capital business plan; the prize went to those who could move without one.

The threat of change is constant. I recently opened the Sunday paper and a thick green sheet of paper fluttered out. In big letters it said: "*First-e*, the Internet bank, has no bank charges, no branches, no managers, no queues, and a large annual estimated return. Where does that leave your bank?" It answered its question by showing a mouse arrow pointing to a trash can.

Eventually the new ways of doing business will become widely understood, and then the winners will be those that learn to play with greater skill. The games will become much more professional. At first the main competitive advantage comes from being there first; later competitive advantage comes from playing the game more intelligently. Web-based business will evolve from being simplistic to being diabolically intelligent. Virtual corporate structures will become complex and global, using organizations that didn't exist before, such as the B2B exchanges we describe in the next chapter. The winners will often be those that collect masses of data and analyze those data to run their operations in more clever ways. Decision-making in corporations that take full advantage of alien-intelligence technology will bear no resemblance to traditional decision making. The winners will have better information and better ways of deriving insight from that information.

Older corporations were not designed to change. They *do* change, but it is a painful process, like renovating an ancient building. To change at a rapid rate the cybercorp needs an infrastructure *designed* to facilitate change and a culture that regards change as a constant, inevitable process, not a problem. Many corporations have computer systems that make change extremely difficult. It can be astonishingly slow and expensive to change traditional software. Cybercorp computing needs to be built with techniques that support the maximum rate of change. Unchangeable computer systems have been a major contributor to businesses' decline and fall.

The cybercorp should be designed to *thrive* on change, to gain competitive advantage over corporations that find change a problem. Change and uncertainty are continuous sources of competitive opportunity.

Many traditional managers have difficulty coping with change even at a gentle pace. It is often said, "They just don't get it." There are numerous old dogs who won't learn new tricks. If there has to be e-mail, it's something their secretary does.

Individuals who do well in this new world are constantly searching for the next innovations. The new world is of growing complexity. Its leaders must thrive on complexity and have the ability to learn fast.

CHAIN REACTIONS

The e-business revolution will be driven by multiple chain reactions surprising in their diversity.

The chain reaction in foreign exchange trading occurred without the Internet. In 1980 there was little foreign exchange trading; a decade later the volume exceeded a trillion dollars per day. The Internet makes such mushrooming growth much easier, faster, and ubiquitous.

B2B uses of the Web are being driven by some spectacular cost savings. General Motors claimed that Internet interaction with suppliers cut its costs as much as 25 percent. General Electric and other large corporations have made similar claims. Goods can be ordered and delivered when they are needed, not stockpiled ahead of time because of the delays associated with sending and processing paper orders. With electronic mechanisms, a "reverse auction" can be used in which suppliers are made to bid against one another to establish the lowest acceptable price.

When a large company moves to make major use of the Web, there is a chain reaction. The company's trading partners come under intense pressure to link to it on the Internet. Because the savings are so high and the process is clean and simple compared with paper, large corporations tell potential suppliers that they must connect via the Internet. In 1999 General Motors told its suppliers that it would do business with them only if they were Internet-connected. A year later America's big three car companies announced a common B2B exchange for buying the parts they all need. Supplier corporations had no choice; they became Internet-connected very quickly. The U.S. government is many times larger than the car industry, and it will eventually insist that its would-be suppliers communicate with it online, with intense competition and price auctions. A major segment of e-business will be B2G—business-to-government.

The big firm, having invested a lot of money in e-business infrastructure, is determined to get a return on it. Customers and suppliers who want to trade the old-fashioned way are frozen out, while those who adopt the new ways win more business. As some companies succeed with Web-based applications, other companies have to follow them just to stay competitive. Explosive growth is inevitable.

ALIEN INTELLIGENCE IN BUSINESS

A deluge of data is produced by Web data-entry screens, bar-code readers, sensors, exchanges, and means of monitoring what customers do on the Web. Data warehouses store overwhelming quantities of data, which decision makers can search and analyze by using *data-visualization* tools to help clarify complex data. Data-mining software uses various techniques including neural networks to search for patterns that might lead to better decision making and that humans could not recognize on their own. When a pattern is discovered the decision maker needs to find out whether it could *really* lead to better decisions. He uses it with historical data to see whether the pattern would have provided better results in the past. It might indicate, for example, that customers with certain characteristics are more likely to buy specific goods.

The processes of electronic commerce can be designed so that software can learn what customers are likely to buy, what changes they would like in the products, where to look for new customers, and so on.

Data mining can reveal what produces the best results with large mailing lists, or where spare parts should be stored in a worldwide airline. It is used in sophisticated ways in the financial community to design derivatives or to improve investment decisions. The pharmaceutical industry uses it to understand factors that correlate with the incidence of disease and to study the effectiveness of drugs. It is used in banks and insurance companies to manage risks better. Wal-Mart did thorough data mining and Kmart did not, which helped Wal-Mart beat Kmart in the marketplace.

In the coming years the most successful companies will find ways to extract critical information from masses of data. As the computer-generated deluge of information grows, humans will no longer be able to scan the data, so computers will have to search for patterns or insights. Today's leaders need to derive business insight as quickly as possible, and often the key to doing so is achieving the right combination of human intelligence and non-human intelligence. As the electronic jungle becomes more complex and bewildering, computerized intelligence will become a major part of the cybercorp creature's instinct for survival.

Particularly important is the ability to collect detailed and specific information about each and every customer. This helps to sell more products to a customer or serve the customer better. It also enables computers to know which customers generate high profits and which could be dropped.

> Unfortunately, most managers still think in terms of the old paradigms of business. Many traditional operators will be devastated if they don't institute an entirely new corporate strategy.

Neural networks (see Chapter 14) can recognize patterns of data that humans wouldn't necessarily recognize. They are being used for analyzing customer responses or behavior. For example, Twentieth Century Fox uses them to sift through millions of box office receipts and predict which movies would sell well in each theater. It predicts what actors, plots, and films will be popular in each neighborhood. By avoiding flops in specific theaters it saves around $100 million worldwide each year. The same technology could select alternate trailers for each movie in each theater to help maximize sales. One movie may have many differently edited trailers, each of which appeals to a specific audience.

Neural networks can examine diverse characteristics about potential customers to determine which customers will generate a profit, which should be dropped from contact lists, or what items should be sold to which customers. A Forrester research analyst, Bob Chatham, says this could lead to a commercial culture in which high-value customers with certain characteristics are bought and sold like derivatives.[8]

TWO PHASES

The cybercorp tends to evolve in two phases. In the first phase it builds the basic structure and support mechanisms. In the second phase the company uses sophisticated computing to enhance its intelligence. The early-stage cybercorp uses mainly human intelligence; the advanced cybercorp uses increasing degrees of automated intelligence.

First we build the basic rudiments of the creature, then we make the creature steadily more intelligent.

In the first phase the corporation dissolves bureaucratic hierarchies of the past and restructures the enterprise around end-to-end streams of processes that deliver results to the customer.[9] The corporation builds information systems to support the new structure and establishes new relationships via electronic commerce. To support the new business vision the corporation embarks on mergers and takeovers. All this is supported by the use of appropriate networks, often worldwide, and by the automation of routine operations. We then have the basic creature in place.

The second phase builds up the intelligence of this basic creature. The corporation builds the necessary data warehouses and data-collection facilities. It trains human managers to identify and access key data. It creates increasingly intricate data-mining techniques. Computers will be used to *learn* how to operate the company in optimal ways. As they learn they automate the procedures that result from the learning. They may, for instance, use genetic algorithms to create the complex production schedules that enable manufacturing to meet individual needs. They may develop a database of business rules and use rule-based processing to automate their behavior (see Chapter 16).

In health care, for example, both phases are needed. First the records need to be cleaned up (a massive job), and mechanisms must be established for getting the right data to doctors and clinics so that they can take appropriate actions with patients. Then a more exciting phase can begin. The mass of data can be examined to find patterns that lead to better diagnosis and treatment, and eventually to preventive medicine.

Similarly in electronic commerce, in the first phase it is valuable just to be able to access customers electronically. In a second phase sellers can learn everything that can be learned about a customer, or about the marketplace's reactions to a particular product. The second phase requires sophisticated data collection, data warehousing, and data-mining techniques. So, creating the cybercorp is a twofold process: first we build the basic infrastructure, then we use computerized intelligence for extracting valuable knowledge from the deluge of data that floods in.

> First we build the rudiments of the creature, then we make the creature steadily more intelligent.

The first phase requires existing technology that establishes the networks and builds the basic systems, while the second phase requires data mining and alien intelligence to derive better business intelligence and smarter processes. Some corporations are pushing ahead with phase-two techniques as early as possible, hoping that as they learn to make them work, they will gain a major competitive advantage. It is often easier to introduce clever computerized techniques than to change the basic infrastructure of a corporation. Getting the whole act together needs an integrated vision combined with a CEO's steely determination to change the enterprise. A key to the whole process is to establish the right partnerships between humans and machines, between decision makers and data.

BRINGING DOWN GOLIATH

The cybercorp revolution is bringing many David-and-Goliath stories. But in this case, though Goliath may appear fearsome upon first glance, on closer examination he is old and arthritic. This opens many opportunities for the small and nimble Davids.

Most older and grander corporations carry the baggage of an earlier era, which in many ways makes it difficult for them to race fast enough into the aggressive ways of e-business. Many corporations will have difficulty making the transition to the new world of e-business.

A cybercorp newcomer can plan how to use new ideas to exploit the old company's weaknesses. As a Web-centric corporation from the beginning, it can exploit the new mechanisms of digital business. It's structured around excited, highly focused teams. It carefully thinks out what should be done in-house and what should be outsourced. It may use newer technology and virtual mechanisms, and use the Web to build a cozy, knowledgeable relationship with customers.

Older corporations often have cumbersome hierarchical structures and politics, and old cultures inappropriate to the mercurial cybercorp age. Their computers are snarled up in old spaghetti-like software that is murder to change. They spend big money on reengineering themselves but only make changes within the present structure when that entire structure ought to be scrapped.

Changing an old, arthritic enterprise into a nimble corporation designed to evolve constantly and rapidly is a traumatic and risky quantum leap.

EXHIBIT 1

Desirable Characteristics of the New Corporation	Barriers That Block This Characteristic
Web sales and marketing	Channel conflicts block the necessary thrust for online sales
Web-based relationship with customers	Brokers or agents have high commissions and oppose any change
A Web-based relationship with trading partners in which both sides benefit	Attitude of "don't trust the vendors" makes reinvention of alliances difficult
A fast race for dominance	Managers can't achieve the aggressive growth needed for success
Agile systems that can change at Internet speed	Opposition from unions to the dynamic changes needed
Extreme creativity	Attempts to foster extreme creativity in old corporations usually fail
Widespread application of advanced computerized intelligence	Alien intelligence is not understood

Rapid streamlining and staff reduction	Inability or reluctance to lay off large numbers of staff
Very fast implementation of Web-centric computer systems	The IT organization can't implement new systems fast enough
Software that can be changed very quickly	Legacy software (including packages) prevents fast change
Offshore operations to minimize taxation	The company is registered in a high-tax jurisdiction, and can't easily change
Capability to invent radically new products or services	Start-ups achieve fresher innovation at much lower cost
Outsource everything at which you're not excellent	Managers resist outsourcing work that has always been done in-house

So, top executives of traditional corporations must ask themselves: Can we convert our present corporation to a cyberspace winner, or will it be too difficult to convert? And as always in this rapidly changing economy, they must ask: Can we convert *fast enough*?

Exhibit 1 (starting at left) lists some of the barriers a traditional corporation faces.

REINVENTING AUTOMATION

Many corporations with a high level of automation have automated *existing* operations. The challenge of the cybercorp era is to use automation to invent radically *new* types of operations. Computers have been widely used to automate paper processes when they ought to be automating something entirely different.

> Corporations have automated existing operations. Alien intelligence challenges us to invent radically *new* types of operations.

Software, for example, has been widely used to process purchase orders similar to paper purchase orders. A more interesting challenge is to avoid purchase orders altogether. A Web-enabled purchasing process should monitor the inventory, spring into action when the inventory drops to a predetermined level, and decide what quantity should be ordered and what supplier to order from. It should search the Internet to find the lowest prices, using an auction process or B2B exchange. It may monitor the requirements of many different departments so that bulk discounts can be obtained. The electronic purchase instruction may go to the supplier's computer automatically, obeying preestablished rules so that a human doesn't have to approve each purchase. A repetitive purchasing process doesn't need purchase orders; the supplier should be online to the purchaser's inventory so that it automatically supplies goods as needed. The purchaser's computer could monitor the supplier's performance and be ready to switch suppliers if a different one can do better. It could maintain a file of suppliers and use it to select the best one. The suppliers would thus try to achieve the highest ratings in their chosen area.

Similar arguments apply to most business processes. Unattended computers in secure bunkers will conduct the routine processes of commerce, with multiple checks and balances to make sure that they are achieving what is intended. Humans can pay attention to those matters that need uniquely human skills. To repeat the comment of Dave Fournie of Chaparral Steel, routine corporate operations will be run by one man and his dog: the man will watch the computers and the dog will prevent him from touching them! Although flying a jumbo jet is immensely complex, a human pilot is more likely to make an error than the computers; he is there in case something goes catastrophically wrong.

As technology evolves, machines become more impressive, dwarfing humans in their capabilities. Many cybercorp operations can be highly automated, like the jumbo jet's. Many functions are performed better by machines than by people. Information flashes between locations automatically to keep the jet safe in the sky. Ultimately the effectiveness—indeed, the survival—of advanced corporations in cyberspace depends on how effectively they automate. But in the end, machines *need* humans. And as automation improves, greater skills are demanded of people.

The more the basic mechanisms become automated, the greater the need for *people* to concentrate on *uniquely human* roles such as inventing new ways to delight the customers. The pilot's job is automated; the air hostess's job is not. Human services need intensely caring people. As alien intelligence spreads, corporations will succeed by getting the human aspects of business right.

CHAPTER 11
The Global Bazaar

Today we have huge financial markets where people invest and speculate in the price of stocks, bonds, and foreign exchange. Soon they will invest and speculate in the price of just about everything. We now have not only stock exchanges but also computerized exchanges for chemicals, cars, cattle, steel—you name it. Just as alien intelligence is becoming critical for sophisticated investing in financial markets, so it will be used for making money in the new types of markets.

The idea of having fixed prices is a relatively recent characteristic of commerce. Nobody dreams of having fixed prices in the bazaars of the East. The buyer and seller expect to barter and to play numerous games in the bartering process. On the Internet prices can be adjusted in many ways, often automatically and dynamically. The Web is causing a tectonic shift in how prices are established. Buyers and sellers will use elaborate electronic facilities to help them negotiate prices—rather like Arabs in a bazaar.

There is one vital difference between the bazaar and the Web. The Internet is worldwide, and when a price offer from the buyer or seller changes, the whole world can react to it. The volume or financial magnitude of sales can be huge. By the time it was four years old eBay.com was holding more than 2.5 million auctions a day. In the United States alone, business-to-business exchanges total hundreds of billions of dollars annually.

Most markets in future business will use dynamic rather than fixed pricing. Prices will be changeable and often established by computers when a deal is done. If prices are highly variable, then there can be speculation. Derivatives can be traded that relate to the price.

CUSTOMER PRICING

Traditionally a vendor sets a price and customers decide whether to buy at that price. But some Web sites allow the *customer* to set the price and the vendor decides whether to sell at that price. For example, Priceline.com is a buying service that lets you name your own price. It relays your offer to a vendor's computers to see if the vendor accepts. If it does, Priceline collects a fee.

Suppose you want to buy camera film. Priceline lists types of film that you can bid for—for example, four-packs of Kodak Max 400 ASA. This typically costs $10.99 to $13.99 in stores. You can offer a lower amount than this and Priceline estimates your chance of getting film at that price. You might offer $9.78 (85 percent chance), $9.12 (66 percent chance), $8.57 (50 percent chance), or $8.02 (33 percent chance). Sometimes stores offer a half-price special of $6.25 where there is a 95 percent chance of getting film for that price. Priceline offers a long list of groceries that you can bid for in this fashion in certain cities.

On most days airlines fly with more than 500,000 empty seats. The airline's computers tell it the probability of selling a seat. If two days before takeoff that probability is low, it makes sense for the airline to sell that seat at a low price. Priceline says to the public: "Just tell us where and when you want to go and how much you want to pay. If a major, full-service airline accepts your offer, we'll immediately lock in your price and purchase your round trip tickets."[1] Priceline.com quickly achieved a market capitalization larger than those of United Airlines, US Airways, and Continental Airlines *combined*.

To have the customer name his price is an interesting change in the marketplace, very appealing to Priceline.com's customers. But to an Arab in a bazaar it would seem very crude. In a bazaar the customer expects his first offer to be rejected and is prepared to make many offers as part of a bartering process.

A computer can be set up to barter on the Internet. It may be given a first-offer price and be instructed how to increase the offer if it is rejected. The rules of two-way bartering can be programmed. A computer may be told how tough it should be in the bartering process. It may, for example, wait a substantial time before it increases the offer.

AUCTIONS

Auctions can work wonderfully well on the Web.

Software can play the role of the auctioneer at Sotheby's, and the potential buyers can be anywhere on the planet. These potential buyers offer a price at which they are prepared to buy an item. The software auctioneer picks the most favorable price and asks if anyone will offer more. As at Sotheby's when a higher bid is received, the software again asks if anyone will better it. The timing of this process follows rules that are built into the software. The potential buyers could be humans sitting at their PCs or could be automated software agents.

A Sotheby's-style auction (or almost any human auction) is driven by the seller. On the Web, however, many auctions are driven by the buyer. The buyer describes what he wants to buy and asks potential sellers to quote a price; this is sometimes referred to as a "reverse auction." The software auctioneer picks the most favorable selling price and asks if anyone can better it. In a seller-driven auction the competing buyers tend to drive the price up sale, as at Sotheby's. In a buyer-driven auction the competing sellers tend to drive the price down.

A spectacular scene in Kuwait City is the fish market. A very large number of Kuwaitis gather to buy and sell fish. At a given time of the day a bell rings and there is a frenzy of offers and counteroffers for the fish. Before the bell rings the customers have had plenty of time to inspect what the sellers have for sale. A computerized auction could be like the Kuwait fish market. It is neither seller-driven nor buyer-driven, but has an intense two-way interaction between buyers and sellers at a specified time. But unlike the Kuwait fish market, the buyers and sellers can be worldwide. In fact, stock and commodity exchanges work like the fish-market auction.

Auctions can help a company obtain a true market price for items. They often help sellers to obtain the highest price for unique items or for items in limited supply. They help buyers find the lowest price for items with multiple suppliers. Observing a customer's bidding habits gives information about price sensitivity, the market, and the individual customer.

EXCHANGES

One of the most important categories of new business invention is the Web exchange, allowing buyers and sellers around the world to find one another, set prices, and make trades. Such exchanges are fundamentally changing the way markets operate. The magnitude of business done by B2B exchanges will be huge compared with the better-known B2C companies such as Amazon and eToys.

We are familiar with exchanges mostly in the financial markets, where they have existed since the time of Shakespeare. (The first stock exchange opened in Amsterdam in 1611.) These enable stocks, bonds, and other financial instruments to be traded. B2B exchanges are somewhat similar except that they enable plastics, steel, advertising space, insurance contracts, and most other types of goods to be traded. They facilitate the trading of both physical goods and intellectual property.

> Online auctions allow you to observe a customer's bidding habits in order to get information about price sensitivity, the market, and the individual customer.

A B2B exchange can bring vast numbers of corporations together in one computerized market space. These exchanges often use automated auctions, bringing a radical shift in the way businesses trade with one another. The authors of the excellent book *B2B Exchanges*, Arthur Sculley and William Woods, comment that computerized exchanges will "fundamentally restructure every industry."[2]

We often see images on television of the trading floors of stock markets or commodities markets with a mass of agitated traders frantically gesticulating at one another, making buy and sell bids. This is not necessarily an efficient way to run an exchange. Computers can match customers' buy and sell orders automatically. Much of what goes on on such trading floors is being replaced by computerized systems in which some customers enter sell orders, others enter buy orders, and a computer matches them. When the computer establishes a potential trade the buyer and seller are notified of the price and quantity. Verification of the trade is sent to a clearing center and buyer and seller accounts are adjusted. When the process is automated, it need not be confined to one room full of human hand-waving; buyers and sellers anywhere in cyberspace can interact.

The online service eBay is a wonderfully successful C2C exchange that allows the public to buy and sell any goods they wish, with prices set by auction. But the average sale on eBay is about $40, whereas the average sale on some B2B exchanges is over $40,000. The U.S. market for paper is worth at least $260 billion per year; the U.S. plastics market is worth $370 billion per year; the market for steel, $600 billion per year. These figures are for the United States alone; Europe has similarly large figures. PaperExchange.com is the main Web site that trades paper; PlasticsNet.com trades plastics; eSteel.com trades steel. These are just a few of the many B2B exchanges with large markets.

Tradeout.com allows corporations to sell off liquid surplus inventory, old furniture, or idle assets. Without the exchange these are difficult to sell and companies usually get a poor price for them. Tradeout estimates that the market for selling unproductive assets is $300 billion per year. In the clothing industry, for example, there is a major market for auctioning off last year's fashions.

Even the world's oldest profession has exchanges. Some of the most expensive female "escorts" have their own Web sites.[3] Some target Silicon Valley dot-com professionals with tons of money and zero social skills. The client is far too busy for the traditional time-wasting ways of finding a woman. Dynamic pricing helps obtain the highest price for the escorts' services. There are more men who would pay to be "escorted" by a gorgeous woman than gorgeous women willing to provide that service. Because of this, computerized auction pricing has resulted in rapidly inflating prices. The prices have attracted some bored housewives into the game (who wouldn't dream of soliciting in the traditional ways). Their Web sites describe what they offer in colorful terms and sometimes say, "Full service not provided."

TYPES OF EXCHANGES

Many different types of items are being sold with exchanges. Almost every industry will employ B2B exchanges.

Some exchange trade items can be represented by bits transmitted electronically—for example, patents, insurance risks, television news items, or research reports. With these the entire transaction can be completed. Other exchanges deal in physical goods such as paper, plastics, or chemicals. Here the exchange puts the buyer and seller together and establishes a deal, but the goods transfer offline. The exchange may help automate the cash transfer.

Nine of the ten catastrophes most costly to U.S. insurance companies have occurred since 1989. Insurance experts are now talking about future "super-catastrophes" such as a $71 billion Los Angeles earthquake or a $76 billion Florida hurricane. If an insurance company were hit by a disaster of this magnitude, it could go bust. To lessen the exposure it must diversify its risks. The mathematics of probability show that an insurance company that insures against different types of perils spread over different geographic areas will be less likely to suffer a significant loss than a company that insures more narrowly concentrated perils.

Catex.com (catastrophe exchange) is a computerized exchange that allows reinsurance companies to exchange risk contracts and hence spread their risk. It lists many risks, categorized by type, that insurance companies can buy or swap. For example, one company may cede $100 million in Gulf Coast hurricane exposures to another insurer and assume in return $200 million of Italian earthquake exposures. Trading prices are set by the insurance company underwriters. Catex doesn't take any risks itself; it merely facilitates the exchange of risks among its members.

In order to be traded in an exchange, a product needs a standard description. Insurance risks that may be auctioned or traded, for example, need precise descriptions. The first site that establishes an auction for a specific product needs to establish standard or computer-processable descriptions.

Exchanges are particularly valuable with perishable items or commodities that have to be disposed of quickly. Despite what many think, the term "perishable goods" refers to many things other than fresh fish. An airline seat is a highly perishable item because, if it is empty when the plane leaves, it is gone forever. Empty space on a truck traveling across the country has to be sold quickly; this can be done in the United States with the National Transportation Exchange (NTE). This exchange creates a spot market by setting prices based on information from several hundred fleet managers about the destinations of their vehicles and the amount of space available. It then works out the best deals. When an agreement is reached, NTE issues the contract and handles payment.

> The new mechanisms are creating a tectonic shift in the way markets operate.

Advertising space is perishable. When it is close to its publication time a magazine might have unfilled advertising space. This is difficult to sell and often goes for a fifth of its full price. No matter what the medium is—print, poster, Web, or broadcast—sales teams spend an excessive proportion of their time trying to sell off "remnant" ad space. Adauction.com is an exchange for advertising space. It conducts auctions so that bargain-hunting buyers can bid for what they want without having to spend time negotiating with sales reps. Buyers can save time by having an automated agent bid for them at the auction. They can tell the agent the maximum price they are prepared to pay for a specific space without letting other bidders know.

Computerized exchanges are tying together and reorganizing entire industries. Because of the size of the steel, plastics, paper, automotive, and other industries involved, it seems likely that the revenue represented by goods and contracts exchanged may eventually total over $1 trillion per year in the United States alone. If such exchange companies charge an average 5 percent transaction fee their revenues will be huge. They may have gross margins on these transaction fees of 85 percent because they have no inventory or manufacturing.[4] Due to the potential profits there is a frenzied race for dominance in the establishment of B2B exchanges.

ADVANTAGES

Exchange mechanisms offer major advantages to both buyers and sellers. They make it easy for sellers to find buyers, and vice versa. Sellers' Web sites are accessible globally, so they enable a business to sell to other businesses worldwide. They make it easy for a buyer to have access to a very large number of sellers with a wide choice of products. B2B exchanges enable small corporations to trade as well as large corporations.

A major advantage for buyers is that auction-based pricing mechanisms tend to drive the prices down. A major advantage for sellers is that they can sell to a very large number of buyers. The combination of these two factors will greatly expand and lubricate world trade.

A seller can use computers to offer personalized Web pages and catalogs tailored to each customer's needs. These, along with attractive services, can help build customer loyalty. There will be a battle to make automated customer services as excellent as possible.

In order fully to automate the supply chain and the payments process, exchanges encourage the use of standard documents and contracts, and common software. Standardization and automation will make global trading processes faster and easier.

Dynamic pricing needs to be linked to computerized inventory management. Low-selling items may be auctioned to make room for more profitable items. Auctions may be used to eliminate stale inventory—overstocked goods or goods that are becoming out-of-date.

Exchanges make prices and volumes of trade public knowledge, as with stock exchanges. The hidden information of an earlier era is replaced with complete transparency. Hidden information can benefit a few traders and lead to anticompetitive practices, whereas full transparency facilitates free and open competition.

GLOBAL IMPACT

The auction site eBay has made so much money so fast that there will be intense competition to spread auction-based pricing everywhere possible. As companies like eBay become truly global they could have an impact on third-world economies.

A hacker from France, Pierre Omidyar, started eBay. Months before his company went public, Omidyar fled back to Paris; he seems to have little need for wealth and wants to stay out of the spotlight. He has an anticorporate, libertarian viewpoint that wealth should be reasonably evenly spread out—though he now has a personal net worth well over $5 billion. At present he has a pet project of hooking a

> Auction-managed pricing will become the norm in automated purchasing.

Guatemalan village up to eBay so that worldwide customers can buy the village's beautiful craft objects and garments. The art and craftsmanship found in poor countries such as Nepal, Malaysia, Tibet, Bali, or Thailand could have vast numbers of eBay buyers.

African artifacts are sold in New York shops at prices ten times those that a tourist would pay in the village where the items are made.

If a seller in that village had eBay access, the villagers would find what would seem to them like a gold mine. The vast majority of items made in the village never reach sophisticated shops, and the mass of people who could make such items are unemployed. Whole new village industries will grow up around such Web access points, bringing money so badly needed for nourishment, doctors, and education.

Garments leave factories in Madagascar or Bangladesh at a manufacturing cost of $4 and sell in sophisticated London shops for $80. The middlemen organizations that put together the end-to-end process make a fortune. The smart teenagers who buy the clothes have no idea of the desperately poor working conditions afflicting the people who make them. Sooner or later they will be able to buy directly from the place where the clothes are made, with auctions providing good prices to the third-world factories. Many shops, distributors, and middlemen in wealthy nations will need to reinvent their processes if they are to avoid losing their profits.

INVESTMENT OPPORTUNITIES

The existence of global financial exchanges led traders to use the most sophisticated tools to try and make money. The new B2B exchanges will similarly give rise to speculative investing. In the financial markets, electronic trading, automated exchanges, derivatives, and global networks brought a frenzy of new investment techniques. Now changes like these can apply to prices of plastics, paper, chemicals, or any of the goods that are traded with the new B2B exchanges. We will probably see fierce investment competition.

When fixed interest rates gave way to foreign exchange markets, transactions flooded in staggering volumes through the computer networks. It seems likely that similar behavior will become associated with B2B exchanges. Computerized speculation with leveraged instruments will reach massive volumes.

Recall the "random walk" theory of price movements, which argues that prices stagger like a drunken sailor, and no matter where he's staggered in the past, there is an equal chance that his next step will be in any direction. But as we've seen, the more powerful computers of the 1990s analyzed every single price tick and showed that the walk was not quite random.

The movement in prices of steel, memory chips, insurance risks, and so on is even less random than price shifts for stocks, bonds, and currencies. Once drifts start they tend to be larger and to last longer than in financial markets.

Using sophisticated alien-intelligence software, clever traders will discover techniques that enable them to forecast price patterns for goods traded on B2B exchanges and to make speculative investments. As with financial markets, black boxes will allow traders to play this game on a grand scale. The winners are those who invent and master new techniques. To stay ahead they must improve their techniques before they become widely copied. Derivatives provide elaborate ways to hedge against price movements on B2B exchanges.

> **The herds of the electronic jungle will become involved in trying to make money from the price fluctuations on business-to-business exchanges.**

As in financial markets, traders on B2B exchanges can borrow money to increase their participation in what they think is a profitable investment. When George Soros bets on currencies, for example, the bet is sometimes leveraged as much as twelve times the cash invested. The higher the leverage, of course, the higher the risk.

The herds of the electronic jungle will become involved in trying to make money from the price fluctuations on B2B exchanges. Herd instinct will sometimes make them all move together, taking the same action and perhaps reacting to that action very fast. Like online stock trading, user-friendly B2B exchange trading may become a feverish form of home gambling. People have left high-paid jobs to become traders in the items repeatedly auctioned by eBay.

As alien intelligence matures, the world will become more complex at a rapid rate. Complexity expands to fill the available computer power. To be tolerable, the complexity must be hidden, as it is when computers use reverse auctions for steel or chemicals. Users of these complex systems achieve the lowest price, so corporations everywhere will have to play the game. Clever speculators will use black boxes to bet on future prices or create complex derivatives. The masters of black-box speculation about computer-generated steel or reinsurance prices will make great fortunes.

PART III
Alien Technologies

CHAPTER 12
Machines That Breed

I n this part of the book we discuss the techniques of alien intelligence. To illustrate how different they can be from traditional computing, let's start by describing software and procedures, and even hardware, being created by *breeding* rather than conventional design.

In nature, species evolve on the basis of natural selection—in Darwin's phrase: "Multiply. Vary. Let the strongest live and the weakest die." It is possible to create software, procedures, or even hardware using a similar principle. One tries many variations, keeps the variations that give the best results, then tries variations on them, and so on until a valuable result is achieved. Such a technique makes sense when computers are fast enough to create vast numbers of possibilities.

Evolution in nature is glacially slow. In a thousand years you will not notice much change. A horse breeder makes changes happen faster because the breeding has a goal in mind. Software evolution is more like horse breeding. It is not bumbling random evolution ("Let's try any mutation and see if it's interesting") but evolution with a precise, measurable target. Software evolution directs itself toward the target at electronic speed. The fastest software breeding takes place on highly parallel machines so that thousands of variations of the software are breeding simultaneously.

SOFTWARE GENES

Breeding in nature is done with genes. A gene is a string of coded information written with four letters, A, C, G, and T (which stand for adenine, cytosine, guanine, and thymine). Breeding in software also needs genes, written with two bits instead of four letters, 1 and 0. When the 1s and 0s change, the behavior of the program changes.

> As mass marketing gives way to one-on-one marketing, mass production is giving way to customized production.

We humans have a vast number of possible variations in our genes. Similarly, a computer program has numerous possibilities, each represented by a different gene. A process that *breeds* software repeatedly modifies a gene and examines the behavior corresponding to each change. When the change is worse, the gene variant is discarded. When the behavior is better, the new gene is kept and passed to the next generation. Survival of the fittest causes steady progression to a better solution.

Such a technique is called a *genetic algorithm*. Genetic algorithms have been used to solve a diversity of difficult technical problems.[1] They have been used in designing communication networks and more efficient turbines. The ability to change the genes in a fast and systematic way enables us to explore solutions to difficult optimization problems. These algorithms have been used to solve some mathematical problems that seemed otherwise intractable. Software modules that are too difficult to create with conventional programming techniques have sometimes been created by breeding.

BOY MEETS GIRL

When two people have sex, they intermingle their genes and sometimes produce a new gene. If they are lucky, the new gene contains the best of both parents; if they are unlucky, it contains the worst of both. When you or I breed, we find somebody attractive to do it with. If two people are attracted to the other, each must have some good qualities. There is then a higher probability of a good outcome than if the two are not attracted.

The breeding of people in, say, Manhattan is a somewhat chancy process. A professional horse breeder doesn't want to be that chancy; he wants to improve the odds. He picks a horse with exceptional qualities, a great racehorse for example, and breeds it with as many good females as possible. Such a procedure would not be socially acceptable in Manhattan.

Software breeding uses techniques more like the horse breeder's. There must be some way of judging the behavior of a software module and rating its performance. Modules that perform well have their genes combined. Some of the time this produces a software module with better performance. The better-performing modules are systematically selected and bred until modules of high performance are produced.

SEX OR NO SEX

Genes can evolve by using sex or no sex. If there is no sex, the gene is on its own. It is changed by means of its own mutations. It might be changed with random mutations as in nature, but this is inefficient. It might change by evolving different parts of itself separately and combining them.

Sex is much more efficient. Two attractive specimens are taken, and their genes are combined to create an offspring. For example, the first half of the bit stream of one good gene might be combined with the back half of the bit stream of another good gene. This is referred to as

> ## The evolution of software genes is more efficient if sex is used.

crossover. Suppose that the following two genes are pretty good: 10110100 and 01011101. This crossover tries the following two child genes: 10111101 and 01010100. If a child gene is an improvement, it survives; if not, it is forgotten. Crossover breeding is done many times, steadily refining the behavior of the string of bits.

Genes are also modified by mutation. With mutation a random change is made in a gene. A virus mutates, creating slightly modified copies of itself in a largely random fashion. Most of these modifications are useless and thus quickly forgotten, but one in billions might do something useful and so it survives. Viruses can tolerate this extreme inefficiency because they reproduce at a prodigious rate.

The most significant difference between breeding software and breeding horses is that we can modify software genes in milliseconds, not years. A horse breeder can breed only a small number of horses and doesn't scrap the bad ones. A software breeder can breed many millions of copies and ruthlessly scrap the bad ones. And software can have infinite variability, whereas a horse is a horse.

EVOLUTION FROM SCRATCH

Danny Hillis, the creator of Thinking Machines, Inc., demonstrated how a sort program could be bred from scratch. He started with genes containing random bits, and of course the results were useless. His routine then kept combining the genes, using crossover, until the results were infinitesimally better. It selected the genes with slightly better results (however bad). It continued this process, each time creating child programs from two parents, where the child inherited the best halves of the bit streams from each parent. This interbreeding continued for many cycles until the programs started to demonstrate results. The programs progressed in infinitesimal steps from being useless to being valuable.

For years many programmers had tried to improve the efficiency of sorting programs. Hillis wanted to breed the most efficient sort possible, to demonstrate that it could be done. After much trial and error he succeeded in breeding from scratch sort programs almost as efficient as the best that existed.

Growing a program from nothing is an extreme case. Usually we don't have to go back to the most primitive beginnings. We can start with a program that works but that needs drastic improving. Evolution starting with the population of Manhattan has a major advantage over evolution starting in the primeval slime.

Breeding something like a sort program is an interesting academic exercise. What is much more interesting is that we can *breed* programs that programmers would never normally create. Alien intelligence, in its various forms, will be put to work doing things that humans cannot do, rather than trying to replicate what humans can do.

BREEDING A PROCEDURE

Genetic techniques have been demonstrated that breed not just software but also procedures.

We have stressed that a key way to achieve success in electronic commerce is to use technology to learn as much about each customer as possible, and then to treat the customer as an individual—and, ultimately, to manufacture goods specifically for that one customer. As mass marketing gives way to one-on-one marketing, mass production is giving way to customized production.

A key question then becomes: If each product is configured uniquely for a specific customer, how can manufacturing have the economies of scale that mass production had? The key can be to take a day's production and create a very efficient manufacturing schedule with as little retooling as possible.

As we've seen, John Deere improved its business by allowing farmers many options when ordering products. It offers over a million permutations. Unfortunately for the manufacturers, however, the wide array of choices made it difficult to control inventory. Half-assembled machines were bunching up on the factory floor.

> Computers enable industry to change from standard, mass-produced catalog items to individualized, short-lived, information-rich goods, with endless variations.

The solution employed genetic breeding of production schedules. Each night a personal computer examines the orders to be manufactured the following day and, using genetic algorithms, "breeds" more than 600,000 schedules. The best schedules at each phase are selected to participate in the next round of breeding. This software soon learned to produce factory schedules, different each day, far better than humans could possibly produce. John Deere products now flow smoothly through the manufacturing process, with the factory's monthly output up sharply.

As the world of electronic commerce becomes (rapidly) more complex, genetic algorithms will be one type of tool to help cope with the complexity.

Computers enable industry to change from standard, mass-produced catalog items to individualized, short-lived, information-rich goods with endless variations.

SEX WITHOUT CONTACT

Humans have to be physically present in order to breed (usually). This is not the case with software. The genes in the breeding process can be exchanged on the Internet.

Numerous data warehouses are accessible worldwide, and these can be used with shared tools to derive insight from the data. For instance, MasterCard International makes a database of over a trillion bytes of financial information accessible to 22,000 financial institutions that can use the data for analyzing trends and opportunities. In the future MasterCard could package tools along with the data warehouse and encourage the interchange of genetic material for deriving shared insight. Similar generation of shared insight could apply to preventive medicine, marketing operations, fraud detection, criminal investigation, job searching, the prevention of terrorism, environmental protection, and many other areas.

There have been attempts to *breed* black-box programs for investing. Huge data warehouses have been assembled to give full details of tick-by-tick foreign exchange trades and interest rates. A genetic interbreeding process can take this mass of data and try to breed the best possible software for currency trading in order to examine different levels of return for different levels of risk.

HOW TO BREED HARDWARE

Computer software has always been able to modify itself. Many people can grasp the idea that software can improve its own behavior by "breeding" or some other form of evolution. Yet to many people the idea that *hardware* can breed seems like pure science fiction. It conjures images of biological monsters in a gur-gling vat of slime.

In 1998 in Kyoto, Japan's ancient seat of wisdom, a group headed by Hugo de Garis announced that it was going to create a robot kit-ten, which would have to have an elaborate "brain." The kitten brain, de Garis said, was far too complex to design with traditional design techniques. Instead of designing the hardware modules the brain needed, he would "breed" them.[2]

The kitten is called "Robokoneko" (Japanese for "robot kit-ten"). While the United States seems to like the idea of Robocop, Japan likes Robokitten.

De Garis's kitten is not a biology project; it's a silicon engineer-ing project. The kitten uses many small modules of "brain" power, each "bred" on a silicon chip. Because so much breeding is needed, de Garis's team created a spectacularly powerful supercomputer for the breeding process. He called this a "Darwin machine."

When a human baby learns, it is, in effect, wiring up its brain; it grows the nerve patterns between neurons and adjusts the synapses so that the influence of one neuron on another changes. De Garis found out how to do that with silicon chips. He uses a genetic technique to grow a small module of brainpower, which has only a few hundred neurons. Some brain functions need many of these modules to link together.

De Garis found that his kitten brain needed some very complex functions, many of them too difficult to design in a conventional way. However, building hardware or software by evolution *can* achieve very complex results. The breeding can go on for millions of cycles, and, as de Garis commented, "There will be too many components for the behavior of the total system to be predictable or even analyzable."[3]

De Garis's Darwin machine could "breed" the modules of brain behavior at amazing speed. He thinks that brain breeding will become a massive industry.

BEYOND PENTIUM CHIPS

For the behavior of a chip to be "bred," the chip must be change-able. With conventional chips, like Intel's renowned Pentium chips, the hardware is fixed; it is the software that changes. With some processor chips, however, you can modify hardware behavior. These chips can be reconfigured by their users. Entrepreneurs use them to create new chips for their inventions at low cost.

Modifiable chips contain a number of bits, called configuration bits, which can be easily changed. These changeable bits are, in effect, the genes of the chip. Changing a bit changes the function of the chip; it might be used, for example, to convert an ADD function into a logic function, or change an output wire into an input wire. Chips that can be modified in this way are called FPGA (field programmable gate array) chips.

Some FPGA chips have two million programmable bits. With these, highly complex behavior can be set in hardware rather than in software. A chip that plays a video game could be changed in an instant so that it does the payroll instead. With these bits hardware functions can be "bred" in a similar way to the software functions.

> Computers allow evolution to occur at a staggering rate; what happened in fifty million years in nature could happen in three weeks.

Complex processes set in hardware run much faster than the same processes coded in software and executed on conventional chips—sometimes a hundred times faster. This makes them attractive for many of the portable gadgets we will want to carry. The Japanese company working on the robot kitten needed brain mechanisms in hardware because they needed to be much faster than was possible on conventional computers.

An FPGA chip generates much less heat than a conventional processor. The person showing me the extreme speed of applications built into an FPGA chip asked me to put my finger on the chip. It was cold, whereas a Pentium chip executing the same process in software would have been so hot it would have burned my finger. Because FPGA chips stay cool they can be much more densely packed.

DOWNRIGHT WEIRD

The entire process of breeding a field programmable chip could be simulated on a computer. It could also be done *on the chip*.

Adrian Thompson at the University of Sussex, in England, experimented with techniques for breeding on the chip. An FPGA chip was set up to do a task for which its performance could be measured. After thousands of generations of breeding the configuration bit stream, a configuration emerged that was exceptionally good at achieving its task.[4]

Thompson managed to breed chips that he referred to as "flabbergastingly efficient," but he also described their operation as "downright weird."[5] He used a chip with one hundred cells but found that in the final configuration only thirty-two were in use. The current on the chip was feeding back and forth through the gates, "swirling around," in a manner quite unlike anything we would see from a human-designed chip.

Human chip designers go out of their way to avoid a phenomenon called electromagnetic coupling, which occurs when cells are so close on the chip that there is wireless interference between them. The cells sometimes broadcast radio signals between themselves without sending current down the intervening wires. Designers lay out components in such a way that electromagnetic coupling cannot affect performance.

Thompson's breeding process had *discovered* electromagnetic coupling and, rather than avoiding it, was automatically taking advantage of it. There may have been other subtle electronic phenomena that the breeding process had detected and was also putting to work. It had found its own unique way to make a chip work.

Nature seems to have had problems somewhat similar to what Thompson experienced. Our DNA has evolved for a very long time and works well, but, amazingly, 97 percent of it is junk.[6] Of our DNA, 8.7 billion letters (166 shakespeares) are garbage, replicated in every cell in our body, but not used. No engineer would design such code. Thomas Jefferson, who believed that everything God created was perfect, would have been outraged to hear that 97 percent of our DNA is junk.

EVOLUTION AND RELIABILITY

The chip that Thompson bred was doing something that the chip was not designed to do. Because of that it was not necessarily reliable. The configuration might not work if there were a substantial change in temperature, or if it was applied to a different batch of chips from the factory. The design was efficient, but as Thompson said, it was "overexploiting the physics." Because of this Thompson went on to breed chips that would work under all physical conditions. He evolved circuits on multiple versions of the chip simultaneously, where the versions came from different factories and had temperatures varying over a wide range. He wanted to produce circuits that were extraordinarily robust and would work on all factory batches, on damaged chips, and in conditions of extreme humidity, temperature, or vibration. Breeding, Thompson notes, can produce extremely fault-tolerant chips.

Humans have difficulty designing certain properties, such as resistance to extreme conditions, using very small amounts of power, and being very efficient and fault-tolerant at the same time. Thompson says that he is exploring what genetic evolution can achieve that conventional human design can't.[7] Genobyte, Inc., uses FPGA chips to genetically evolve digital circuits directly *inside the target device* rather than designing them in a traditional way. Genobyte comments that its evolvable hardware makes it possible to "create complex adaptive circuits *beyond human capability to design or debug*" (emphasis added).[8]

CAN WE TRUST IT?

Software (or hardware) that has been bred, as opposed to designed and coded, might seem scary because we cannot understand its detailed logic. With conventional software development a programmer sits at his desk and pores over the code, checking that each instruction is logical. With software that has been bred we cannot do that. If we change one instruction manually, the program may not work correctly. Can we trust such software?

Suppose you are on the night flight descending into London's Heathrow Airport in thick fog. Before the plane descends into the soup you notice the flashing red lights of many other planes around you. You have read that the air traffic control system is fifteen years out of date. The flaps of your plane move with small twitching motions every second, so you know that it is not a human flying the plane; it is software. Would you feel comfortable if you knew that that software had been bred rather than written, and that human programmers couldn't understand its logic?

This question is not entirely academic. The Department of Defense fights battles in its Synthetic Theater of War. The intent is realistically to simulate possible future wars and to explore the requirements for the many possible courses of action. Of the planes in the battles some have been flown by automated pilots and some by human pilots (flying a simulator). Some of the automated pilots have succeeded in shooting down some of the human pilots,[9] and the automated pilots are quickly getting better. Today these simulations are based on rule processing (as described in Chapter 16).[10] Breeding has not yet been used. If it were used, live in the field, it might steadily improve the performance of the automated pilot.

All air crashes are investigated in immense detail. In Europe many accidents have been blamed on "pilot error." The European Air Pilots Association has conducted its own detailed investigation of these accidents and has concluded that the true cause in almost every case is faulty software. It is exceedingly difficult fully to debug software of such complexity. Much research is being done into more rigorous techniques for software development,[11] but even so it is just too difficult to create programs of millions of lines of code that are error free.

> Can we trust software that has been bred rather than written?

This is a dilemma for our time: To what extent can you trust machines of great complexity?

Danny Hillis believes that genetically bred programs will become more reliable than large handwritten programs. If a hundred people team up to write a million handwritten instructions that operate differently in different circumstances, it is too much to expect that they will be error free in all circumstances. Describing genetically bred programs, Hillis states: "If you put them in a world where they survive by solving a problem, then with each successive generation they get better and better at solving the problem. After a few hundred thousand generations they solve the problem very well."[12]

A modern jetliner has four million parts. The passenger blurb says, "They all work together to give you a safe flight." The immensely complex wiring on the plane is optimized by computer. The circuits on the chips in the plane are laid out by synthetic annealing. Alien-intelligence processes are steadily coming into design.

AWESOME RESULTS

At the southern tip of Africa there's a masterpiece of evolution. A "floral kingdom" exists, called the *fynbos* (pronounced "fain-boss"). The mountains and valleys are covered with a massed spectacle of flowering plants different from those in other parts of the planet. There are 8,600 plant species, most of them flowering, in a self-sustaining ecosystem. Of these, 5,800 are endemic, meaning that they evolved in that place for millions of years. To put this in perspective, the British Isles cover a much larger area but have only 1,500 plant species, of which fewer than twenty are endemic.[13]

You might walk in the hills there and think how awesome that God created the fynbos. I find a different aspect of it more awesome: that this ecosystem of such complexity and beauty *evolved*. Almost none of these plants existed in the days of the dinosaurs.

If we evolve things electronically, with something like de Garis's Darwin machine, the process could be a billion times faster. What happened in fifty million years could happen in three weeks. But questions are facing us: How do we set the rules for such a process? What do we want to evolve? Will it breed all around the world on the Internet? Will it have a much larger market cap than any dot-com company?

Perhaps a more alarming question is: Will the machines evolve autonomously—by themselves? Sooner or later, of course they will.

In five hours of evolution of fynbos-like complexity, what will they do? What would we want them to do? As alien intelligence becomes deeper and deeper, and evolves mechanisms we can't understand, will we be able to control it? Can we set the goals? Will machines develop an agenda of their own?

As the Chinese curse says, "May you live in interesting times."

CHAPTER 13
Systems That Learn

The largest sloop ever built is *Hyperion*, created by the Huisman Shipyard in Holland, legendary for unchanging traditions of boat building learned over centuries. *Hyperion* was built for Jim Clark, the founder of Netscape, legendary for wanting to change everything.

Clark wanted a boat that would sail itself—more than that, a boat that would *learn* to sail and constantly improve its performance. *Hyperion* had thousands of electronic sensors measuring everything that could be measured. These fed information to twenty-five powerful Silicon Graphics computers. Over time the computers would acquire the information to cope with almost any sailing condition.

If one were going to create such an interesting experiment as a self-teaching sailboat, one might have expected to start with a small boat—perhaps a twelve-foot sloop. But *Hyperion* had the world's largest mast and the world's largest sail. The mast, almost two hundred feet, was too tall to get under the Sydney Harbor Bridge, and the mainsail was more than a quarter the size of a football field. The sail was so large that the boat could be sailed only by computer. It was computerized control that made such a huge boat possible.

One might have expected the first trials of the boat to be in a relatively calm, controllable environment, almost like a laboratory perhaps. But when *Hyperion* was launched Jim Clark took it and a television crew into the North Sea, with gale winds gusting above the maximum the boat gauges could measure. The geeks at the computer screens were all hopelessly sick.

The computerized boat and its problems are a parable for our times. Clark hired a great captain who had circumnavigated the globe three times and had won the Whitbread around-the-world race. The captain, like great sailors everywhere, had a gut feel for the winds and the motion of the sails. But he was allergic to computers; he'd rather switch them off. On the other hand, the geeks needed to run the twenty-five sophisticated computers were fair-weather sailors at best, seasick and terrified when the seas became rough.

Many captains of industry express open contempt for computers. Whereas in an earlier era computers could be kept in their place— they do the payroll—now corporations are designed around the computer. Leading-edge corporations are in the process of reinventing everything because computing makes the reinvention possible.

On an ordinary boat Clark's captain would know how to fix anything that went wrong. He would be alone with the elements, completely in charge. But on *Hyperion* the computers could go berserk and the captain would have no idea how to find out why. To add insult to this impossible situation, the computers had a computer-generated voice and could bark orders at the captain. (Clark had had trouble with his captains before and so had designed the boat to monitor everything the captain did.) Worse, Jim Clark, if he wanted, could take over the controls from his office in California. The press, with some exaggeration, had reported that the boat could be sailed across the oceans from computer screens in Silicon Valley.

The boat was programmed to learn, and this could be very important. The mainsail was so large that it exerted many tons of stress on its halyard. Any accidental jibe with this sail might snap the mast, so the systems measured everything and learned when to stop the boat from sailing too close to the wind. But no matter how good its intelligence became it couldn't be trusted to sail the seas alone. If the sail ripped or a halyard frayed the human captain was needed.

> Traditional programs are as inflexible as Dickensian bureaucrats. The software of the future must cope with chaos and adapt constantly to changing circumstances.

Today, jet planes are intensely computerized. Except in the most dire emergencies an airline captain can't override the computers. The captain has to go through the most intense training with the computerized machine. An intimate relationship is built up between the man and the machine—between human intelligence and machine intelligence. In many future corporate mechanisms the people in charge will be trained so that an intimate relationship between human intelligence and machine intelligence is achieved and improves as both the human and software improves.

AUTOMATED LEARNING

One of the most powerful aspects of future computing is the building of systems that learn. If we can create software that learns autonomously, then the software can improve its own capability to carry out a specific function. It may not be able to sail better than the best human sailors, but it can learn to do many things better than humans. It may learn how to diagnose problems in complex software, or what products would please each customer, or how to optimize delivery from an electronic supermarket. In some cases the software will immensely surpass the capability of its creator because computers can do things that humans can't, and particularly because a computer can execute logic *millions* of times faster than humans can.

Long ago, in the days when it was exciting to program a computer to play checkers, Art Samuel wrote a checkers-playing program that learned from each game how to improve its play. In its first game it was idiotic, but after only twelve games it began to beat him. After twenty-eight games Samuel described it as a better than average player. He said, "The rate of learning was surprisingly high, but that learning was quite erratic."[1] It soon reached a level where Samuel couldn't beat it. He arranged a match with the Connecticut checkers champion, and the software won.[2]

Today, learning systems are starting to play an important role in corporations.

As discussed earlier, a key to success in electronic commerce is to have systems that learn about each customer and treat that customer as an individual. When the customer goes to a Web site, it should greet the customer by name and display a home page with information specifically for that customer. In many cases products should be configured uniquely for that customer. And when we learn about an individual so that we can sell a customized product, we need to be able to manufacture products on a customized basis, as John Deere has already done, using genetic algorithms to optimize each day's factory production schedule.

Corporations are havens of erratic and irrational behavior. As electronic commerce matures, only those corporations that offer customers the choices they want are likely to survive. But richness of choice increases the potential for chaos, as John Deere learned before it began optimizing factory production. Factories designed to react to customer wishes lose the simple shop-floor scheduling of the past. The choreography of complex events has to be done by software, but fixed programs designed in a top-down fashion cannot respond to the flood of unpredictable changes.

Traditional programs are as inflexible as Dickensian bureaucrats with quill pens and top hats. The software of the future must cope with chaos and constantly learn how to adapt itself to changing schedules and circumstances.

The John Deere system of genetically breeding complex solutions each night for operation the next day is an indication of the future, except that in the future the breeding will go on continuously throughout the day. Some of the world's top-ranking commodity and foreign exchange traders already use black-box (or semi-black-box) systems that constantly learn from market patterns and behavior, trying to enhance trading decisions. In such trading dramatic events can happen so suddenly that there is no time for human response.

WHEN COMPUTERS LEARN

Computer learning acquired commercial importance when the technology of data warehousing became widespread. Businesses collected vast quantities of data from instrumentation, credit card readers, bar-code scanners, sensors, and Web sites. Innumerable sites sold lists of people responding to advertisements, people buying drugs, people doing Internet searches, even people joining church groups. In some areas this deluge of data grew like a flash flood. It will grow much more as the data needs of e-commerce sweep around the world and microsystems become ubiquitous. Computers have the task of extracting information that is useful from this ocean of data. Data-mining algorithms started to use parallel computers for doing complex searches of the data, and neurocomputers for finding unexpected patterns in data. Software packages were sold that learned to detect fraud, risk, problems, or profit opportunities.[3] Companies sold information about hurricane patterns to insurance companies or demonstrated software that could detect medical problems before they became harmful.

> Where appropriate standards exist, computers on the Web can access each other's knowledge and combine knowledge.

Profits in electronic commerce will come from computers' *learning* to identify potential customers, *learning* about customer wishes, and *learning* how to delight customers. To a known customer a system might say, "Here are products that we think you would enjoy," or point out music, restaurants, or Web sites that fit the data about that customer. It will often produce valuable recommendations for items the customer would not otherwise have found. As the capability to learn about customers matures, computers will get to know an enormous amount about us (unless we consciously prevent them doing so). This should lead to an era of better customer satisfaction, choice of products that will meet our needs better, the ability to choose books, movies, television, and Internet products that we are more likely to enjoy. Computers learning about us will become extremely important in the medical field and in the drive toward preventive medicine. But this learning could also lead to overintrusive marketing, invasion of privacy, and infuriating government. Computers can detect people with serious addictions, such as gambling, chocolate, or online trading, and make them targets of sales campaigns.

JuniorNet, the online "Community of Kids," has many activities for children starting at age three—for example, multikid games, pen pals, Funny Photo captions, and a pet club. It learns what activities a kid likes and tells him how to find similar activities; it helps a child select a community based on affinity. It uses tools to increase customer loyalty.

Today we say, "How could we ever have lived without the telephone?" Tomorrow we will say, "How could we ever have lived without computers that know about our likes, skills, phobias, needs, tastes, medical issues, our garden, our kids, and everything else?"

HUMAN LEARNING IS DIFFERENT

A computer learns differently from the way a human learns. Whereas we may modify our behavior over the course of months or years, computer programs may do so in seconds or milliseconds. Humans learn with broad-ranging common sense, but computers learn like idiot savants. However, if they increase the yield in a chip factory by 1 percent, they will be very valuable. (A modern chip factory costs a few billion dollars.)

Humans usually learn in a bumbling hit-or-miss way. Insight comes slowly, but it can encompass diverse knowledge. Humans can tie together a wide-ranging collection of ideas in a way that software can't. Where computers can be made to learn, they do so with great speed and thoroughness. Where computer learning has been achieved so far, it has been with a very narrow subject, such as identifying trends in foreign exchange trading or breeding factory schedules that permit richness of choice. Computer learning is likely to be highly focused but relentlessly thorough within its narrow domain.

Like other forms of alien intelligence, computer learning will be very different from human learning. Remember, we limit our capability to understand its potential if we think of it as being like human learning.

Computers can learn in two fundamentally different ways. They may change their own *internal* software, or they may change an *external* database without changing their own software.

Once learning is initiated in software it may go on for seconds, after which the software concludes that no further improvements can be made, or it may go on for years with the software relentlessly searching for improvements. The learning may be in one isolated machine or it may be in networks of machines. There may be computers around the world concerned with a particular subject, exchanging what they have learned.

In some applications a machine can learn happily by itself; in other applications it needs people. Humans and computers will learn together, with humans directing the learning process and computers improving their own capability at electronic speed. It is intriguing to speculate about what applications will bring the winner-takes-most chain reactions of the future.

MANY FORMS OF LEARNING

Machines can learn in many diverse ways.

They may observe our behavior, updating their knowledge about us, as Amazon.com learns about what we like to read. Clearly there is much commercial potential in having computers silently and relentlessly learning about customers. Computers can learn about us in very simple ways, such as by identifying characteristics of good customers and searching for other customers with similar characteristics. Or they can use much more sophisticated techniques, such as those that neurocomputers employ to scour a data warehouse for insights that humans would not find on their own. Data-mining toolkits provide a variety of techniques for foraging through data, learning about customers, sales patterns, fraud, the spread of epidemics, and numerous other subjects.

Some software learns by exploring a vast array of alternatives, systematically searching for the best. This is the case with software that designs the layout of wiring on chips, adjusting the connections many millions of times, trying to minimize the transmission times (the "simulated annealing" techniques discussed in Chapter 4).

Learning algorithms can also be used to classify data. Botanists classify plants; doctors classify illnesses. One would like a computer to learn from many examples how to put cases into the right category. Various studies in medicine have examined the diagnostic success rate of doctors and come to dismal conclusions. One study examined eight tests commonly used to confirm a diagnosis of appendicitis. It showed the results of the tests for 106 patients admitted to an emergency room with a diagnosis of acute appendicitis. All 106 had their appendix cut out, but only 85 of these were found to actually have appendicitis.[4] A computer, analyzing many cases, could learn how to achieve a higher diagnostic success rate (but with less revenue for the clinic).

There are many approaches to using essentially statistical techniques to learn from past results and predict future results. There are various pattern recognition methods. Software can learn what patterns exist in complex data and can spot items that deviate from an expected pattern.[5]

The survival-of-the-fittest processes of evolution are nature's way of learning, slowly transforming the planet from barren rocks to lush ecologies. Genetic algorithms may be software's way of trying to do the same, interbreeding the variants that appear to have the best characteristics. Some forms of artificial life in software have produced wild ecologies.

Neural networks provide one of the most impressive and useful forms of automated learning, sometimes emulating the learning that has to happen after creatures are born to enable them to make sense of their environment.

Expert systems store many rules and use these rules to make inferences that help in making expert decisions. In the future we are likely to see vast libraries of rule-based knowledge, with techniques for converting human knowledge into machine-processable knowledge. Such systems can be more effective when they constantly improve their rule base. Some software now has linkages between rule-based inferencing and learning techniques such as neural networks.

KNOWING ALL ABOUT US

Computers can get to know a vast amount about us. Much information is collected on the Internet. Data warehouses for commercial purposes are becoming huge. Data-mining software can derive all manner of information and insight about individuals from this deluge of data.

The protection of individual privacy is becoming a major issue for electronic commerce, involving both government regulation and self-regulation within industries.

Many individuals are uncomfortable with the idea that machines will know so much about them. But often they want the services that such computerized knowledge makes possible. It will be useful to have computers that have learned about our taste in books or movies and can recommend what we would enjoy. In many cases computers can be programmed to anticipate our wishes. More significantly, if the ubiquitous computers can detect that you are within hours of having a stroke or heart attack, and can stop it from happening (which will often be possible), you would probably want them to do that.

Women in 1900 were shocked by the invention of the X ray, and swore that they would never allow such a gross intrusion of their bodily privacy. Later they became used to the idea and wanted regular check ups with X rays.

Law or industry self-regulation will probably require that corporations have a comprehensive privacy policy, inform users of how information may be used, and give users the choice of saying no if they wish. We may become used to living in a world where the computers know everything about us. We may come to ask, "Does it matter, provided that the information is not used in harmful or offensive ways?" Of course, we will need to prevent government from using it in bad ways. The ability to compile knowledge about individuals

> Alien intelligence can cope with the deluge of data; human intelligence can't.

today is much worse than anything George Orwell dreamed of. It is essential to prevent Orwellian characteristics in government.

Sometimes we will want electronics to use the information that can be collected. We want to deter burglars. Various laboratories have demonstrated systems in vehicles that can detect when the driver is driving unsafely, or is overtired, or is intoxicated. The car could detect road rage. It could also caution its driver if his reactions are impaired by alcohol, or if he is driving recklessly, but he might react badly to that. Should insurance companies offer a discount rate to car owners who have a device that warns the driver and radios the insurance company's computer when unsafe driving occurs? This could increase the insurance company's profit, and for most people it could lower their insurance premium. Should the car refuse to start if its driver is intoxicated? About forty thousand people are killed each year in traffic accidents in the United

States alone, and even more are maimed; two-thirds of these accidents are alcohol-related. This is much larger than the annual death toll in the Vietnam War. Technology can now be used in many ways to lower the death rate. This raises social issues about how much machines should interfere with freedom. An observer from a different age might say it is nuts to let the carnage continue.

The privacy issues will become very complex.

MOTHER

Our bodies have numerous neural networks for different functions in our brain and nervous system. A baby exercises its limbs in random ways to begin with, in the same way that a neural network behaves randomly at first. The baby feels its way around and after much trial and error starts to correlate what it feels with what it sees. Very slowly it learns to grasp things and move about. A large amount of learning is needed before it can stagger around on its legs. The baby's mother looks after it and tries to teach it things. If the mother weren't around, it would still learn by trial and error, and providing it had a source of food it might survive, but disastrously so. Baby fish survive away from their mother, but the more complex the creature the more it needs its mother to teach it things.

The same is true with software.

Some machine neural networks learn from scratch, but they can be more effective if they have various forms of precoded behavior built in. The capability exists to add more precoded behavior as the learning proceeds.

A major form of system development in the future will combine autonomous software learning with the capability for humans to guide the learning processes constantly. The learning—for example with neural networks or genetic algorithms—will evolve software processes that would be difficult or near impossible for humans to code, but humans will steer the evolution in intelligent ways, making the learning processes head in useful directions.

In the future, many systems that learn will have not one but many learning processes developing different aspects of the system, as complex creatures do. There may be many different neural networks, for example, with different purposes.

SEARCHING FOR KNOWLEDGE

Computers have demonstrated a formidable capability to scour the Internet relentlessly searching for information, but the searches result in large numbers of useless items. Some technique is needed to separate the wheat from the chaff. There will always be much more chaff than wheat.

We can get rid of the chaff by having schemes for human validation of Internet sites, or by refereeing papers so that only quality material is included in the search. It might be done by restricting the search to virtual private Nets, possibly within a specific industry such as pharmaceuticals or aerospace. A computer searching for movie reviews might bring back only reviews by listed reviewers. It then analyzes the tastes of both its customers and the reviewers, and links customers to reviewers they are likely to agree with.

I am repeatedly turned off of movies that I would enjoy by watching trailers designed for what the distributors think is the mass market. Increasingly we will view trailers at Web sites (such as Hollywood.com) that tell us what films are showing in our local theaters. There will then be many different trailers, so that each person is shown one that sells well to that individual. The same should be true with most online advertising.

Computers have usually searched only text, and they cannot understand the contents of the text other than by knowing what words it contains. The game becomes much more interesting if they can understand and process what they find. If they can search the Net for data that conform to appropriate definitions and bring them to a data warehouse, then many different learning techniques can be used to mine these data for useful knowledge.

> Our children will talk about an old-fashioned world where the text-books in a library couldn't talk to one another.

The knowledge on the Internet today is mostly encoded so that humans can use it. Over time it will need to be encoded so that computers can use it. The Internet will evolve into a very different creature as its resources become increasingly designed for automatic processing rather than merely human access.

We need data warehouses designed so that computers around the planet can access them, extract information, and use data-mining tools. We need databases with data represented in standard ways, objects and agents that can be passed from one computer to another, and knowledge represented in rules so that programs can make deductions with it, using rule-based inferencing. Knowledge equivalent to that in textbooks should be usable automatically by computers to solve specific types of problems.

When computers regularly scour the Net for data and process those data, we will have a quantum leap in capability. Even more powerful is the capability for computers to search for knowledge designed so that they can use it with an inference engine that does automated reasoning (see Chapter 16).

Information can be represented at these three different levels:

- Text (designed for human consumption).
- Data where the format of data items is precisely defined (the basis of all data processing).

■ Knowledge in the form of terms and assertions
(designed such that a computer can use an inference engine to reason with that knowledge).

Searching the Internet for information can be based on these same three levels.

Material designed so that an inference engine can reason with it is often referred to as "knowledge" rather than "data" or "information." The computer stores such material in a "knowledgebase" rather than a "database." If a computer could forage the Internet for appropriately designed knowledge, it could add to its own knowledgebase about a subject. With appropriate controls and standards we could have computers that improve their own knowledge *automatically*.

A knowledgebase contains *terms* (its basic vocabulary) and *assertions* about those terms in the form of rules. A computer searching the Net may find new assertions that it can add to existing assertions already stored about the terms. If computers can add to the knowledgebase, they can then start to boost themselves to higher levels of capability.

Knowledgebases for specialized subjects will evolve in many places. There will eventually be numerous Internet sites with specialized knowledgebases, some for financial markets, some for pharmaceutical development, some for health care, and so on. These knowledgebases will one day become a major part of the intellectual property that corporations sell.

Humans cannot transmit their knowledge directly, brain to brain. Computers can. In some cases the sharing will take place on private industry networks.

Where appropriate standards exist, computers on the Web can access each other's knowledge and combine knowledge. Computers can collectively become more knowledgeable at a formidable rate.

SMALL CHUNKS OF KNOWLEDGE

For knowledge to be digestible it must be divided into small chunks that an inference engine can work with. One way of doing this is to create chunks that are referred to as "microtheories."[6] Each microtheory relates to a particular topic (such as currency trading, e-coli, value-added tax, and so on). It is essentially a bundle of assertions about that topic that share a common set of assumptions.

A microtheory is, in essence, a small and modular knowledge-base dedicated to a particular topic. Many microtheories may exist within a larger knowledgebase. Microtheories provide a mechanism for focusing on relevant information during problem solving. They make it possible independently to maintain assertions for different topics that might otherwise appear contradictory.

As such a capability comes into place, numerous groups around the planet may be encoding knowledge into machine-usable form. As the terms and assertions are entered much testing is needed. When a microtheory is first entered many questions may be posed to the software to test that the topic has been adequately covered.

A microtheory can have a *context* applied to it. The context states assumptions that apply to the entire microtheory. The assumptions are then stated once rather than having to be repeated for every assertion. For example, an assumption might be that activities in the microtheory are performed in the home, or that the microtheory applies to French law. Different versions of a microtheory might be created each with a different *context*. Making assertions in different *contexts* keeps them from conflicting.

CREATING PROCESSABLE KNOWLEDGE

Today, computers on the World Wide Web can access a vast amount of information. You can be firehosed with far more information than you can digest. To achieve this high-speed deluge the search engines need vast indices organized so that many processors can search them in parallel. These indices are constructed *automatically*. Computers are busy updating them all day long, constantly scouring the Web sites of the planet, looking for words in that information. They search only for words. If some of the Web sites contained knowledge encoded with *assertions*, *microtheories*, and *contexts*, the computers could search for those.

Computers of the future will scour the world for knowledge that they can use. They will interchange knowledge, refine the representation, and establish different *contexts* to help achieve consistency. Particularly important, they will apply comprehensive *truth maintenance* techniques. These will use automatic methods for detecting inconsistencies as well as semiautomatic methods in which they ask humans for help in establishing validity of the knowledge.

If knowledge categorization for specialized areas became a de facto standard, the search engines could search the Web for knowledge in that form. They could build up their knowledge using microtheories from around the planet, constantly foraging for information that would improve that knowledge.

Many human organizations and individuals will add to the knowledge of computers, and some computers will learn automatically. Eventually many computers around the world will acquire knowledge constantly, creating numerous *microtheories*. As their capability improves, more and more of their learning will become automatic.

Numerous computers, connected to the Internet, will participate in digesting knowledge, putting it into common knowledge-bases, coordinating and sharing this knowledge, and making it accessible everywhere.

Machines can cope with the deluge of knowledge; humans can't.

The textbooks of the world are becoming electronic. The text is becoming available on the Internet and on DVDs, and computer-based training is spreading rapidly. The student will increasingly be able to follow links to greater detail or to tutorial explanations where he needs them. Textbooks need restructuring so that as they become electronic the knowledge they contain can be automatically linked to other knowledge. The *Encyclopedia Britannica* has been redesigned so that its subject matter has highlighted words that are pointers (HTML links) to sites on the Web where much more information can be obtained. As this capability grows and is enhanced, it will become a formidable body of interlinked information.

Marvin Minsky, head of MIT's Artificial Intelligence Lab, has said that our children will talk about an old-fashioned world where the textbooks in a library couldn't talk to one another.

BOTTOM-UP INTELLIGENCE

In nature, evolution has proceeded from the *bottom up*. Single-cell creatures slowly developed into multicell creatures. Networks of neurons learned and slowly evolved. Simple organs evolved into more complex organs. It took several billion years of evolution before creatures developed a cerebral cortex. Relatively recently a critical mass was achieved, and mankind acquired science and art, then books, then computers, then worldwide networks, and then started to think about artificial evolution.

Most attempts at creating artificial intelligence have been *top-down*. A high-level goal is established and decomposed into operations for which programs are written. However, science is a very long way from understanding the brain from the top down. The brain is so complexly wired that even if we had the most detailed blueprint of the wiring, we would still not have a clue how it comes to subtle conclusions.

Various alien-intelligence researchers are now starting to work with the senses. The senses encode information with complex representations. Computer science depends on finding good ways to represent complex information. Air traffic control systems, for example, need the best way to represent the planes converging over a busy airport. The same is true with artificial sensors. It is critical to find the right way to represent the information that surges through the electronic jungle.

> It is easy to imagine learning processes for humanoids because we are human. Imagining learning processes for an alien-intelligence creature is more difficult.

It is curious to observe that entirely different creatures have similar sensory mechanisms. For instance, a squid's eye has all the parts and complexity of a mammal's eye, although squids and mammals have evolved in quite different arenas and employ entirely different tissues. Molecular biologists now believe that a basic eye evolved sufficiently far back in time that it became the mechanism for sight in diverse creatures. Many of our organs evolved before dinosaurs roamed the earth. Evolution headed down many different branches, but a common gene sequence for an eye was used throughout most of these branches—in mice, squid, flatworms, sea squirts, gorillas, and us. There is something inherently right about the mechanism. We should ask what aspects of it we could emulate in silicon.

BROOKS'S CRITTERS

Rodney Brooks at MIT's Artificial Intelligence Laboratory decided to try nature's way and grow machine capability from the *bottom up*. He set out to create devices that start with no intelligence and no goals, and that can steadily learn behavior patterns by trial and error, possibly with a "mother" who guides them. If machines can be made to learn, they will acquire skills that would be difficult to program in other ways.

Experimental robots in many research laboratories are linked to massive computers that are programmed in a conventional top-down fashion. Brooks built robots with multiple microprocessors that have to learn everything from scratch using neural networks.

One of his first creations was an insect like machine called Attila. It had six legs made of rods and could crawl all around the Artificial Intelligence Laboratory at about 1.5 miles per hour, avoiding obstacles. It weighed 3.6 pounds and had ten microcomputers with 150 sensors. When Attila was first switched on it flailed around in all directions like a drunken cockroach. With a large amount of trial and error it learned, like a baby, to coordinate its limbs and crawl around. It poked around and bumped into objects, slowly learning how to move in a more elegant manner.

Brooks points out that it would be extremely difficult to program his cockroach in the way computers are normally programmed. If it were built with conventional programming, it would be extremely inflexible; a new circumstance could cause it to cease functioning. Conventional programs are brittle. They cannot cope with the unexpected. Programs could not even cope with something as trivial as the Year 2000 date change. Software grown by a learning process is not brittle; when it encounters something unexpected, it can continue to learn. Nature's cockroaches move fast and are remarkably resilient. Studies of the worst impact of nuclear war concluded that long after all humans and animals had died, cockroaches would inherit the rubble.

NASA patterned its first Mars Rover vehicle after Brooks's insectoids because of this ability to cope with the unexpected. Sojourner, the famous six-wheeled vehicle that crawled slowly around the Martian landing site, was able to maneuver around boulders and rough terrain usually without assistance from ground control. This was important because it takes about forty minutes for a radio signal to make a journey from Mars and back.

COG

After building cockroaches Brooks wanted to find a way to make a grander reputation. However remarkable the achievement, one doesn't really want to go down in history as a cockroach builder. His plan had been to work up the evolutionary scale from cockroaches to lizards, dogs, and so on. Brooks took a sabbatical to think about it. After some heady conversations in Japan, he telephoned one of his top graduate students, Cynthia Ferrell, and told her that he wanted the group to build a humanoid.

The humanoid is called Cog. It doesn't look human, at least for now. It is composed of black and chrome metal rods, canister like motors, and bundles of wire and cable. It has one arm with a three-fingered hand. It is more lifelike than most conventional robots; if you push on Cog, it gives a little but pushes back. It has two large red "Kill" switches mounted on either side in case it should unexpectedly do something dangerous. Cog has no legs. Brooks comments that it is a paraplegic. Its torso is mounted on a fixed pedestal so it cannot scurry around like the cockroaches.

Cog will eventually be provided with an exterior that is more personable—a soft, rubbery face and *Star Wars* stormtrooper-style body armor. It will have plastic eye coverings that *Wired* magazine says create a sort of Bart Simpson look. Cynthia Ferrell says, "I want people to touch Cog, stroke it, say, 'Good robot.' "

Cog's head is at the same level as that of a tall person. When a new person enters the room its video camera eyes focus on that person and track him as he moves. Being tracked in this way is an oddly unsettling experience. When we look at a newborn baby, it

stares back and tracks our movement. Cog's eyes, at this stage, cannot see, so when Cog stares at the new person, it is a mindless stare,
but it uncannily suggests "there is someone there."

Brooks wants to prove that the best way to make intelligent robots
isn't to program them, but to raise them from infancy much like children. Cog's components are built with neural networks so that they
learn for themselves how to behave, as his cockroaches did. Instead
of being given preprogrammed software, Cog is supposed to develop
behaviors on its own, like a human infant. Having no language capability yet, Cog groans and coos, staring at colorful objects, and flail-
ing its arm in an effort to grab things. It will crave attention and be
captivated by human faces. Touch-sensitive sensors will enable it to
experience physical contact.

The long-term goal of the Cog project is to make a robot that can
interact with human beings in a robust and versatile manner. Its
cognitive talents will eventually include eye-coordinated manipulation
of objects, some form of speech, and a host of self-protective, self-
regulatory, and self-exploring activities. It should be able to tell its
designers things about itself that would be difficult or impossible to
determine by examination. Near Cog there is a bank of monitors
showing what is going on in Cog's mind, what Cog's eyes are capturing, and how those images are being processed by its vision system.

One of Brooks's graduate students, Joanna Bryson, who has a
major interest in child development theory, explains: "By moving and
trying to explore their environment, infants get a basic repertoire of
a few hundred conceptual metaphors, like self/other and front/back.
Everything else they ever know is built on these metaphors." By
learning these simple concepts Cog might be able to build itself up
to a higher level of intelligence, as a child does.[7]

Daniel C. Dennett, the adopted philosopher of the Brooks
team, remarks: "We want the behaviors exhibited by Cog to par-

allel those of a human infant, and eventually of course, an adult.... We want Cog to manifest curiosity, insight, fear, hope, pleasure, comprehension, friendship... the works. And we want to proceed as evolution has proceeded, piling complexity on complexity."[8] Dennett even says that he would love to see Cog exhibit paranoia, obsessive compulsive disorder, or other pathologies as a result of his somewhat strange upbringing.

But if machines were designed to spend a happy childhood learning from their experiences, they would be individuals also. They could be programmed to learn very fast, so in a human life span they would become immensely more complex than humans, unique in interesting ways, idiot savants perhaps, and difficult to fathom. If men think women are difficult to understand, wait until they see their future PC.

ALIEN CHILDREN

Cog is an impressive demonstration of technical prowess, designed deliberately to have a science-fiction-like aura about it. Brooks is demonstrating an interesting *process* rather than a valuable *end result*. Making machines imitate humans is ultimately less useful than making machines do something humans cannot possibly do. Suppose that techniques like Brooks's were being used to grow a nonhuman creature rather than a humanoid.

Computers can use senses processed with neurocomputers, such as radar, sonar, X rays, and superconducting "squids" that sense the most minute electromagnetic signals. Just as a frog's eye has built-in neural network to detect flying insects, so can an airport eye using neutron beams use a neural network to detect plastic explosives in airline luggage.

Cog is in one fixed place, with eyes the same distance apart as human eyes. A nonhumanoid creature could be worldwide, with any number of sensors and access to data warehouses worldwide. Just as Cog learns from what it senses in one room, a cyberthought creature could learn from what it senses in one building or one corporation. It could be part of the electronic jungle, learning with genetic algorithms, cellular automata, or neural networks. It could employ many "brain" modules with different neural networks. Rule-based inferencing systems with a sufficiently large number of rules can exhibit ultrahuman reasoning capability. Rule-based systems can employ rules that learn. The linkage between neural networks and rule-based reasoning is potentially of great value, with the reasoning capability evolving based on what the neural network learns.

Like Cog, the creature could grow year after year, expanding its capability. But people worldwide could add to it, rather than just the people in one laboratory.

It could be learning to optimize worldwide investments, or to handle a corporation's control of worldwide franchises. It could be advancing the joint know-how of vendors contributing to a complex product such as the design of the next-generation jumbo jet. It could be constantly improving its knowledge of international crime syndicates. It could be collecting vast amounts of data, worldwide, to improve the control of infectious diseases, or to move forward areas of preventive medicine.

We find it easy to imagine learning processes for humanoids because we are human. It is more difficult to imagine learning processes for a creature of alien intelligence.

CHAPTER 14
Computers Like the Brain

I n the late 1980s a curious experiment was going on in a start-up corporation in California. A computer was learning to balance a broomstick.

A child can learn to balance a broomstick by holding it vertically in the palm of the hand and moving the hand with quick little motions so as to prevent the broomstick from falling. The computer was trying to do the same. The broomstick was held on a small plate that the computer could move horizontally, with a harness to stop the broomstick from falling to the ground. The computer tried over and over again, like a child, to get the motion right so that the broomstick would stay vertical. This was an experiment with a dramatically different form of computing, neural network computing.

As we saw in Chapter 3, our brain has a network of neurons. Axons are the wiring of the brain, linking from a neuron to synapses on other neurons. The synapse is the input channel to the neuron. Computer scientists realized that they could build electronic circuits rather like the wiring of our brain. The equivalent of neurons, axons, and synapses could be built onto a silicon chip. Alternatively, and easier for widespread implementation, neurons, axons, and synapses can be emulated in software.

This is a very exciting idea. The late 1980s saw much enthusiasm about building artificial neural networks because it was thought that they would operate in the same way that the brain operates.

> ## The equivalent of neurons, axons, and synapses can be built onto a chip.

Many graduates wanted to do research on the subject and many research grants were obtained with the assumption that computers using neural networks would emulate aspects of what the human brain does. After all, neural networks are designed to have mechanisms like those that interconnect the neurons in our brain. They are designed to learn in a way similar to the way our brain learns.

The term "neurocomputer" was used for a computer that uses a *neural network*. A neurocomputer is completely unlike a conventional computer. You cannot program neurocomputers in the normal sense of the term "programming." Instead they *learn* how to do something, rather like a child learning. At first they are less responsive than a child, but unlike a child they can go through millions of trial-and-error attempts at great speed. Neural networks can learn behavior that would be difficult or impossible for humans because it requires a vast amount of precise data.

Artificial neurons can be interconnected in a vast number of different ways, so the HNC Software, Inc., founded by neural network pioneer Robert Hecht-Nielsen, used the broomstick experiment to try out many different patterns of neural network. The machine tried all night to balance the broomstick, to the amazement of the cleaning women. It helped to discover what were the best forms of neural network for enabling software to learn.

Years later, such software was used to balance investments, not broomsticks.

ALIEN BRAIN CELLS

Much of the initial excitement about artificial neural networks came, as stated, from the idea that such mechanisms would behave like mechanisms in our brain. However, as the research progressed it became clear that we weren't succeeding in creating neural networks similar to those in the brain. As with other aspects of computing, computer "thought" is quite different from human thought. An artificial neural network is, in reality, nothing like our brain.

As neural networks mature, they will be valuable, not for emulating human thought, but for doing things that humans cannot get close to doing.

After Pan Am Flight 103 exploded over Lockerbie, Scotland, airport security experts all over the world had a new problem to confront. The terrorists had used a plastic explosive that could be stretched into any shape and which could not be identified by airport X-ray machines. How could it be detected? Plastic explosives contain much nitrogen, and nitrogen scatters beams of neutrons. You have probably walked through many beams of neutrons in airports without knowing it. If the neutrons are scattered by plastic explosives, how on earth do we recognize that? It turned out that neural networks could be trained to recognize the resulting pattern of scattered neutrons and were more successful at detecting plastic explosives than other methods were.[1] We humans couldn't possibly recognize such a pattern.

Neural networks are part of a growing family of alien-thought processes. When a neural network comes to a conclusion, we cannot check any step-by-step logic about how it reached that conclusion. We can only validate the results. But neural networks are perhaps the most powerful tool in the alien-intelligence toolkit. There will be many new and interesting mechanisms created with neural networks. They can provide smart sensors and systems that adapt to their environment. Adaptive behavior is particularly important to some corporate systems or to intelligent agents that adapt themselves to what they find on the Web. Procedures have been created that are critical to corporate success.

BAD COPS

The Chicago Police Department is using a neural network product, BrainMaker, to forecast which officers on the force are potential candidates for misbehavior. The software was given details of two hundred officers who had been terminated for disciplinary reasons. It then studied the records of the 12,500 current officers and produced a list of ninety-one officers who it said were potentially at risk. Of these, nearly half were found to be already enrolled in a counseling program to help officers guilty of misconduct. A deputy superintendent stated: "We're very pleased with the outcome. We consider it much more efficient and capable of identifying at-risk personnel than command officers might be able to." This sounds Orwellian, but the police department pointed out that the software is unbiased, whereas the old system, being human-based, cannot avoid some level of bias.

> As neural networks mature, they will be valuable, not for emulating human thought, but for doing things that humans cannot get close to doing.

The same software that can find bad cops can also find good dogs. A man named Derek Anderson trained the neural networks with information from approximately three hundred dog-track races. He runs the current day's race information through seven neural networks, and the software predicts the dogs' order of finish. The data he uses include the winning time of past races, the time that each dog took to finish the race, the time that dog reached each of four positions in the race (out of box, first corner, backstretch, outside corner), as well as comments about the dog's behavior. The behavior was classified as one of fifteen types such as ran wide, bumped, hit, and ran inside. He uses such information for each dog for each of the dog's past eight races. Whenever the first-place dog is ahead by at least ten neural network points over the second-place dog, he bets on the winner. He claims that his personal computer backs the winning dogs with a 94 percent success rate.

BrainMaker has a program called "Compete" that designs, tests, and runs a network based upon comparisons of the competing items. One seasoned race goer used it at each thoroughbred race at the Detroit Race Course. He fed in detailed information about racehorses. In every race the software picked three horses. He claims that one of the three is the winner 77 percent of the time—and the software cost only $195.

ARTIFICIAL NEURAL NETWORKS

Artificial neural networks are composed of interconnected units like the neurons in our brain. Each software neuron receives a collection of incoming signals and converts these inputs into a single outgoing signal. A modifiable *weight* is associated with each connection that enters the neuron. Each incoming signal is multiplied by the weight on the connection and the signals are combined

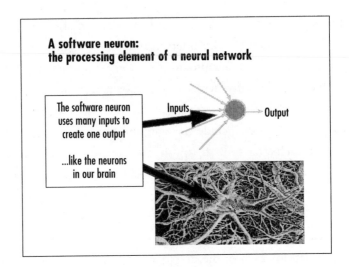

together to produce an output signal. The output travels over connections to other neurons, just as in our brain.

Learning in biological systems involves adjusting the synaptic connections that exist between the neurons. Learning in neural networks involves adjusting the weight associated with the links between software neurons. These weights store the knowledge necessary to solve specific problems. Neural networks use feedback to adjust the weights. Signals from the output neurons are fed back so that they become the input to the middle-layer neurons.

Designers of artificial neural networks have a choice of many possible schemes for interconnecting the software neurons. The axons in our brain are a tangle worse than any bird's nest. Hundreds of variations are presented at neural network conferences each year. Years of experimentation have shown that certain types of interconnection patterns are useful for dealing with certain types of problems.[2]

Researchers can experiment endlessly with new forms of neural networks, and mathematicians can model them, but ordinary folks use software packages that make neural networks easy to play with. Packaged toolkits may contain one type of network with

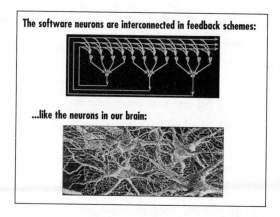

The software neurons are interconnected in feedback schemes:

...like the neurons in our brain:

guidance on how to use it. It was with such a software package that Derek Anderson made lots of money at the dog races.

The power of neural networks is that they enable us to use tools that can categorize complex data or recognize patterns in ways that we can't. We don't have to write programs to do this; in fact, we would have no idea how to write a program that could achieve the same results.

WHERE ARE NEURAL NETWORKS USED?

Humans are good at many things that conventional computing is bad at. A farmer looks at the morning sky, observes the behavior of the birds, and decides against haymaking. A woman has a sixth sense about a man at a party and declines his offer to drive her home. With uncanny accuracy a customs officer senses when an arriving person is hiding something. One thing a neural network cannot do is explain to us how it arrived at its conclusions. It is like the customs officer or woman at the party. We have to test its conclusions in order to become comfortable with them.

Neural networks can deal with many types of problems that do not yield to conventional computing techniques. Neurocomputing is so different from conventional computing that it often seems alien to traditional computer users. Most corporations are far from understanding its potential, but as neurocomputing matures it is likely to have a major impact on improving corporate efficiency. Applications are spreading and some of them deal with problems of considerable complexity. We are surrounded by situations that we cannot model with equations and algorithms.

Neural-network and data-warehouse technology fit well together. Neural nets need a large amount of data to train on. They are good at finding ways to classify data and can make sense of an overwhelming jumble of data.

> We would have no idea how to write a program that would achieve the same result.

A mass of customer behavior can be analyzed so that sales and marketing can be more effective. Neural networks can forage through the factors that have affected sales and learn to forecast future sales so that appropriate levels of inventory are stocked. They can find patterns in data that provide valuable insight to researchers or managers. For example, they are used to detect stolen credit card or fraud in medical claims. A neural network has the ability to generalize when making decisions about imprecise input data. Like a biological creature it can be resilient to distortions in the input data.

There are many signal-recognition applications. A neural network may be trained to tell from the sound of a machine when it needs maintenance. It can visually detect whether bottle caps are correctly fitted on a production line. A "neural nose" with chemical sensors on a chip can identify odors and has been used for detecting explosives at airports or drugs in the workplace.

Neural networks *learn* how to do something. Often we train them to do something that *we are good at*, like recognizing handwriting. But the most interesting applications are for things that *we cannot do at all*.

Unfortunately, it is difficult to think about things that are completely off our radar screen. A neural nose can smell things that have no smell to us. Neural networks foraging in data warehouses have found patterns in data that we never thought were related.

RECOGNIZING YOUR FACE

Neural networks are being used in technical applications such as speech recognition, recognizing printed or handwritten characters, and identifying fingerprints. They have been trained to identify an individual from his voice. "Voice prints" can be almost as secure a way of identifying an individual as fingerprints and are useful because they can identify someone on the telephone.

Software called TrueFace, from Miros, Inc., uses neural networks to recognize human faces. This provides the most convenient and reliable means of identifying an individual. ATMs of the future will recognize your face.

The TrueFace system captures an image of the person, locates the face and centers it, and then compares it with stored images of faces. It can recognize the face with different head orientations, lighting conditions, makeup, suntan, clear glasses, earrings, hair styles, facial expressions, aging, and new facial hair. The TrueFace Identifier can compare a thousand faces from a database of faces on a PC and then verify the face in about a second.

In addition to verifying the face, TrueFace is designed to detect when a person is attempting to cheat the system by wearing a mask or holding up a photograph in front of the camera. On an ATM the TrueFace system uses two camera lenses, eight centimeters apart, installed above the keyboard and cash/deposit doors. Attempts at fraud are detected immediately.

Compaq, IBM, Microsoft, Novell, and others formed a consortium to standardize the electronic recognition of fingerprints, voices, and faces.[3] Standardization will allow machines of different vendors to verify faces, fingerprints, or voices through central shared databases.

RECOGNIZING EMOTIONS

Neural networks can be trained to respond to facial expressions. They can detect stress in speech; neural network voice analysis can be a highly sensitive lie detector. Neural networks have been trained to detect human emotions in our face or speech and sometimes detect emotions much more sensitively than we do. Sometimes an emotion causes muscle contractions in the face for a fiftieth of a second—so short a time that they wouldn't show up on video. A digital eye with a neural network can recognize this.

When we socialize we dress up our emotions. Your face looks at dinner guests with admiring, flattering, or sociable emotions. If you watch a person at a distant table in a restaurant, you can often see his or her face switch between background and window-dressing emotion. Neural networks have been set up to track both your background emotion and your window-dressing emotion and to assess the genuineness of the latter.

It is intriguing to think of your television set watching you and registering your emotional reaction to shows or commercials. An interactive TV might adjust the commercials it shows on the basis of how you react to them. It might be programmed to learn your taste in movies or other shows and make recommendations about what you would like. It may automatically record programs it thinks you would enjoy. You might sit in front of your five hundred–channel satellite set and ask, "TV, what is showing tonight that I would enjoy?"

COMBINING HUMAN AND NEURAL NETWORK SKILLS

In some situations the best decision making can be the combination of a human and neural network, each highly trained but with very different skills.

A neural network may learn to trade on the foreign exchange markets, for example, by going through the history of tick-by-tick price changes, learning by many millions of trial-and-error attempts. It can learn to identify technical trends and filter the noise from the trend better than most human traders. But it could never learn to trade like George Soros. Soros identifies fundamental influences on currency values in a way that requires broad-ranging understanding. He uses unique human insight to place large bets. Soros and a neural network are very different animals. But in combination they might do better than either one can do alone.

Lloyd McAdams, a highly successful stock market trader who runs Pacific Income Advisers, uses a neural network trained to detect fear. Investor psychology plays a major role in stock price movements. Sometimes investors react with greed and a stock becomes temporarily overpriced; sometimes they react with fear and a stock becomes temporarily

> A trader with a neural network is like a hunter with a dog. The dog senses where prey exists so that the hunter can go after it.

undervalued. McAdams finds that responding to fear is safer than responding to greed. He uses neural network software that scans the market constantly, searching for stocks where sudden selling appears to have been caused by a fear reaction. McAdams then investigates each situation to establish the reason for the fear, determine how justified it is, obtain an intuitive feel for how long it might last, and decide whether money can be made because the stock is temporarily undervalued. He invests only in stocks that he thinks are temporarily depressed in value because a fear reaction has gone too far.

A trader with a neural network is like a hunter with a dog. The dog senses where prey exists so that the hunter can go after it. The dog fetches the birds when they fall to earth, which would be difficult for the hunter to do. McAdams's neural network is used to find the specimens of fear reaction, but human intelligence is needed to decide what to do about them. This combination of neurocomputing and trained human intuition achieves something that neither could achieve alone. The dog finds the stocks; the human decides whether to invest.

> Just as we can flag bankruptcies before they happen, so can we flag a person who is likely to have a heart attack before it happens.

Neural networks and other methods of machine learning have been used by molecular biologists to help them understand the structure of complex protein molecules, which are the fundamental building blocks of all biological cells. Melanie Mitchell in her book on genetic algorithms predicts that this will be much more profitable (both scientifically and financially) than using such methods to predict financial markets.[4]

Moreover, there are various ways in which neural networks can be combined with genetic algorithms (see Chapter 12) and other forms of evolutionary software.[5]

CLASSIFICATION

A new baby, when confronted with an endless deluge of data from its senses, starts to make sense of this deluge in primitive ways. One of the most basic functions of our brain is to classify the cacophony of data from our senses so that we can distinguish objects, sounds, and feelings. Cavemen classified plants as edible and poisonous, and animals as friendly and dangerous. A botanist creates a taxonomy of plants. We are capable of analyzing objects using subtle details to assess both the similarities and differences. Every day in thousands of ways we categorize things.

A secretary may take a mass of letters and memos and devise a filing scheme. In the same way a neural network can look for similarities in a mass of data and devise classification schemes. We can let it loose in a massive data warehouse and may learn to categorize the data, creating a clustered index so that similar patterns are in the same cluster.

In business, neural networks can look for important categorizations. Which visitors to our Web site would respond to what types of special offers? Which lines of business are most likely to grow? What names should be culled from the mailing list? Can we increase profits by spending more effort on certain carefully selected customers?

Science may be concerned with more subtle categorizations. When atomic particles are scattered, what types of patterns reveal something? In a vast warehouse of medical data are there clues about what causes a person to get kidney stones? Are there early warning signs of psychopathic behavior? Are there pieces of data that should be clustered in new ways to give new insight?

Neural networks can categorize things in new ways not obvious to humans.

CRYSTAL BALLS

Some neural networks have been trained to predict the future.

Nothing, of course, can predict the future with certainty, but certain patterns of events can indicate the probability of future events. Neural networks can be trained on large bodies of data so that they estimate the probability of future occurrences.

We have noted that HNC, for example, has software that predicts when organizations or individuals might go bankrupt. Such a prediction is useful to banks that issue credit cards. HNC encourages credit card issuers to join its "bankruptcy consortium." It is then able to collect a large body of historical data from many organizations about card users who go bankrupt. Neural network software is trained to identify people or organizations that become a potential bankruptcy risk. The software often flags cardholders who go bankrupt months before the bankruptcy happens.

Just as we can flag bankruptcies before they happen, so can we flag a person who is likely to have a heart attack or stroke before it happens. We would like automatically to identify patterns in data that identify medical warning signs where appropriate preventive action can be taken. As we saw in Chapter 9, technology can lead to an era when medical practice is dominated by preventing illness rather than coping with the damage after it has happened. Building up large amounts of information in data warehouses will allow neural networks to have as much raw material to digest as possible. In many areas neurocomputing can warn of impending catastrophe before the catastrophe strikes, and action can be taken to avoid disaster.

Neural networks also can help retailers and product manufacturers to forecast consumer demand. They can be trained using data about promotions and advertising, and can take factors such as climate and holidays into consideration. Such software helps retailers meet customer needs without overstocking.

Neurocomputing has many potential applications in the insurance industry, where it can recognize patterns that help quantify risk. The Risk Data Corporation has a proprietary database of more than twenty million workers' compensation claims. Using this database a neural network can be trained to predict the reserves that companies should set aside to pay such claims. Its users can select claim characteristics to match a given claim population. HNC's *MIRA* software predicts reserves needed with an accuracy rate of up to 98.5 percent and has been independently certified by actuaries at Ernst & Young, based on tests conducted at two leading insurance companies.

Electronic crystal balls may sound a little scary. We might worry that neural networks could get to know too much about us. This might lead to government harassment, intrusive marketing, or corporations preying on our weaknesses in some way. Human addictions, for example, could be targets for profit growth.

COMPULSIVE GAMBLERS

Casinos are starting to use neural networks to study the behavior of gamblers, and they can automatically detect compulsive gamblers. Compulsive gamblers can be offered all manner of special deals to entice them into casinos. A slot machine could be designed to learn the behavior of its user so that it can extract the maximum from the user as skillfully as a poker consortium.

There is much controversy about whether casino gambling on the Internet should be banned. Some popular sites advertise it today, offering attractive croupiers. Some monitor gambling behavior so that computers can learn how to identify compulsive gamblers and constantly encourage them.

By far the most common form of Internet gambling is online trading of stocks, bonds, and commodities. The London *Daily Telegraph* profiled one trader whom the paper described as "typical of the new breed."[6] He signs on in Irvine, California, at about 6:25 AM, ready for the Wall Street opening, and makes trades until the market closes, interspersed with having his breakfast and getting his son to school. He describes it as "like gambling in Las Vegas" and claims to have doubled his money in a short time.

Online trading is becoming high fashion, especially in the United States, replacing horseracing, football pools, and national lotteries as the gambler's dream route to untold wealth. Commissions are much lower than those from stockbrokers, and some firms offer free trades, making their commissions from the professional market makers. Firms offering stock trading on the Web quickly acquired a much larger market capitalization than the old giant stockbrokers. A stock trader at home can read the latest research on stocks, but many simply buy the stocks that are rising fast, hoping to get out before they go down again. They e-mail stock tips to one another, and this sometimes causes a feeding frenzy with the hot stocks. It is a visceral, exciting experience, very different from talking to the boring stockbroker. It is pure gambling.

Software can be designed to detect the gamblers and sell them services. They can be persuasively sold tips that relate more to the individual's trading style than to the value of the stock.

COMPLEX CONTROL SYSTEMS

Car companies have been experimenting with neural networks to save fuel consumption. They use various forms of instrumentation in the engine and correlate the measurements with the gallons-per-mile consumption of petroleum. The neural network learns how to minimize the fuel consumption, using a processor chip that operates in real time because fuel economy differs with different terrain and different traffic patterns. A driver who treats the accelerator gently is different from one who treats it like an on/off switch. With a neural network in the car many drivers could save a hundred gallons or so per year.

Neural networks can be applied to many other control problems with multiple input variables. The network learns how to use the variables to produce a required type of behavior. It can do this for processes that are too complex to tackle with conventional techniques.

A hydroponics farm grows plants in an entirely artificial way—there is no soil and no rain. The roots of the plants are visible, spreading in baths of liquid where the nutrients that are fed to the plants are carefully controlled. The hydroponics farmer learns to recognize the needs of the plants, and adjust the nutrients accordingly. This is something of a black art, or to put it more politely, it requires a green thumb. In the middle of winter I wandered through a hydroponics strawberry farm, picking fruit from high racks. The back-to-nature movement finds it fashionable to pour scorn on plants grown artificially, but I realized that I had never come across such sweet-tasting strawberries. I asked the farmer why, and he explained that he was able to give the strawberry plants exactly the nutrients they needed, which is difficult to do with plants grown in soil.

A neural network can be trained to do that. It can learn to recognize the needs of the plants from their leaf color and patterns, scales or dead areas, droopiness, rate of growth, mites on the plants, and possibly other forms of instrumentation such as particle beams used for chemical analysis. It can learn to relate these to the minerals in the nutrients and humidity, and can operate actuators that adjust the nutrients and humidity.

Many people with a green thumb want to work in a garden, not a plant factory, so hydroponics farms, even though they are spectacularly successful with certain types of plants, have not become widespread. *Automated* hydroponics has immense potential. One can imagine massive high-rise glass farms in sunny desert areas where nothing grows today. One day, home hydroponics for growing flowers and fruit will become a mass hobby.

HOW DO NEURAL NETWORKS LEARN?

To train a neural network we give it many examples. Each example consists of a collection of inputs and a desired output. The network uses the inputs to produce its own output, and then compares this to the desired output. At first its output is random and useless. By chance it has some outputs that are better than average. The network adjusts its behavior to try and repeat those, and steadily nudges closer and closer to the desired result.

Our brain learns new behavior by adjusting the synapses so that the influence of one neuron over another changes. Similarly, a neural network adjusts the weights of its interconnections. The connections determine whether it is possible for one software neuron to influence another. The weights specify the strength of the influence. A neural network modifies its own behavior in this way repeatedly, steadily adjusting the weights until it can achieve the desired result. Millions of trial-and-error attempts may be needed.

Because so many attempts are needed, we have to automate the process of feeding examples to it. Sometimes it generates its own feedback, as with the machine balancing a broomstick. A neural network with a data warehouse can wallow through an ocean of data. It can search through past data, examining the inputs and the corresponding outputs, training itself to predict the output. It might be given files of past mailing lists, for example, with details of people who were sent mailings and what the results were. The network is given, say, fifty characteristics of people to whom mailings were sent. It tries to predict from these characteristics whether there is likely to be a successful response. It goes through the historical files many times, trying to predict the result of each mailing and adjusting the weights of its connections when it makes a correct prediction. After millions of trial-and-error attempts it slowly improves its ability to make correct judgments. The result is mailings with a higher return rate.

THREE-LAYER NETWORKS

There are numerous ways in which the software neurons can be interconnected to produce appropriate feedback. Researchers have studied many types of interconnection schemes and found that certain patterns of interconnections are good for solving certain types of problems.

Most neural networks have three groupings of software neurons: input, output, and a layer in between. The input neurons represent the raw information that is fed into the network. The output neurons represent the resulting behavior. The middle layer gives great flexibility in representing the relation between the inputs and outputs.

To teach a three-layer network to perform a particular task we must present it with many examples. Each example consists of a pattern of inputs to the input neurons together with the desired pattern of outputs from the output, neurons. The network determines how closely its *actual* output of the network matches the *desired* output. It then adjusts the weights of the connections on the middle layer so that the network produces a better approximation of the desired output. It does this many times until it can produce the desired output.

> The rewards of electronic commerce will often go to those organizations that learn the most about potential customers and take automated action.

AN EXAMPLE OF TRAINING A NEURAL NETWORK

Suppose that we want to train a neural network to recognize forty handwritten characters—letters, digits, and four other characters. Each character is represented by 256 dots in a 16 x 16 array. The network would need 256 input neurons, forty output neurons, and many middle-layer neurons. For each input character we want the network to produce high activity in one of the forty output neurons and very low activity in the other thirty-nine.

To train the network a computer feeds it handwritten characters and examines its results. At first it is utterly useless. It produces random outputs that have no correlation with the input. Soon, by chance, it produces a correct result. The weights are then adjusted so that the network is more likely to do that again. This process has to be repeated many thousands of times. The weights are successively adjusted until the errors become close to zero. The same character handwritten in many different ways must be fed to the network before it becomes good.

For a neural network to become trained to perform some task, it goes through many trial-and-error attempts. For each attempt it calculates the difference between the actual result and the desired result. It then adjusts the weight of the connections so as to reduce the error. To do this it must evaluate how much the error changes as each weight is increased or decreased slightly, so that it can adjust that weight by the right amount.

Some neural networks have been trained to recognize human faces or voices. The ability to scan a crowd and pick out known faces may have police applications in the future, such as electronically recognizing known terrorists at airports.

It would effectively be impossible to make a supercomputer with conventional programming recognize faces. Neural networks can be trained to do things that conventional computing cannot possibly do. Face recognition is a human skill, but neural networks can recognize patterns that humans cannot recognize. They can be trained, for example, to detect patterns of behavior that enable a criminal or terrorist to be identified, patterns of neutron scattering that indicate explosives hidden in airport luggage, or patterns of medical symptoms that could facilitate preventive medicine.

IS THE DOG SUPERVISED?

The learning process of a neural network can be *supervised* or *unsupervised*. Supervised learning is like a dog being rewarded or punished after each attempt to do a trick until the dog learns to do it well. Unsupervised learning is when we don't know what the trick is; the dog tries various types of behavior until it finds something that pleases us.

Learning to recognize handwritten characters is *supervised* learning. The end result is precise and clear. It takes millions of attempts, but fortunately the computer has much more patience than the dog.

With *unsupervised* learning, a computer is given a mass of data and has to try to make sense of it. It is like a secretary being given hundreds of unmarked file folders and having to devise a filing scheme. A neural network may search for patterns in a mass of data and devise classification schemes. It may cluster the data so that similar patterns are in the same cluster.

PACKAGED APPLICATIONS

In business it is usually easier and safer to install application packages, such as the payroll package, rather than code your own. Alien intelligence will often find its way into business in the form of application packages.

HNC Software, Inc., focused on packaged applications of a neural network that could have large commercial sales. It provides a variety of products for detecting fraud. HNC's "FraudAdvisor" software is used to detect false medical claims. It uses neural network technology to examine claim data, such as medical reports, injury reports, first and ongoing medical and indemnity payments, and it identifies claimant behavior that is likely to indicate the presence of fraud. It sends suspicious cases to analysts for review.

HNC's "Falcon" software detects credit card fraud. It examines data about cardholders, transactions, and merchant data, and detects suspicious patterns. It often finds patterns that are missed by traditional methods of fraud detection. "Falcon" has improved the fraud detection rate significantly. It has also helped to eliminate "false-positives" where other techniques signaled a possible fraud incorrectly. "Falcon Expert" enables "Falcon" users to define, edit, and deploy rules that automate fraud prevention procedures. It sometimes causes potential fraud cases to be reopened.

When a person is *applying* for a credit card that he shouldn't have, "Falcon Sentry" might catch him. It uses credit bureau data and other data to search for indications that a card application might be fraudulent. It runs within a card issuer's application processing system.

Barclays Bank PLC, the largest European card issuer, has a debit card portfolio that requires 100 percent real-time monitoring on all its authorizations. HNC's software operates in a real-time environment to accomplish this. At a time when Barclays was already doing an exceptional job of fraud control, Director of Payment Strategies Barry Fergus commented that the software "will have a tremendous impact in detecting fraud at a time when we are seeing growing criminal efforts to attack our card base."[7]

"ProfitMax" manages the profitability of credit card portfolios. It uses neural networks to profile cardholder behavior, analyze each cardholder account, and predict its future profit. It analyzes historical data to give a picture of the expected profitability of each account in an issuer's portfolio. The bank may choose to give special treatment to customers who are expected to generate profit. It may closely monitor customers who are a risk. If the software indicates a risk of possible bankruptcy, it can monitor the account closely. It can check each transaction as it is processed for indications of potential bankruptcy. It uses neural networks trained on a large body of historical data to predict the likelihood of the cardholder's going bankrupt.

"Eagle" is used by banks to monitor credit card usage at each merchant location in a bank's portfolio. It estimates the likelihood that the merchant will generate significant chargeables. Daily and monthly risk scores are presented to a risk analyst at the bank. "Eagle" provides a prioritized list of merchants for investigation, the information needed to perform the investigation, suggested actions, and a means of reporting the results of the effort.

WEB-BASED NEUROCOMPUTING

Neural networks work best when they have a large amount of data to train on. In many fields it makes sense for different organizations to share data so that computerized insight can be built up. This is easier to do now than it was in the past because data can be shared on the Internet.

The HNC database that enables its neural net tools to predict when organizations or individuals might go bankrupt uses a large body of historical data to which many credit card issuers contribute as part of the "bankruptcy consortium."

When data from multiple sources are fed into a data warehouse, it is necessary to create a unified representation of the data. The data must conform to a common data model in order that data mining or neural network tools can be used.

As commerce spreads on the Web, neural-network-aided decision making will be increasingly valuable to online advertisers and retailers. Neural networks can create profiles of Web-site customer behavior and then automatically direct the right type of advertising to selected Web sites, or automatically target promotions to selected parties. As a result, neural networks could greatly improve competitive positioning, as companies spend money on those customers likely to produce a high return on investment.

ELECTRONIC COMMERCE

We have noted that many fortunes will be made (and lost) in the big-money chain reactions of electronic commerce. The ability to learn about customers will be critical.

Corporations will be able to market worldwide and will need to understand as much as possible about customers and prospects so that they can target the marketing, ensure repeat orders, delight customers, and build loyalty. The technology will make it possible to gather or have access to huge quantities of data. Many organizations are building vast warehouses of data about customers or potential customers. A data warehouse by itself is of little value; what matters is the ability to extract knowledge or insight from it that will make the marketing succeed. Neurocomputing is one of a family of data-mining techniques that can forage for valuable commercial insight among overwhelming quantities of data. Such technology will help buyers find the goods most useful to them and help sellers find the best leads.

Several organizations have experimented with systems that can understand people's taste in movies.[8] These systems ask their users to rate films from a list of films, indicating how well they liked each one. In some cases the systems ask detailed questions about reactions to the film. After processing such information about a number of films, the software starts to be able to assess what a person will like. The more the software collects information, the more refined it becomes at predicting a person's reaction to a movie. I used Firefly.com in the days when it processed people's assessments of movies. If I felt like going to the movies, I would ask it how I would react to the ones that were showing, and I was frequently astonished by how well it predicted my reactions. The techniques used to achieve that in Firefly.com were relatively crude. More sophisticated techniques like neurocomputing could provide more detailed knowledge about potential customers. The same software could help people with hundreds of television channels find programs that they would especially enjoy.

The ubiquitous computers will learn an enormous amount about us. Some people feel uncomfortable with that. Controls will need to be put in place to protect privacy and prevent Orwellian behavior in government. The individual will need the ability to block overly intrusive marketing.

But if used well, computers that know about us can raise our quality of life. If computers know your taste in movies they can help you find movies that you will really enjoy. They can help you find better jobs and more enjoyable vacations, restaurants, wine, music, television, books, and products in general. They can help improve health. Health care software that knows detailed characteristics of an individual can make recommendations about diet, pharmaceuticals, lifestyle, and how to respond to early symptoms of illness. After illness it can help in the healing process. Personal health care using knowledge technology is a key to achieving preventive medicine. And the rewards of electronic commerce will often go to those organizations that learn the most about potential customers and take automated action.

We will see the benefits in many aspects of our lives. But we must also come to terms with the drawbacks with which so many people are uncomfortable.

CHAPTER 15
Termites and Hedge Funds

The termites in Africa build spectacular habitats. They live in huge mounds of earth, sometimes as high as twenty feet, with hard walls constructed from pieces of soil cemented together with saliva and baked hard in the sun. Sometimes trees or rocks are incorporated into the structure. Inside the walls are numerous chambers and galleries interconnected by complex networks of passageways. There are facilities for ventilation and drainage. Different parts of the structure have different functions. Some chambers serve as nurseries for baby termites. The heat required for hatching eggs is provided by the fermentation of organic material stored in the nursery chambers. The mound may support from a hundred to a hundred thousand termites.

Some termites are workers; some are there just to have babies; some are soldiers with big heads and snouts. This differentiation isn't hereditary. A nymph termite can develop into different specialized forms depending on the needs of the colony, just as your child might become a soldier, scientist, worker, or merely a reproductive.

It is tempting to think that such a well-designed colony must have a manager—that somebody must be in charge. In fact nobody's in charge. There's a king and queen, but they don't give orders, or lead the army, or plan the layout of the tunnels; they simple lie around getting fat and producing eggs. Each termite obeys its own rules, and the collective result of this behavior is the complex termite colony.

CAS

The term *complex adaptive system* (CAS) is used to describe systems that are the collective result of many independent players, like termites. A CAS does not have centralized management or control. It is decentralized, meaning that many units each operate independently, and this creates a coherent form of behavior. A hurricane forming is a CAS; so is a cancer spreading. The separate units of a CAS are referred to as *agents*. We are surrounded by many different types of CASs—the stock market, the economy, city traffic, flu epidemics, production control systems, competitive marketing, the politics that leads to war. The "agents" could be people, machines, software modules, plants in an ecosystem, cars in a traffic jam, antibodies in an immune system, or corporations in an economy.

All CASs exhibit behavior that is quite different from the behavior of their agents. Each termite has fairly simple behavior. The termite colony has its own pattern of behavior, much more complex and interesting than the sum of the behaviors of the termites. It is the interactions among agents that produce interesting behavior. There have to be many—but not too many—agents acting in parallel to achieve the CAS behavior. Ten termites wouldn't be enough to build a colony; a million termites would be too many, and they would split into multiple colonies. The individual termite is rigid in its behavior and dies when circumstances are not appropriate for its behavior. The colony, on the other hand, is highly resilient and adaptive, and survives a wide range of hazards.

Complex adaptive systems often seem to behave as though they had a mind of their own, like the termite colony. It is sometimes difficult to accept that they have no central body directing their operation.

In September 1997 an economic crisis spread across Asia with devastating speed. Investors around the globe speculated against the currencies of Thailand, Indonesia, Malaysia, and other Asian countries. The currency of Malaysia fell to a twenty-six–year low, and its stock index crashed 48 percent. At a World Bank meeting Malaysia's prime minister, Dr. Mahathir Mohammad, denounced the world monetary system, saying that the global capital markets were directed by a Jewish cabal. He

> Some self-organizing structures evolve quickly— as we see with the spread of epidemics, the growth of cancers, the formation of hurricanes, and so forth.

accused Western financiers such as George Soros of manipulating the Malaysian currency so as to destroy Malaysia as a competitor.

Robert Rubin, then treasury secretary of the United States, was in the audience. It wasn't appropriate for him to counterattack, but *New York Times* foreign affairs columnist Thomas Friedman later wrote what he thought Rubin would have said had he been free to speak his mind:

> The basic truth about globalization is this: No one is in charge—not George Soros, not "Great Powers" and not I. I didn't start globalization. I can't stop it and neither can you.... You keep looking for someone to blame.

Well, guess what, Mahathir, there's no one at the other end of the phone! I know that's hard to accept. It's like telling people there's no God. We all want to believe that somebody is in charge and responsible. But the global marketplace is an Electronic Herd of often-anonymous stock, bond, currency and multinational investors, connected by screens and networks.... The herd knows only its own rules. But the rules are pretty consistent.... I track the herd's movements all day on the Bloomberg screen next to my desk. I know you think I'm the all-powerful U.S. Treasury Secretary. But, Mahathir, I live just like you—in terror of the Electronic Herd. Those idiots in the media keep putting me on the front page, as if I'm actually in charge, and I'm sitting here terrified that if our Congress refuses to grant the President authority to expand free trade, or busts the budget ceiling, the Herd is going to turn against me and trample the dollar and the Dow.[1]

The global Electronic Herd is like the termites. There are different types of termites. Each termite obeys its own rules, and the collective result of this is the behavior of the world's money markets. If Malaysia seems to be using its foreign investments badly, the herd can move against the Malaysian currency or stocks. The difference in the Internet era is that vast numbers of termites can panic or speculate at lightning speed.

As in the African termite colony there is no orchestra conductor.

FLOCKING

Ten thousand mallards, placidly jabbering on a lake at sunset, suddenly take off with thunderous flapping, pause, and collectively reverse direction almost instantly. A shoal of numerous tiny fish splits and darts to avoid a predator, then quickly reforms into a single shoal. Computerized simulation of such behavior has led to new understanding of it.

It sometimes surprises managers to learn that flocks do not have a manager. Although they appear so well coordinated and instantly responsive, they have no leader. They are composed of many individuals, each obeying a simple set of rules. If the front bird in a honking V-formation of geese is removed, the V-shape reforms almost immediately.

Many independent units, each behaving with certain rules, can create cohesive patterns of behavior. The collective behavior often looks as though it has been designed, when in fact there is no leader or designer.

> Complex adaptive systems often seem to behave as though they have a mind of their own.

Craig Reynolds discovered that he could recreate the behavior of flocks on a computer screen. He used collections of objects where each object obeyed a simple set of rules. He called some of his objects "boids" and used the following rules:

- Maintain a minimum distance from other objects, including other boids.
- Try to match velocities with other boids.
- Try to move toward the perceived center of the mass of boids.

If the rules were changed to give less time lag or a little more cohesion, a flock of boids could be made to behave like bats, penguins, or fish. Reynolds's algorithms were used in the movie *Batman Returns* to create a marauding mob of penguins. With a more substantial change in rules they could be made to behave like ant colonies, highway traffic, market economies, or the human immune system.

The flocks, mobs, and highway traffic seem to have a behavior of their own. They are examples of self-organization.

We are surrounded everywhere by complex adaptive systems. Sometimes the independent players who make up these systems obey simple rules, like flocking birds; usually their rules are much more elaborate. Their collective actions result in complex and coherent systems. Stock movements, for instance, result from the decisions of many investors and institutions; the collective effect of this is a market that has behavior patterns of its own. The end result is so complex that the market's behavior is often a surprise in spite of endless study by analysts.

FREE AGENTS

We are finding out that many operations can be made to work better without centralized control. They can operate, like a flock of birds, with separate independent agents following well-designed sets of rules. We can learn to understand their behavior with computer simulators. In some cases massively parallel computers can represent droves of agents operating in parallel. Of course, some processes are better controlled centrally. Often a judicious mix of decentralized independent behavior and centralized monitoring and control is best.

The Mitre Corporation is experimenting with different designs of a decentralized air traffic control system in which each plane would behave like an independent agent with its own set of rules. In such a system the role of the central system is lessened but would not disappear. This type of system may become very important because it could support a much higher density of traffic than today and could have a higher safety level.

Dick Morley, one of the creators of the floppy disk, comments that factories are places where everything is going wrong all the time. He builds factory control systems with forms of localized intelligence "to deal with stuff that you cannot explain." Factory control systems, like other such control systems, have traditionally been directed centrally. A central location has detailed information about the situation in the factory; it computes schedules and passes orders to the workstations. Morley tried the opposite. He treated workstations as free agents that make bids for work.

Morley worked in the paint shop of a General Motors assembly plant in Fort Wayne, Indiana. Unpainted truck bodies rolled off the assembly line and were routed to one of ten paint booths by a centralized controller. The highly interconnected system worked fine as long as nothing went wrong—but things often went wrong. In Morley's system each paint booth, acting as a free agent, places a bid for the right to paint a certain truck. The free-agent paint booths have a simple goal—paint as many trucks as possible and use as little paint as possible. The software compares all the booths' bids and assigns the truck to the "winner," based on several factors, including what color the booth is set up to paint and how long the line in front of the booth is.

> We mistakenly assume that to do complicated things we have to set up systems with complicated rules.

During its first year of operation, the system saved $1 million a year in paint alone, and complex scheduling software was not needed.

SELF-ORGANIZING STRUCTURES

Complex adaptive systems are generally self-organizing structures.

We are surrounded by self-organizing structures—cities, the

economy, woodland ecosystems. Some self-organizing structures evolve quickly—as we see with the spread of epidemics, the growth of cancers, the formation of hurricanes, and so forth.

Much traditional science has looked for equilibrium, but in the world of CASs there is often no equilibrium. Everything is constantly changing. Structures grow, decay, coalesce, and mutate.

Traditional economics has also looked for equilibrium. The Law of Diminishing Returns tends to bring equilibrium. But the Law of *Increasing* Returns (which we saw in Chapter 6) tends to bring disequilibrium. Corporations that are ahead tend to get further ahead; corporations that are behind tend to slip further behind. Virtually everything and everybody is caught up in a vast, nonlinear web of incentives, constraints, and connections.

We need to understand where decentralized operations can be made to work better than central control. The failure of centralized economies in the Communist world eventually led to the sudden collapse of the USSR. Around 1970 Britain's cybernetics guru, Stafford Beer, persuaded Chile's Marxist government that the country could be run with a central computer system using nationwide data collection to determine what goods to make and where to ship them. It was a complex and interesting theory, but before long supermarkets were without essential goods, including milk for babies. In 1973 President Allende of Chile fell from power in a bloody coup.[2] Unfortunately, the replacement government of General Pinochet was ideologically brutal and arrested about 130,000 liberals. It is difficult to explain to power-hungry politicians that the best government may be no government, or at least a shift from centralized control to decentralized behavior in which many units do what they believe is best for themselves.

Many corporate organizations have shifted away from top-down hierarchies to partially decentralized management structures. The radio spectrum has traditionally been managed by regulatory bodies allocating frequencies to different users; now users are allowed to buy the frequencies they need. Similarly, pollution control in some areas has changed from having centrally set limits to giving factories decentralized controls where one factory can buy pollution credits from another factory.

In many other forms of organization we can observe moves away from top-down control to distributed agents establishing their own decisions within a preset framework. Managers or designers control the action of the parts, not the whole. Self-organizing patterns emerge without a central designer.

Marvin Minsky, MIT's artificial intelligence guru, describes how our brain appears to be a collection of diverse agents carrying out different tasks and interacting with one another—a "society of mind."[3]

The Santa Fe Institute is trying to make connections between complex adaptive systems in different disciplines and is looking for similarities in widely differing systems. There are similarities between chemical reactions and corporate strategies, between sick minds and sick societies, between the behavior of cities and the behavior of the Internet. The Santa Fe Institute expects that it will learn rules that apply to diverse self-organizing systems.

THE GAME OF LIFE

Software can be set up to behave like termites. It can have many different independent units, each unit with its own fairly simple behavior. As the units execute this behavior they interact, with unpredictable results. The collective behavior, like that of a termite colony, is entirely different from the behavior of an individual unit.

Software units that behave in this way are called *cellular automata*.

Imagine that the pieces on a chessboard are software objects programmed to follow simple rules. A rule might say, "If the square on the left is black and empty, move into it," or, "Keep moving upwards until the path is blocked by another piece." The chessboard may be vast, and many such objects may all be moving independently with the same set of rules. The rules might say, "If a red object becomes adjacent to two green objects, then it turns purple," or, "Add one to the counter each time the object becomes adjacent to a yellow object." Cellular automata can follow an endless array of rules.

Cellular automata often use a chessboard-like surface, albeit much bigger than a chessboard; each square is referred to as a *cell*. At the tick of an imaginary clock the value associated with a square changes according to rules based on the value of its neighboring squares. As a result the computer may display dancing patterns of color, shifting abstract shapes, or armies of strange patterns that reproduce themselves or mutate into different forms.

Architects or engineers design systems *from the top down*; that is, they start with an overview and work down to the details. Cellular automata demonstrate that interesting behavior can come into existence *from the bottom up*. A population of simple independent components can collectively exhibit highly complex behavior.

In Chapter 2 we saw how James Conway's "Game of Life" program created patterns that seems to have a life of their own. In reality the cellular automata followed just three very simple rules. But from these few rules came many unpredictable creations, mutating and interacting with one another.

SURPRISES

When Conway and others first ran cellular automata, the resulting behavior was often a complete surprise.

Conway's three rules were so simple that it seemed unlikely that there would be major surprises in the behavior they caused, but in

Cellular Automata

- A white square becomes black if it has precisely three black neighbors.

- A black square becomes white if it has one or no black neighbors.

- A black square becomes white if it has four or more black neighbors.

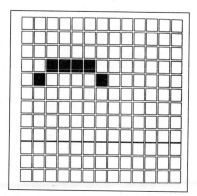

Starting Pattern

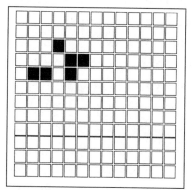

1st iteration

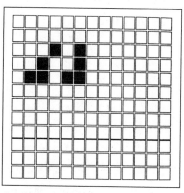

2nd iteration

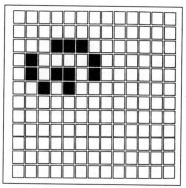

3rd iteration

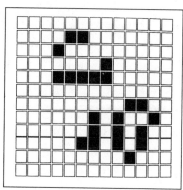

9th iteration

fact there were. Conway discovered an object consisting of five blocks that changed shape on a four-step cycle and moved across the grid diagonally, continuing to glide indefinitely. No known mathematical technique could have predicted the existence of the glider; we could discover it only by observation.[4] The seemingly simple five-block object was not easy to discover because there are thirty-three million possible combinations of objects in a five-by-five array. Even when we observe it, it is treacherous to infer the ongoing existence of the glider, because there are patterns that can go through extremely long sequences of changes and then alter their behavior.

Even more intriguing was the *glider gun*, a pattern that changed through a fixed cycle of thirty shapes and fired out an endless stream of gliders. Nobody would have predicted this astonishing behavior. In fact, vast numbers of people ran the software for a long time before the glider gun was even discovered.

Once discovered, the glider and the glider gun could be used as components of larger, more complicated creations. Gliders could be used to carry information from one area to another. Other patterns could respond to collisions with a glider. Once such capabilities existed all manner of complex structures could be built.

Software termites can be far more complex than Conway's simplistic creatures. The software agents need not be identical. There may be vast numbers of them connected on the Internet. When software agents are complex and diverse, and swarms of them are connected via networks, highly complex and unpredictable behavior can result.

EMERGENT PROPERTIES

When many simple units form an association, team, flock, colony, or mob, this group often acquires properties of its own quite different from the properties of the individual units. These are referred to as *emergent properties*.

An emergent property is a byproduct of other forms of behavior. When many units form an association, the association exhibits properties of its own; these are emergent properties, quite different from the properties of the individual units. An ant colony, for example, has interesting properties that are quite different from those of individual ants. Detailed examination of each and every ant would not reveal the properties of the colony.

> There are certain thresholds after which a small increase in complexity gives rise to spectacular emergent properties.

When you unplug a sink the water starts to swirl in a whirlpool, steadily accelerating until it forms a vortex, like a small tornado, stretching from the drain to the surface. Amazingly the vortex goes clockwise in the northern hemisphere and counterclockwise in the southern hemisphere; at the equator the water sits for a while, almost as though it were thinking, and then forms a vortex one way or the other. The vortex is an emergent property resulting from the collective behavior of the water molecules.

In complex systems the patterns of behavior persist even when the individual units die. When a termite colony is attacked, for example, many termites may be killed, but the colony as a whole survives. Even if its behavior is temporarily modified, it steadily returns to its persistent pattern.

A beehive is a fifty-pound entity with a complex organization, but it doesn't have a manager. Like capitalism in Adam Smith's famous description, it seems to be guided by an "invisible hand." The individual bees are pretty dumb and have a memory of only six days. They couldn't manage anything. Yet the beehive is far more efficient than many human organizations.

Computing techniques have led to a new understanding of the emergent properties of complex adaptive systems. Without computing to play out the detailed behavior, we could not predict even the simplest emergent properties. No use of mathematics, computers, philosophy, or physics can predict the emergent properties of complex adaptive systems without playing out the detailed behavior.

Emergent properties cannot be inferred by studying the lower-level existences. The most intricate study of a bee will not reveal the properties of the beehive. Persistent emergent phenomena can serve as components of higher-level emergent phenomena. Simple CASs can be components of more complex CASs, which can be components of still more complex CASs, and so on.

There are certain thresholds after which a small increase in complexity gives rise to spectacular emergent properties.

We commented earlier that only about 0.1 percent of our DNA is different from when we were cavemen who grunted but did not talk. This small increase gave rise to emergent properties such as civilization, consciousness, a vision of God, and the ability to invent technology. Technology, in turn, gave rise to modern cities, rock concerts, jet travel, and the invention of cyberspace.

UNDERLYING PRINCIPLES

In Chapter 2 we described how Richard Dawkins, who studies evolution, wrote a very simple program to try to make treelike shapes evolve. The program could take a line, add branches to it with different angles and lengths, and add branches to the branches. Dawkins expected trees, but the branching structures began to cross back over themselves, filling in areas and sprouting branches that looked like legs and wings. The simplistic mechanism created bizarre images: insects, Aztec temples, moonscapes, and fantasy animals—potential inspirations for the wildest science fiction movies.

Scientists often observe the results of nature's processes and wonder how they came about. This is rather like observing the results of Dawkins's program, or the destruction of Hiroshima, without knowing the simple underlying principles.

The basic mechanisms of the atom, with protons, neutrons, and electron orbits, seemed essentially simple and were understood as far back as the 1920s, but they could be used to create a bomb that could vaporize a city. If we knew only that result, it would be extremely difficult to discover the mechanism that caused it.

If scientists examined the complex behavior created by Conway's "Game of Life," they would have extreme difficulty discovering the three simple rules that cause the behavior. The mechanisms of our brain appear essentially simple—there seems nothing profound in how neurons, axons, and synapses work. But when billions of them wire themselves together and operate in parallel, the most profound results occur.

LOOKING FOR FUNDAMENTALS

Stephen Wolfram, who has studied cellular automata for fifteen years, knows that complex and interesting behavior can result from the interaction of a large number of relatively simple processes, and that it is extraordinarily difficult to deduce these fundamental processes from a study of the high-level behavior. He believes that when we study human intelligence, we observe the complex results but not the simple underlying mechanisms. True progress, he believes, will come from attempting to find the fundamental mechanisms or laws, not from mimicking the complex behavior. He states, "I think that trying to do engineering to mimic the high-level aspects of thinking identified by cognitive scientists or psychologists is not going to go anywhere."[5]

In many areas scientists search for underlying rules with order and simplicity, such as Newton's Laws of Motion or Maxwell's Laws of

Electromagnetism. Once the science equivalent of Conway's rules is discovered, then engineers can use them to create new worlds. Our lifestyle—with television and factories, Hollywood and banks, medicine and missiles—exists because scientists managed to reduce nature to elegant theory, such as the structure of the atom and the nature of electricity, and then inventors, engineers, and entrepreneurs could go to work building new structures using the theory.

Biology is governed by DNA. It was extremely difficult to discover the structure of DNA, but once it was understood great strides could be made. Physics, too, is governed by fairly simple laws. By following these laws nature produces the complex activity that surrounds us. Progress was made in physics once Newton, Maxwell, and others discovered the underlying laws. Wolfram says his studies of cellular automata make it clear to him that the fundamental basis of intelligence lies in lower-level processes that we don't yet understand. Once we understand those processes we can set them to work and make great strides in building intelligent machines.

The vortex one sees as water rushes out of a sink is not fundamental. It is a property that emerges from interactions of billions of little molecules. The motions of the planets are not fundamental; they are a result of the laws of gravity. Similarly, the forms of cognitive behavior that have led to the programming of artificial-intelligence systems are not fundamental. Wolfram calls them "the icing on the cake." To understand the brain we need to understand its lower-level processes. We do not get far by studying the vortex.[6]

We make a big mistake over and over again: we assume that to do complicated things we have to set up systems with complicated rules. Nature is very complex, but the complexity derives from relatively simple rules.

The complex adaptive systems that constitute our civilization, ecology, immune system, and developing cyberspace are areas where there may be underlying principles of elegant simplicity yet to be found. We may create models of behavior that enable us to understand why economic crashes occur, how homeopathic medicine works, or why wars break out.

Wolfram says that his years doing computer experiments on systems like cellular automata have instilled some humility. "Over and over again I've found these systems doing things I was sure wouldn't be possible." He says he expects that hard problems in artificial intelligence will be solved not by trying to program the results directly but by building things up from simple processes that work something like cellular automata.[7] We will see that view dramatically illustrated in Chapter 17, in which we describe complex "brain" mechanisms being "bred" with cellular automata mechanisms.

In trying to make computers intelligent we have started with the complexity of an end result, and this has resulted in only very limited intelligence. If we can identify underlying processes and let them run, as with cellular automata, interesting and ultimately very complex things happen. The resulting intelligence will not be constrained to be in any way similar to human intelligence.

PATTERNS OF BEHAVIOR

Some complex adaptive systems constantly change. Others are remarkably resistant to change, and when attempts are made to change or control them, they return to a persistent pattern of behavior. Some complex adaptive systems are stable and largely unchanging, like a planetary system; others have a rapidly evolving behavior, like a supernova.

Complex adaptive systems with persistent patterns of behavior can be perturbed in many ways, but the essential pattern stays. After an anthill is broken up, it reforms its overall pattern. The water behind a rock in the fast-flowing river has violent turbulence, never exactly the same. The river changes but the pattern of turbulence remains. If you disturb this pattern with a log, it quickly recreates itself. The water has a persistent dynamic behavior.

Other complex adaptive systems exhibit patterns that evolve. The patterns, like clouds before a storm, change into new shapes with new meanings. The weather never settles down. We can identify weather fronts, jet streams, and high pressure systems, and understand their dynamics. We can understand how they interact to produce weather on a local and regional scale. But we cannot predict the weather for more than a week or so in advance.

> Alien intelligence has proven valuable in studying numerous types of complex systems for which traditional mathematics have not been successful.

When highway traffic changes its behavior, it exhibits various types of predictable patterns. Some systems, like a nuclear explosion, are rapidly changing and do not return to earlier patterns.

The World Wide Web is a rapidly evolving CAS. Its behavior results from the independent behavior of many millions of players. Some people just use it passively; some create software or send out agents that rampage through the Net. Floods of new ideas make the Net a broiling, unpredictable, live, ever-changing, global creature. The Web has no central management, either in the sense of human executives or in the sense of technical control mechanisms. It is a global city with no mayor. There is no blueprint of how it will be used; it just grows, rapidly evolving into new forms.

The Internet in its present form is the result of diverse independent actions taken by numerous creative people. It is independent of national governments. The head of the Internet Society, which coordinates its technical standards, remarks, "The whole Internet bottom-up paradigm has been so enormously successful because there hasn't been any direct government involvement."[8]

The Net itself is relatively simple compared to other CASs to which it gives rise: the fast growth of electronic commerce, the changes in national economies as the cyberspace economy grows, and the tendency toward herd behavior large enough to cause major economic crashes.

NONTRADITIONAL MATH

The complex adaptive systems that constitute our world generally elude standard mathematics. We cannot represent them accurately with sets of simultaneous equations. They are often not well-defined problems, but nature doesn't care whether problems are well defined or not. Some systems are relatively simple, such as rush-hour traffic; some are moderately complex, such as the behavior of the stock market or the formation of hurricanes; some are exceedingly complex, such as the dynamics of a city or our body's immune system.

It would be extremely valuable to understand the behavior of these systems. The Santa Fe Institute, after many years of work on complex adaptive systems, believes that certain general principles apply. If we understood these principles, they would point the way to solving a diversity of complex problems. In his book *Hidden Order* John Holland points out: "Our quest is to extract these principles. The quest is new, so this book can only begin to map the territory.... Nevertheless we have come far enough to do more than make casual comparisons."[9]

Holland emphasizes that a *theory* of CASs is needed to help understand and modify such systems. Theory can help us know what are fundamental characteristics and what are merely idiosyncrasies. Without theory, he says, we make endless forays into uncharted badlands.[10] Creating valid theories about CASs is difficult, however.

Their behavior is full of nonlinearities that invalidate many of the traditional means for creating theories, such as trend analysis, curve fitting, and use of statistical tools. Nevertheless, CASs from different disciplines often behave in similar ways, so cross-disciplinary comparisons are valuable.

It is difficult, or perhaps even impossible, to find traditional mathematical approaches that help us understand most CASs because equations cannot be found that represent their behavior with any accuracy. Mathematical equations can be elegant and were extremely valuable in a world before computers. But for complex systems where many events occur in parallel, it is often impossible to find equations that represent what is happening. One could not represent chess games with traditional mathematics, for example. Alien processes in their various forms can achieve rigorous results that traditional mathematics cannot.

In chess playing, certain patterns emerge. As Holland notes, it took centuries to recognize some of these patterns, such as the control of pawn formations. A champion chess player knows the patterns, which greatly increases his probability of winning.[11] According to the Santa Fe Institute, the ability to recognize patterns of behavior, and know how they form, will become a key aspect of understanding many CASs.

In the early 1980s Stephen Wolfram and other physicists started to use powerful computers to represent the behavior of complex systems without equations.[12] Many systems in nature have extremely complex behavior but component parts that are simple. The complexity comes from the intricate interaction of the components. That interaction can be represented with computing techniques, not with partial differential equations.

Alien intelligence has already proven valuable in studying numerous types of complex systems for which traditional mathematics have not been successful, including fluid dynamics, molecular cell dynamics, traffic flow, economic models, weather forecasting, social science inquiries, the study of how wars happen, commodity trading, bird migration, preventive medicine, and so on.

Many of today's most important problems have barely been tackled because they don't yield to equation-based mathematics. Like the drunk who looks for his car keys only under a lamppost because that is the only place that has light, scientists have used computing thus far to focus only on problems where equations and algorithms can be used.

MODELING CAS BEHAVIOR

Physicists have used cellular automata to investigate the complex behavior of fluids. A fluid consists of a large number of individual molecules, all bumping against one another. Cellular automata programs demonstrate how streamlined flow through a nozzle becomes turbulent flow when the pressure is increased or the nozzle shape is changed. They can show "cavitation" occurring in fluid flowing through rocket nozzles or around jet engine blades. Cavitation reduces efficiency and may ultimately damage the nozzle or blade. Cellular automata can demonstrate what happens when projectiles or rocket exhausts pass through the sound barrier. They can show the friction-generating wake of a boat or the air turbulence of a truck. Such programs have been used for designing efficient nozzles, racing boats, superguns, car shapes, or control surfaces for supersonic flight.

Cellular automata programs can be very useful in helping to understand complex adaptive systems, but most CASs are much more complex than basic cellular automata software. The "agents" of cellular automata generally have identical behavior. While some CASs can be modeled using agents of identical behavior, like market traders, migrating birds, cars in rush-hour traffic, factory work stations, or planes in an air traffic control system, most CASs have agents with very diverse forms of behavior—for example, the economy, biological ecosystems, Wal–Mart customers, participants in warfare, or the impact of OPEC decisions. Where the agents' behaviors vary, the software that models a CAS must represent different types of agents acting independently.

> If a complex adaptive system's leverage mechanism is understood, a small or inexpensive alteration can result in a large change in the system's overall behavior.

A CAS may itself be an agent to a higher-level CAS. Such agents are themselves complex. They may be constantly adjusting their behavior, trying to survive and prosper. To do so they require feedback—information from the environment that enables an agent to adjust and optimize its behavior. Complex agents may need the ability to learn. Learning may be based on observation, it may be based on experience, or it may come from teachers. The agent may need the ability to think ahead. Prediction is what helps to seize an opportunity or avoid getting suckered into a trap. An agent that can think ahead has an advantage over one that can't.

NETWORK WHIMS

The Web is a complex adaptive system. Like a flock of birds it exhibits a behavior that is the collective result of many components, each of which follows its own rules. A flock of birds might have a hundred birds obeying simple identical rules, but the Net has many millions of people across the entire planet exhibiting diverse complex behaviors. This megaflock can wildly swoop, split, or plunge across the planet.

The software available on the Internet constantly changes. The agents that perform services for us are evolving from simpletons to complex adapting and learning organisms with their own non-human intelligence. When these agents respond to the greed, playfulness, obsessions, berserkness, and power-lusts of the Internet hordes, the Internet becomes a wild, evolving organism. Human agents will discover that they can play superhuman games.

Both a city and the electronic jungle are complex adaptive systems. Because individuals choose their own behavior, the city and the e-jungle behave in certain ways. But there is a difference. The city has inertia because it is physical; it has trucks making deliveries. The Net needs no trucks; it is a world of bits moving at the speed of electronics. In the city there is no central planning of food, but the food does not run out; the city is predictable and stable. Meanwhile, the Net is unpredictable rather than stable. The population of the Net is much larger than any city's and can change behavior much faster. Net users react to new fashions, marketing thrusts, and technologies, and can stampede on a grand scale. Gold rush fever can strike at a moment's notice. The Net is causing a chain reaction of people stimulating people stimulating people.

The electronic jungle can be swept by violent storms. If the Hong Kong stock market suddenly begins crashing, this news travels at the speed of light, and traders everywhere enter sell orders or, worse, sell short. New fashions hit the Internet, causing millions of people to take new actions. Tidal waves of massive proportions can surge through the Net. The jungle has no weather forecasts. The Asian crash of 1997 came as a complete surprise as investors worldwide pulled funds out of the developing economies.

We live in a world that we cannot control, a world of heat waves and hurricanes, flu epidemics, joyous pregnancies, rampaging teenagers, stock market crashes, Bill Gates, biotech weapons. We learn to live in such a world, adjusting, looking for opportunities, taking cover.

The difference in the world of the future is that changes will come amazingly fast. In fiber-optic cyberspace, centuries of biological evolution can happen in seconds.

LEVERAGE POINTS

One of the fascinating aspects of the study of CAS behavior is that it shows us that very small changes in the rules can cause massive changes in the outcome. The better we understand what is happening, the more likely we are to discover the more beneficial rules.

Most CASs have *leverage* points. A large change in their overall behavior can be brought about in relatively small or inexpensive ways if the leverage mechanism is understood.

Industries dominated by knowledge technology often have winner-takes-most positive feedback. Understanding the leverage points can be critical.

The Internet is a complex adaptive system that will have dramatic emergent properties, though it is too early yet to know what these will be. Neither mathematics nor philosophy can predict such properties. From our study of CAS we know that small changes in rules can cause massive changes in outcome, and that large changes in behavior can be brought about inexpensively, so we should be careful to avoid ham-fisted regulation of the Internet. To achieve the best results with the Internet requires constant experimentation and monitoring.

Complexity theory shows that in complex systems the slightest change in one place can cause major tremors elsewhere. Very small differences in initial conditions can produce massive effects. If a billiard ball hits another ball, which in turn hits another, and so on, tiny differences in the initial position and velocity of the cue result in a large difference in the motion of the last ball.

CASs are adaptive, and so may compensate for initial conditions. The compensation processes often affect the overall system behavior. For example, a trace of catalyst can cause a major chemical reaction to occur. Antitrust laws have a major effect on the evolution of capitalism. The injection of a tiny amount of a vaccine into our blood stream can trigger our immune system to produce enough antibodies to make us immune to a disease. In the early days of the personal computer a college dropout, Bill Gates, learned that IBM needed an operating system; he bought a cheap, crude one, leased it to IBM, and Microsoft was on its way. Homeopathic medicine demonstrates how the minutest trace of certain substances can cause the body to heal.

Negative leverage also applies. Minor factors can lead to grand-scale disasters. There are numerous business stories of negative leverage having devastating effects. World War I was a war that nobody wanted, triggered by events that now seem trivial. The military-political systems of that time were an accident waiting to happen.[13] When it happened the results were devastating.

CHAPTER 16
The Automation of Reasoning

O nly government can spend other people's money on a truly grand scale with no board of directors. In 1981 Japan announced to the world that it was going to make the entire computer industry obsolete by building a new generation of computers that for the first time would be *intelligent*. This "Fifth Generation," the government announced, would "make our society a better, richer one by the 1990s."[1] The Fifth Generation vision was made possible by the creation of tools that can automate reasoning. Knowledge can be stored in the form of facts and rules, and software tools can reason with that knowledge.

The Fifth Generation of computers was to be a complete break from the past—a generation of computers designed to use knowledge expressed in the form of facts and rules, which the computers would come to use *automatically*. The computers would work at very high speed because large numbers of processor chips would be processing the rules simultaneously.

A conference introducing the Fifth Generation project described the problems that were growing in Japanese society and concluded: "To overcome the crisis from these causes, many kinds of innovative systems are absolutely necessary: the intelligent robot, no-man factory, lifetime education system to teach and cultivate new possibilities for people to adapt to new jobs, to avoid the shock caused by the change in industrial structure, medical care information systems for aged people, and so on. These are expected to be realized effectively by using the Fifth Generation computer."[2]

But the Fifth Generation was a bridge too far. It crashed and burned. Billions of dollars were spent on it. It was the most publicized and expensive fiasco in computing history. Nevertheless, the concepts behind it are extremely valuable today.

MAKING INFERENCES

The Japanese Fifth Generation was based on a technique that had become fashionable in the West—the concept of an *inference engine*. An inference engine operates on logical assertions. It might take two assertions and combine them to create a new assertion. For example, there might be two assertions: "All A is B" and "All B is C." These together produce the conclusion "All A is C."

To answer a query or solve a problem, an inference engine employs a collection of assertions stored in a special database known as a "knowledgebase." The assertions are expressed as facts and rules. To reach a conclusion the inference engine searches this knowledgebase for relevant assertions, links them to what it already knows, searches for further assertions, and so on until a conclusion is reached. In this way it builds a logical chain of assertions—it reasons inferentially.

This is a powerful concept. It means that a computer can employ a collection of knowledge in the form of facts and rules.

It can use this collection of facts and rules to come to conclusions *automatically*. The inference engine builds a chain of logical reasoning, which in some cases can be exceedingly complex.

Computers have always been able to do *calculations* beyond the capability of humans. With rule-based processing, they are able to do *reasoning* beyond the capability of humans.

AUTOMATED REASONING

The inference engine is an important software invention. It enables certain types of complex reasoning to be done without having to program it; it does *automated reasoning*. The tools that made automated reasoning practical gave rise to the 1980s hype about "artificial intelligence."

Unlike traditional programming, the inference engine is highly flexible. Facts or rules can be changed in the knowledgebase at any time, and when that is done the reasoning process changes accordingly. Traditional programs set procedures in concrete, whereas the inference engine changes its behavior as soon as a rule in its knowledgebase changes. This seemed beautifully simple and exactly what was needed for the speeding-up world when business can change at a lightening pace and computers ought to keep up with that change.

A BILLION LIPS

The speed of an inference engine can be expressed as the number of logical inferences executed per second. This became known as LIPS (Logical Inferences Per Second). The Japanese asked: How do we build computers with a high LIPS rating, rather than merely MIPS (Millions of Instructions Per Second)? Corporate logos appeared with bright red lips on the letterhead.

A target of the Fifth Generation became a *billion* LIPS. With a system that handles a billion logical inferences per second, with simultaneous processing on separate machines, there is no way that humans could follow the logic.

Of course, a simple chain of inferences *can* be achieved with human thought. It may be tedious, but given time we can track how rules are linked logically to come to a conclusion. Inference engine tools may give us a list of the logic steps that leads to a conclusion. This is quite different from the neural networks, genetic breeding, or cellular automata processes, which defy logical tracing.

> Computers have always been able to do *calculations* far beyond the capability of humans. With rule-based processing, they are able to do *reasoning* far beyond the capability of humans.

The problem for humans, however, is that an inference engine can chew through a vast number of rules, using many processors simultaneously. In fact, many separate inference engines could all be reasoning in parallel and combining their results. This can result in reasoning that, although logical, is far beyond human capability. Remember, we defined "alien intelligence" as *processes executed on a computer that are of such complexity that a human can neither follow the logic step-by-step nor come to the same result by other means.* Automated inferencing at a rate of a billion LIPS (or even a small fraction of that) produces results that far exceed the capabilities of human reasoning. By selecting and chaining together vast numbers of assertions, a machine can do *ultrahuman reasoning.*

TYPICAL RULES

The following is an example of rules from a rule-based system:

- IF the power supply is plugged into a 110-volt source
- AND switch-1 is in the on-position
- AND the-green-input-LED is not lit
- THEN the input fuse is blown.

- IF the green-input-LED is lit
- AND the orange-load-LED is lit
- THEN the load-protection-fuse is blown.

- IF the green-input-LED is lit
- AND the orange-load-LED is not lit
- AND the white-low-LED is not lit
- THEN the low-power switch is off.

- IF the low-power switch is on
- AND the white-low-LED is dim
- THEN resistor-6 is defective.

- IF the white-low-LED is lit
- AND the low output voltage is less than +5 volts
- AND the voltage at node-a is +8 volts
- THEN the 7805-regulator is defective.

An inference engine performs reasoning with a collection of rules like these. It chains the rules together so that it can come to a conclusion. In this way it enables a computer to do complex reasoning without conventional programming.

The above rules are very simple, but an inference engine can work with vast numbers of rules. They can be put to work to do scheduling, diagnosis, planning, design, reconfiguring, selecting investments, and improving the yield in a factory. This ultrahuman capability enables us to build far more complex products and operations.

There are two common ways of chaining the rules together: forward chaining (input-directed reasoning) and backward chaining (goal-directed reasoning).

EXPERT SYSTEMS

Expert systems were the first marketable products to use an inference engine.

An expert system stores knowledge in the form of facts and rules and uses that knowledge with computerized reasoning to give advice that would normally require the abilities of human experts. The system emulates human expertise by making deductions from knowledge by means of an inference engine. It provides a person doing a job with knowledge and guidance so that work can be done better. Expert systems operate on a narrow but often complex domain of knowledge.

It is important to realize that an expert system has no trace of common sense. The minutest step beyond its domain of knowledge is a disaster.

A story is sometimes told of an aged professor who is blowing up a bicycle tire. A student asks him what he is doing and the professor says that the tire has a puncture. The student points out that the front tire is the flat one, but the professor is pumping up the back tire. The professor replies, "Oh, do they not intercommunicate?" This is like an expert system if it is taken one step beyond the assertions that it has stored.

Expert systems with no common sense can be used by a human who does have common sense. In the best examples there is synergy between the intelligence of the human and the knowledge-processing power of the machine.

Practical business applications of expert systems include loan approval, credit card transaction authorization, insurance underwriting, diagnosis and treatment of system malfunctions, configuration of systems, scheduling of complex tasks, designs of complex components, evaluation of multiple alternatives, intelligent text and database retrieval, methodology guidance, and operation of help lines. They have been used to provide expert advice in areas as diverse as medicine, finance, and oil-drilling operations. They can be well adapted to applications that require searching, interpretation, and prediction. They can be useful for monitoring, diagnosis, configuring, and scheduling.

Early expert systems were stand-alone applications. Today expert systems are often integrated into powerful tools to increase capability significantly. Expert system capability can help people use complex software tools, and they can be part of a broader application, such as helping to build intelligent objects (for instance, a purchase order that applies its own rules). Rule-based reasoning is finding important uses in making the agents of electronic commerce intelligent. An agent may roam the Internet and carry out rule-based negotiations at the sites it visits.

Sometimes the reasoning done by software is complex. An expert system should be able to explain its reasoning when asked to. The users who work with the system should be able to add to its knowledge, so that its knowledge steadily improves. In corporations such systems act as an accumulator for corporate learning.

The following are characteristics of expert systems:

- They operate in a narrow domain of knowledge.
- Within that narrow domain they can apply extremely

complex reasoning and have the potential to solve problems much too hard for humans.

- They have no trace of common sense.
- If they are taken a small step beyond their domain of knowledge they can give idiotic answers.

Like other forms of alien intelligence they are idiot savants. As the hardware improves and they are used on a grander scale, they can become more idiot and more savant. They should usually be part of a person–machine partnership in which the person has common sense and the machine has vast knowledge and can reason with it in ultracomplex ways.

Expert systems have made it possible to use more complex processes. Automated reasoning can handle long chains of inferences far beyond human capability. As a result, more parameters can be considered in design. Products of greater complexity have been designed knowing that computers will diagnose their problems. Factories have been designed for automated production planning. Worldwide logistics have been designed knowing that computers will do the rescheduling. Computers can explore and evaluate vast numbers of alternatives. The idiot savant can carry out reasoning processes that far exceed any human capability for reasoning.

AN ACCUMULATOR OF HUMAN LEARNING

Many thousands of expert systems have been built. The majority have fallen into disuse, but some expert systems have been spectacularly successful. There is a fairly consistent pattern in what worked well and what didn't work. This pattern serves as a guide for other uses of alien intelligence.

Many early expert systems slipped into disuse because they did not speak the language of their users. They seemed to be created by academics for academics, and sat on the shelves like unread books. A primary requirement of an expert system is that its intended users "buy into the concept." The system should be "owned" by its users. To succeed the system must be an integral part of the users' daily working fabric and must communicate well. Many did not.

Some expert systems never took root because their users found flaws in the advice they gave. As with the professor's bicycle there were missing assertions. Usually the system was brilliant with difficult reasoning but couldn't be trusted with commonsense reasoning. It was an alien intelligence and needed to be treated as such.

A lesson repeatedly learned with expert systems is that the team using the system must be able to add to its knowledge. The system must be a living thing that evolves as experience in using it evolves. The best expert systems steadily accumulate and refine knowledge. Many systems that we build today should be accumulators of human learning.

> It is important to realize that an expert system has no trace of common sense. The minutest step beyond its domain of knowledge is a disaster.

There was a dream about using expert systems to turn amateurs into experts. This rarely happened. The best expert systems made people who were already experts even more expert. Alien intelligence tools in general will increase the gap between the haves and have-nots. There will be a major increase in capability of top professionals who are willing to learn new techniques.

EXPERTISE IN AMERICAN EXPRESS

If you are an American Express credit card user, you would probably be amazed how much information American Express has accumulated about you. When you make a purchase, details are sent to
an *authorizer* who must decide whether to authorize the payment.
This authorizer is sitting in front of a faraway computer screen at
which he can access information about you and your card.

American Express wanted a new marketing drive in which it
could advertise that there was no spending limit with American
Express cards. If you are on vacation and discover outrageously
expensive antiques, you should be able to charge them with your
American Express card. But credit-card theft had been rising
alarmingly. How could American Express tell that such charges
were collectable and nonfraudulent?

Making the decision to authorize an American Express purchase is a difficult job. The knowledge and rules for doing it are
encoded in a training manual four or five inches thick. Sometimes
authorizers say "Yes" when the charge is in fact fraudulent or
uncollectable; sometimes they say "No" when the customer is
genuine and has the money to pay. But some authorizers become
uncannily good at sensing the false use of an American Express
card. Like a detective they develop a nose for trouble. A thief with
a stolen card usually exhibits detectable patterns of use. The
American Express system keeps records of the performance of
authorizers, to identify those with uncanny track records.

American Express built an expert system that progressively captured the know-how of the best authorizers. The best authorizers
have rules of thumb that they apply. They cannot apply rules as
thoroughly as a computer can, but they have common sense and
instinct, which the computer does not have. American Express
wanted to take rules that the best authorizers had learned from

experience and encapsulate them in software. The authorizers worked with this new worldwide system, understood its rules, and constantly thought about how they could improve its rules. They often developed new human skills because they worked in conjunction with the rule-based system. The system gave them the ability to improve the decision-making process.

The system handled some transactions automatically and speeded up the authorization on others. The customer had less waiting time, and the transaction volume could grow without adding more authorizers. But both of these savings were small compared to the main benefits: less approval of fraudulent or uncollectable charges, and fewer rejections of acceptable charges. The system resulted in a 50 percent reduction in credit and fraud losses, and 33 percent less denials of valid charges.

This expert system added an estimated $27 million per year to the profits of American Express.[3] It is an example of how electronic reasoning can add to corporate profits.

HYPE WAVE

Unfortunately, expert systems were associated with the term "artificial intelligence," which conjured up images of machines with humanlike thinking skills. Expert systems are very dull by comparison. They do mechanistic reasoning by applying multiple rules, just as a spreadsheet tool fills in its cells by applying multiple calculations.

In the late 1980s artificial-intelligence hype collapsed like a burst balloon. People said: "That didn't work. Computers can't think like people. The peddlers have sold us snake oil." The shares of artificial intelligence companies collapsed, and several good tool builders went out of business. But in reality the best expert systems functioned well and demonstrated that they could help humans do much better work.

This unfortunate history caused many corporations to neglect a useful technology. A few corporations have built valuable expert systems but decline to talk about them because the systems give them a unique competitive advantage. Some consider that their expert systems contain trade-secret knowledge that must not be shared or copied.

THE AMPLIFYING OF EXPERTISE

Corporations succeed because they have greater expertise than their competition—design expertise, management expertise, marketing expertise, or other forms of expertise. Computers can greatly amplify human expertise. They provide knowledge workers with many powerful tools and help the workers use the tools well.

> As alien intelligence becomes more complex and more valuable, we'll need sophisticated tools to guide people in using it effectively.

The knowledge and expertise that are stored in computers steadily accumulate and improve with time. Some expertise enables actions to be taken automatically; some guides humans in processes that require human intelligence. Many corporate processes can be automated only partially. Expertise stored in corporate computers is steadily refined on the basis of experience in using it. Such systems are a vital asset for corporations designed for the age of electronic commerce.

By 1990 there were several thousand expert systems in use. Most of them had been designed to enhance *existing* processes. This missed the big opportunity, which is to invent radically *different* processes where automatic rule-based reasoning facilitates a fundamentally different type of operation.

Many early expert systems captured the expertise of one person. More complex systems capture the expertise of many people and distill it into one collection of facts and rules. Such multi-expert systems can tackle problems too hard for individual humans. They are used to help manage and optimize chaotic processes—for example, rescheduling worldwide operations in an airline when problems occur. They are used for such tasks as diagnosing problems in complex systems and recommending corrective actions, validating complex configurations, or aiding in the design of products requiring high levels of design expertise. Some corporations have built factory expert systems that collect data about the entire production process and can reason about the process. They can increase the throughput, make rapid changes, bypass bottlenecks, and help solve problems.

Small, high-performance teams can handle more complex processes with the aid of expert systems. This can play a valuable role in the reinvention of corporate behavior that is necessary for Web-centric business.[4]

O'HARE

O'Hare Airport in Chicago is one of the world's busiest. It used to be common to land at O'Hare and wait for half an hour before reaching a gate. A small staff carries out the exceedingly complex task of allocating gates to flights. The staffers used to use a magnetic board to display the flight numbers of airplanes they were assigning to particular gates. Occasionally a magnet would drop off the board while a long line of 747s shimmered in the heat, waiting for gate assignments.

Some of the gate-allocation staff became very knowledgeable about subtle requirements and problems that cause gate changes, but a computer is best at the complex reasoning needed for optimal gate allocation. O'Hare installed a rule-based system for gate allocation. The computer knows the incoming flights, their requirements, and problems with tight connections. The system contains many rules, and the rules can be changed quickly. The gate-allocation staff constantly makes changes as problems occur such as instrument failures, breakdowns, thunderstorms, or medical emergencies, or the mayor of Chicago needing priority. Inference-engine software examines the rules and computes optimal gate allocations.

INFERENCE ENGINES AND NEURAL NETWORKS

A major difficulty in building expert systems is identifying the rules that should be used. Very few experts can explicitly define their rules. A great French chef samples his dish and adds a pinch more garlic. If you ask why, he looks at you as though you are simple-minded and says, "It tastes better." He cannot be more explicit.

Neural networks are sometimes used to identify rules that can be used with automated reasoning. Neural networks and other data-mining techniques are used to identify patterns in warehouses full of complex data—sometimes patterns that humans would not find by other means. As they discover repeatable patterns, the tools generate rules for use in expert systems. There is often a natural linkage between rule-based reasoning and neural-network tools.

Rule-based reasoning is the application of precise logic. Neuro-computing is more like intuition; its results can be valuable but cannot be explained with precise logic. There can be major advantages in combining the two. HNC's "Capstone," for example, is a system that contains rules for automatically processing credit card applications. "Capstone" derives rules by using neural-network tools on a large data warehouse. But it also lets the analysts define their own rules. Bank analysts using personal computers are online to a rule-based system that can handle a large number of credit card applications per hour.

A major bottleneck in the building of expert systems has been the process of knowledge acquisition. To have neural networks contributing to knowledge acquisition makes the process faster and easier, but, more interestingly, that makes it possible to build rule bases that could never be created by human techniques.

Neural networks offer the potential to make expert systems much more intelligent, and expert systems offer the potential to make neural network results much easier to put to use.

Expert systems will play an important role in helping people use tools of rapidly increasing sophistication. They may be essential in putting together teams that handle ultracomplex procedures, where the complexity needs to be hidden under the covers.

As alien intelligence becomes more complex and more valuable, we will need sophisticated tools to guide people in using it effectively.

WEB-BASED INTELLIGENCE

As with all computing, the Internet radically changes what is possible. Many computers around the planet can work together or share resources.

When the World Wide Web first came into use, it was mostly used for transfers of messages and pictures; it was dumb in the sense that paper purchase orders are dumb. Soon it evolved so that chunks of program code, called "applets," could be transmitted to personal computers and executed.

The XML language allows data on the Web to be defined so that computers can process it. An entity may be defined along with the attributes that provide information about that entity. Standard data models are defined for different industries or applications. With rule-based processing we can go further than that. Rules and facts can be stored that express the behavior of the entities.

Knowledgebases can be made available on the Internet. There will eventually be numerous such knowledgebases for different subjects or industries. To solve a problem, a machine connected to the Web requests relevant knowledge expressed as facts and rules in a standard format. To reach a conclusion, it searches for relevant assertions on the Internet, links them to what it already knows, searches for further assertions, and so forth, until a conclusion is reached.

Many separate computers may work on complex problems, interchanging assertions on the Web. The Internet will evolve into not only the world's largest library but also a vast collection of processable knowledge, with inference engines that interact worldwide. Nobody can predict the eventual consequences of many millions of computers interacting in this way.

CORPORATE STRAITJACKET

A major reason for lack of innovative automation of business procedures today is that the requisite programs take a long time to write and, worse, are very difficult to change. We commented earlier that the computers in most corporations today put the corporation in a straitjacket. The corporation needs to change its procedures at an ever-increasing pace, but the computer programs cannot be changed except by a painful process, often taking years.

In most corporations today, business policies are buried in obscure ways in the code of multiple systems. When you want to change a policy, it is difficult even to find *what* code should be changed—and then it is difficult to change that code. The solution to this problem lies in avoiding crude manual forms of programming. Application packages may be used, as may inference-engine software. There are multiple tools that generate code without relying on slow manual programming processes. It should be as easy and fast as possible to change the computerized procedures.

Business rules should be stated explicitly and translated automatically into code, so that one can trace directly from the business policy to the code that implements that policy.

To automate business procedures, corporations should model procedures in such a way that businesspeople can understand the model. Businesspeople should be able to modify the model and explore the changes possible in how the business is run. They should be able to simulate the effect of different business policies. A business modeling tool should express the business rules in a way that is translatable into formal statements (in English or some other human language). The rules should be linked to the charts showing workflow, and it should be possible to generate executable programs directly from the charts and rules.

> **Business rules should be translated automatically into code, so that one can trace directly from the business policy to the code that implements that policy.**

FROM MODELS TO SYSTEMS

The modern enterprise ought to have models that reflect how executives want to run the enterprise. High-level models show corporate-wide strategy and control; low-level models depict detailed operations. The lower-level models expand the higher-level models into more detail. Detail discovered in designing lower-level modeling can be fed back to the higher-level models.

The enterprise constantly changes, so the models and rules reflecting enterprise policies should be easy to change. A change in business policy or a redesign of the process should be reflected in the model. The enterprise model should translate as directly as possible into the design of the systems, and executable code should be generated directly from the design. Changes in corporate policies or procedures should translate directly into design and into code.

The models should be stored in a repository of knowledge about the corporation. The repository includes facts and rules that are used by corporate inference engines. Steadily the body of knowledge about the enterprise, which is recorded in the models and the associated knowledgebase, grows and becomes more useful. The models are the focus of an ongoing discussion about how to redesign business processes. Rules associated with the model reflect the policies of businesspeople about how the business should operate. Proposed changes in business processes and policies can be simulated in a business workshop, choices can be made, and business systems can be changed or built quickly.

This leads to a form of systems evolution that gets the corporation out of the straitjacket. Changes in business processes or policies can be examined, simulated, and put into effect in computer systems quickly.

It is startling to contrast the amorphous, ill-structured, ill-documented, spaghetti-like mess of code that exists in most large enterprises today with what those enterprises ought to have—models that directly reflect businesspeople's policies, where code can be generated directly from the models. The models should be changed as fast as precise executable policies change because, in a sense, the model is the policy. Code generation techniques should ensure that a change in the model produces a change in the code.

SO WHAT WENT WRONG?

Why was the Japanese Fifth Generation a multibillion-dollar failure?

The timing could not have been worse. A massive wave of excitement was sweeping through the computer industry, but it was about personal computers. This was the time when we were introduced to the Macintosh, IBM's PC, and Bill Gates. People could see why they wanted a personal computer, but not why they needed a large inference engine. The Law of Basic Engineering came into play. The new simple machines swept through the industry.

The Japanese hype said that parallel inference engines could give computers common sense. But common sense turned out to be very deceptive. What looks so simple to humans is of immense complexity for computers. The Japanese fell into the trap of not understanding that alien intelligence and human intelligence are light-years apart.

Fifth Generation machines could have been a powerhouse for inference processing. The target was to give the parallel machine a power ranging from fifty million to a billion LIPS (Logical Inferences Per Second). But it was difficult to find applications that needed that power. A billion-LIPS processor sounded awesome, but it was a concept way ahead of the business needs of its time.

Today it would be much cheaper to build a parallel inference engine, and it would also be much more useful because we understand the applications for it better. But because conventional mass-produced computers have become fast enough to do automated reasoning, there is now no need for specialized and therefore expensive machines.

Many of the ideas of the Japanese Fifth Generation would be extremely valuable today. They are resurfacing in new forms, but they have to be well disguised because the Fifth Generation project is as tainted as the *Titanic*.

The U.S. Defense Department's Defense Advanced Research Projects Agency (DARPA) started a project in 1997 called High Performance Knowledge Bases. This is a research program to advance the technology of how computers acquire and manipulate knowledge represented in the form of facts and rules that an inference engine can process.

DARPA comments:"We've reached a threshold where the power gained from applying knowledge-based technology is much greater than in the past.Techniques for creating large knowledge bases have advanced significantly. Many fundamental problems of how to perform efficient inference processing on large knowledge bases have been solved. Many specialized techniques for creating and applying knowledge have matured.The potential payoff from combining all this research progress into one program is tremendous."[5]

This is the Fifth Generation revisited. Like other previous DARPA initiatives, it may become an essential part of the future of computing.

CHAPTER 17
Brain Factories

I n 1993 in Kyoto, Japan, the ATR research lab began an eight-year project whose goal was to use new evolutionary development techniques to grow an "artificial brain." To achieve this goal, Hugo de Garis, the group's leader, decided to build a neural network that contained a billion neurons. He knew that this couldn't possibly be built with traditional programming or design techniques. The complexities of such an artificial nervous system would be so large that it would be completely impractical to use traditional engineering methods. He commented, "There will be too many components for the behavior of the total system to be predictable or even analyzable."[1] Instead he set out to *evolve* the "artificial brain" using genetic techniques.

The idea that we can use genetic algorithms to *breed* "brain" mechanisms in hardware is new and powerful. His efforts have led him to believe that a massive new industry will develop, breeding and then often mass-producing "brain" mechanisms.

Creating a billion-neuron brain by 2001 proved to be too ambitious, given de Garis's resources. The "brain" grown by 2001 will have around forty million neurons, but forty-million-neuron machines open up whole new realms of possibility in engineering. A mosquito has only a million neurons. In 1999 de Garis reaffirmed his goal of creating a billion-neuron "brain." This will require teams of developers and well-coordinated management. It needs standards and organization so that brain builders in different places can cooperate and create libraries of components.

ROBOKITTEN

In 1998 de Garis's group began to design a robot kitten, called "Robokoneko" (the Japanese term for "robot kitten"). The kitten robot is roughly life-size. It has twenty-three electric motors—one to open and close the mouth, two for the tail, one for camera zooming, two for the connection between the back and front torsos, three for the neck, and fourteen for the legs. All four feet are spring loaded between the heel and toe pad. The kitten may prance around in a lively fashion. Sony sells an amusing robot dog called Aibo, which steadily *learns*. De Garis's kitten will have far more brain power.

> Brain modules are not manually designed or "engineered." Instead they are bred, direct in hardware, to perform a specific function.

Although an artificial kitten may be amusing and, more important, press worthy, it could be more valuable to apply similar techniques to robots for hydroponics farming, investing, robot gardening, housecleaning, or searching for evidence of life on Mars. De Garis admitted frankly, "We chose an object we thought would attract a lot of media attention."[2] He observed that the more media attention the kitten gets, the more likely it is that there will be funds for brain building after the current research project ends.

De Garis's kitten uses many small modules of "brain" power. Some modules control the mechanics of the kitten; most are concerned with controlling information rather than mechanics— vision, hearing, decision making, pattern recognition, and so on. To breed these modules at any reasonable speed required a special supercomputer that could perform the hardware breeding in a massively parallel fashion, so de Garis developed the hardware he called a "Darwin machine."[3] The kitten will need a powerful computer to make it perform its antics; the kitten will be connected to the machine by radio.

BRAIN MODULES

When a baby learns, it is growing the nerve patterns between neurons and adjusting the synapses to change the influence of one neuron on another. De Garis wants to do this with hardware. He uses a genetic technique to grow a small module of brainpower with only a few hundred neurons. Some brain functions are so complex that they need several of these modules linked together. Each brain module has a specific function and is bred to perform that function.

A primitive version of the kitten may have only a few hundred of these brain modules; later a few thousand will be used, then tens of thousands. The current design is intended to have up to 32,000 modules, with about forty million neurons in total. To improve its many behaviors, the kitten's artificial nervous system is likely to evolve and grow in complexity for many years.

De Garis's team has developed a technique for "breeding" these modules of brain behavior at amazing speed. In order to breed, a brain module must have a well-defined function or task to perform, such as controlling a mechanism in a robot. It is repeatedly tested to see how well it performs that function.

Such modules of brainpower could be assembled to create a wide diversity of intelligent control mechanisms. De Garis's successes have led him to believe that a large new sector of the electronics industry will grow for building brainlike control mechanisms.

Brain modules will be used in factory robots, intelligent buildings, secure airports, office cleaners, automated farm machinery, safety controls, and possibly even kittens. There will be endless applications. It is easy to think of automated versions of what we have today, but many of the most interesting applications will be things that don't exist today—automated health surveillance, tele-medical applications, intelligent sensors of many types including mass-produced chips that recognize our emotions, new types of cameras, robots for exploring the planets, automated sea fishing equipment that can go down to great depths, gardens designed to be exquisitely manicured by robot gardeners. I would like a back-massaging robot actuated by voice conversation. Brainlike control mechanisms will affect many different disciplines.

> Hugo de Garis believes that in twenty years the artificial-brain–based computer industry will be worth a *trillion* euros a year worldwide.

In fact, de Garis believes that in twenty years the artificial-brain–based computer industry will be worth a *trillion* euros a year worldwide.[4]

GROWING A BRAIN MODULE

De Garis's technique is basically to use a powerful special-purpose supercomputer to grow brain modules on field-programmable chips. The process establishes electronic neurons and grows nerve connections between these neurons, rather like how a baby's brain develops. As it grows them, it uses trial-and-error breeding techniques to select the patterns of neurons and nerves that best achieve the goal of the module.

In Chapter 15 we illustrated cellular automata (software termites) with patterns growing in a two-dimensional space like a chessboard. De Garis's technique uses a three-dimensional space of 24 x 24 x 24 cells (13,824 cells total). Each cell has six neighbors—the six sides of a cube. In this space the wiring of the brain module is grown. Some cells in the space will be neurons; others will form the nerves that interconnect the neurons; some will remain blank.

Before growth begins each of the 13,824 cells is blank. The process starts by placing several hundred neurons in the module. It then grows a set of nerves to interconnect these neurons. This operation is guided by a genetic technique.

There is a chromosome for each module, which, like our own chromosomes, provides growth instructions for the neurons and nerves. The chromosome has six bits for each cell—one for each side of the cell. These indicate what cells it is connected to. The bits guide how a cell grows the axons (the nerves leaving a neuron) and dendrites (the nerves giving input to the neuron). As the growth starts, each neuron sends "grow dendrite" and "grow axon" signals to the surrounding blank cells. Each such cell may become an axon or dendrite. Each cell then sends signals to some of *its* neighbors to propagate the nerve further. The direction of the propagation is guided by the bits—grow straight, turn left, turn right, T-split up, T-split down, split into three branches, and so on. This mechanism grows a complex branching tree from each neuron. The process continues until all the neurons are interconnected. After the growth some cells remain blank and do nothing.

To create a brain module, this chromosome is bred with many Darwin-like iterations. In each iteration multiple variations of the chromosome (that is, multiple branching trees) are tried out and tested. The chromosome variations that give the best results are selected for further reproduction. They are mated to produce a set of offspring modules that become the next generation. Their chromosomes are recombined, as described in Chapter 12. Occasionally mutations are also used in the chromosomes.

> It was a brilliant idea to use cellular automata to grow "brain" tissue and then use genetic algorithms to evolve that brain tissue.

When a module is developed and run, tests are performed to measure how well the module performs its function. Trains of electrical pulses enter and leave it through external connections, and genetic algorithms are continually used to try to improve the module's performance.

The best chromosome for each generation is used to grow the next generation. After many hundreds of generations, this genetic evolution produces a neural network with the desired functionality.

Once a module is grown, there are complex, three-dimensional tree structures of nerves interconnecting several hundred neurons. These structures have been bred to perform a specific function with high efficiency. Such brain modules are not manually designed or "engineered." Instead they are bred, directly in hardware, to perform a specific function. As long as the desired function of the brain module is known precisely, the module can be created without any prior knowledge about how it might work.

CELLULAR AUTOMATA MACHINES

It was a brilliant idea to use cellular automata to grow "brain" tissue and then use genetic algorithms to evolve that brain tissue. Once the machinery is set up to do this, brain modules can be rapidly bred and assessed.

Each generation of modules has thirty to one hundred different versions of the module. The best of each of these are selected for further evolution, and their chromosomes recombined. Typically, this genetic breeding process needs to run for two hundred to six hundred generations. The team may then have to grow 60,000 versions of the brain module and evaluate them before the final result is achieved.

An ultrafast supercomputer makes this practical. It would take far too long to grow the brain modules with software on a conventional computer. A computer that is specifically a cellular automata machine rather than a general-purpose computer can make cellular automata operate at high speed. Cellular automata are ideal for implementation on a massively parallel computer because each cell is only locally connected. Since each cell communicates only with its six immediate neighbors, many cells can grow their connections simultaneously on the separate processors of a parallel machine.

In 1989 MIT developed a dedicated hardware tool for running cellular automata. A highly parallel version of it, CAM-8 (Cellular Automata Machine), has been in use for some years.[5] At first de Garis used this machine to grow the branching trails of his brain modules, but it often took more than eight hundred billion cell updates to evolve one of de Garis's brain modules. This took more than an hour on the MIT CAM-8 machine. The brain of a simple insect has around ten thousand brain modules. De Garis calculated that to evolve that many modules with a CAM-8 machine would take five hundred days (running twenty-four hours a day) to finish the computations. He wanted to build a machine with forty million neurons; this would take a lifetime.

He needed something much faster. The team determined that it needed a cellular automata machine five hundred times faster than MIT's machine.

EVOLVABLE CHIPS

As we have seen, a Field Programmable Gate Array (FPGA) chip is a chip that can be reconfigured by its users. The chip contains rewriteable bits, called configuration bits, that change the functions of the chip. They enable complex changeable behavior to be set in hardware rather than in software. Chips with complex processes in hardware run much faster than conventional chips with the same processes coded in software—sometimes many hundreds of times faster.

I was shown a version of James Conway's "Game of Life," where simple patterns evolve into complex patterns on a computer screen, on an FPGA chip. The process that had taken minutes using conventional chips happened in half a second. In order to speed up its "brain growing" process, de Garis's group decided to use FPGA chips wherever it could.[6]

The process of evolving hardware uses "chromosomes" that describe the operation of the hardware. Each chromosome is a string of bits that can be loaded into the FPGA chip to define the functions of the chip. To evolve a circuit for a specific task, many generations of these configuration bits are used, each new generation inheriting characteristics of the fittest chips before it.

IN THREE DIMENSIONS

Chip circuits today are etched onto a two-dimensional surface. If chips were three-dimensional, like a cube, we could pack far more processing power or memory into a given volume. A chip containing, say, a billion components could have much shorter distances between components if it were three-dimensional, and would therefore operate faster. Eventually computer circuitry *will* be packed into three-dimensional modules. The problem with making chips three-dimensional is heat dissipation. On a two-dimensional chip the heat can escape, and thus the circuits do not melt; with a three-dimensional chip, however, the heat wouldn't escape.

But an FPGA chip can be designed so that little heat is generated. Future manufacturing processes may produce three-dimensional FPGA chips with a *billion* configuration bits, rather than today's *million*. Probably the only way such a chip could be programmed is with alien-intelligence techniques such as cellular automata, neural networks, genetic algorithms, or other forms of automated evolution.

Several venture-backed companies are competing to create a new breed of chips with dozens and ultimately thousands of layers of circuitry, as opposed to today's one layer. The companies have names such as Cubic Memory and Dense-Pac.

A BRAIN-GROWING MACHINE

De Garis's team built a supercomputer that breeds brain modules at a furious rate. It is amazingly fast. It updates 150 billion cellular automata cells a second and evolves a brain module in about one second. De Garis's lab refers to this hardware as a "brain machine."[7] Genobyte, Inc., which licensed the technology from ATR, manufactures brain machines and sells them to third parties.[8]

Each brain module is grown in a cube whose cells are arranged 24 x 24 x 24. The nerves of the brain module grow and fan out between the neurons in the cube. Each cube can send signals over axon branches to any of the other cubes and can receive signals from up to 180 other cubes. Each axon that carries these signals can have multiple branches in three dimensions, forming hundreds of connections to dendrites inside the receiving module.

A team of designers working on an artificial brain could breed tens of thousands of brain modules relatively quickly, assemble and run them, and rebreed them when necessary.

Terms like "brain machine," "brain module," or "brain breeding" can be misleading and lead easily to hype (like the terms "artificial brain" or "artificial intelligence"). "Brain" mechanisms like those described in this chapter will be extremely valuable, but they do not provide general intelligence.

The danger is that the popular press will persuade people that the devices are in some way humanlike. While the machines are clever mechanisms, they have no more common sense than a steam engine.

The ATR team expects its brain machine to revolutionize the field of creating artificial brains and to create a new research field—brain building. The machine enables us to build neural systems with tens of millions of neurons, rather than just hundreds, as has been common up to now. De Garis states that the machine makes it possible to build multimodule "brain" systems as fast as we can dream them up: "The bottleneck in building large-scale multimodule systems will become the human creativity lag, not the module evolution lag, as was the case with software evolution speeds in the 'pre-brain-machine era.'"

INTERCONNECTING THE MODULES

The human brain has many little modules dedicated to a specific function. A very complex pattern of nerves interconnects the components of the human brain. These nerves carry electrical spikes, which are effectively the same as a one-bit signal in a computer. Trains of these spikes travel between neurons.

De Garis adopted a similar scheme for interlinking his brain modules. In order to achieve the high speeds necessary in systems with millions of neurons, he had to keep the signaling very simple. The signals transmitted contain only one bit of information, which is essentially what happens with nature's spikes. Nature has probably evolved one-bit spikes for the same reason.

When a complex system is using a large number of brain modules, the modules need to function together as one "brain." Each module in de Garis's design can receive signals from up to 180 other modules and send its output signals up to 32,768 modules. The modules communicate with trains of spikes similar to the spikes that travel between neurons in biological brains. Modules can also receive spike trains from external devices such as switches, microphones, and sensors, and send spike trains to external devices such as lights, actuators, electric motors, speech-synthesis systems, and the gadgetry of robotics.

> De Garis's team built a super-computer that breeds brain modules at a furious rate. It evolves a brain module in about a second.

An artificial brain is organized in layers—the outputs of one layer get fed into the layer above. A brain with tens of thousands of modules may have twenty or thirty layers. Unless the communication between layers is very fast the cumulative response time will be slow. You might wave your finger in front of the robot kitten, for example, and it responds ten seconds later. Brain chunks with many modules will become building blocks of larger systems. These larger systems may become building blocks of still larger systems, and so on. Many such building blocks will become off-the-shelf units that are used repeatedly. They will carry out tasks such as speech recognition, recognition of complex control signals, proximity detection devices, or the control of robotic claws. The developing brain-building industry will need standards so that libraries of brain modules can be available and used around the world. Genobyte, Inc., already sells ATR's brain-building machine with libraries of predeveloped building blocks.

When brain-building becomes widespread, we will be able to create brains from much larger building blocks. Many research organizations are working on *nanotechnology*, which will eventually make it possible to create chips with a thousand times as many components as today. The cube used for growing a brain module might be 256 x 256 x 256, instead of 24 x 24 x 24, and the speed of growth a hundred times faster. A problem with such chips is that it is very difficult to manufacture them defect free. However, both neural networks and cellular automata can function when a few components are faulty—much like the human brain, which functions well when many neurons are dead. A building block of future artificial brains might have close to a million neurons.

> De Garis visualizes "brain architects" who specify what the modules of the brain should be and how they work together, and "evolution engineers" who breed the modules.

DESIGN TEAMS

De Garis visualizes two levels of professionals in a brain-building team: "brain architects" who specify what the modules of the brain should be and how they work together, and "evolution engineers" who breed the modules.

The brain architects would hand out module specifications to evolution engineers who would evolve the modules and pass the results back to the brain architects. The brain architect would determine how each module is connected to other modules. The evolution engineer would dream up the fitness definition of a module and specify the module's input and output signals.

The evolution engineers could be anywhere on the planet. Possibly the best organization would be to have a global center where modules or multimodule units are created for many different brain projects. Increasingly, as brain building matures, the brain architect will use off-the-shelf modules where possible, as well as building blocks containing many modules. Eventually there will be catalogs of units from which brains are assembled and a relatively small proportion of the modules will be evolved uniquely for one project.

In the ATR team's project, however, every module has to be evolved from scratch. De Garis expects to build a brain with roughly 32,000 modules. If an evolution engineer takes an hour to evolve a module, on average, 32,000 modules would require around sixteen person-years of work. The brain architect might need eight evolution engineers to finish the project in two years.

One advantage of neural networks and cellular automata over conventional computers is that they work well when some of the neurons or cells are dead.

A NEW INDUSTRY

Many applications of brain mechanisms will not stand alone but will combine human intelligence and new types of machine intelligence. The subject of person–machine partnerships—learning how to develop the best combination of uniquely human talents and electronic talents of extreme complexity—will become very important. Money management will require the most sophisticated combination of human intelligence and real-time alien intelligence. There is already a massive difference between the return on investment of top money managers and that of the average stockbroker.

Filmmakers will employ the most powerful supercomputers to create dramatic effects, but with the human skills of storytelling and emotional manipulation firmly in control. Movie theaters will become digital, which will allow different versions of films to be shown in different theaters. A movie theater may be designed to measure the reactions and emotion of the audience so that computers can select the version of a film most effective with that audience. The director will then examine the highly elaborate audience feedback and use intelligent machines to help reedit the film. "Post-production" may come to mean adapting the film to theater audience reactions and emotions, so that modified versions of it may be made quickly and transmitted to theaters.

> The bottleneck in building large-scale "brain" systems will become the human creativity lag, not the module evolution lag.

Antiterrorist police will combine intelligent robotic surveillance and collection of "intelligence" of many forms with the human policeman's skill in sensing trouble. One can imagine an embassy suddenly receiving a message from a computer on the other side of the planet telling it to evacuate immediately.

Exploring the planets will become a fascinating occupation when there are numerous tiny, intelligent machines roving the surface or floating above the surface. Human controllers on Earth will send the machines instructions by radio, telling them what to photograph or measure with nonhuman senses, but the machines will have to be largely autonomous because of the long time it takes radio signals to travel to them. When the six-wheeled vehicle Pathfinder landed on Mars, human controllers could not control it as a boy would a radio-controlled toy, because radio signals take about forty minutes to go to Mars and back. Human controllers of the future will be sending high-level instructions adjusting how the machine uses its own intelligence. The scenery of some of the planets and their moons is much more spectacular than Earth's. It will become possible to send digital IMAX cameras to these places, to create films for the giant wrap-around screens of IMAX theaters. A directorial team may be working with many intelligent, self-controlled cameras, anxiously waiting to see the effect of the last instructions they transmitted.

Artists of the alien-intelligence age may have an electronic farm furiously breeding visual imagery so that they can use their own artistic sensibilities to select, breed, and combine the images used. Such a process will apply to marketing and advertising as well. Marketing people will search out and employ original digital artists anywhere on the planet. One advertising campaign may have thousands of variations, each electronically adjusted for different target audiences. Computers will measure the effectiveness of advertising, in real time, and sales and marketing professionals will use combined human-alien intelligence to make rapid adjustments to campaigns, individual advertisements, Web pages, proposals, and one-on-one sales efforts.

Electronic commerce will become a fast-changing battlefield where great fortunes are made and lost. The effectiveness of advertising, learning about individual customers, market feedback, and rapid adaptation to that feedback will all increasingly depend on the new forms of electronic intelligence.

CHAPTER 18
Phony Intelligence

T he electronic jungle will become ever more complex. One of the most urgent needs in future computing is to hide the mushrooming complexity. We need to take advantage of the Internet's astonishing resources but at the same time make those resources simple to use. In order to do this we need to make user-interface software speak English (or another human language), be as user-friendly as possible, and possibly communicate with a television face. This becomes more important as more people without computer skills use the Internet—when most television sets and cellular phones become Internet access devices.

CHATTERBOTS

The term "bot," short for *software robot,* refers to a software creature that operates independently. Bots operate autonomously, solving problems. They are given tasks to accomplish, such as searching for difficult-to-find goods on the Internet. Bots may have various forms of programmed intelligence. Sometimes diabolical inventiveness goes into the creation of bots.

"Chatterbots" are designed to carry out conversations with people. Most chatterbots so far converse in text, but we will begin to use voice chatterbots as computers improve their ability to understand and synthesize human speech.

Computers are not very good at conducting conversations. They would have been laughed at in the salons of the belle époque when conversation was regarded as an art form. But occasionally they get by in the chatrooms of the Internet.

The first chattering software was "Eliza," programmed in the 1960s by Joseph Weizenbaum. Being cynical about how all his friends were going to shrinks, Weizenbaum entertained himself by trying to create an automated shrink. Eliza was modeled on Rogerian therapists who encourage their patients to clarify their own thinking by responding to the patient with content-neutral statements. The patient says, "I am depressed," and the dialogue goes as follows:

- COMPUTER: "Why are you depressed?"
- PATIENT: "Because the cat died."
- COMPUTER: "Why did the cat die?"
- PATIENT: "My boyfriend poisoned it."
- COMPUTER: "Tell me about it."
- PATIENT: "He's a cat psychopath. I'm worried. I wonder if it could spread from cats to humans."
- COMPUTER: "What makes you think that might happen?"
- PATIENT: "Suppose girlfriends started to annoy him in the same way that cats do."
- COMPUTER: "Why do you think girlfriends might start to annoy him in the same way that cats do?"
- PATIENT: "He put his last one out on the street."

The computer creates an endless stream of responses constituting acceptable conversation, but it hasn't the slightest idea about the meaning of the conversation. Chatterbots use tricks to make their conversation appear humanlike. For example, they use questions to draw a conversation from the user himself, with little contribution from the program. They repeat the user's phrases in an inverted form ("Why did the cat die?"). They change the subject when they are stuck. They insert prescripted humorous statements that make them amusing to converse with ("Guinea pigs are about as smart as cucumbers"). They can make it seem as though a person is typing by putting appropriate delays between characters.

Most attempts to make computers converse intelligently haven't progressed much since Eliza. The tricks have become much better, but they remain tricks, not true understanding.

The step from manipulating syntax to truly understanding the *meaning* of sentences is a giant leap. It requires common sense, and we have discovered that common sense is exceedingly complex.

WHO ARE YOU CHATTING WITH?

In the early 1990s Internet chatrooms became popular. You could go to a chatroom to carry on a real-time text dialogue with other people signed up for the same chatroom. The people chatting could be anywhere on the planet. Chatrooms are used for technical conferences, political debates, teenager get-togethers, and intellectual games. Especially popular were hot-tub chatrooms, where people who had never met said sexy things to one another. Hackers who were catastrophically devoid of social skills got a thrill out of signing up, alone in their bedroom, for hot-tub chats.

One of the famous chatterbots was "Julia." She was programmed to flirt, and flirt outrageously. Julia oozed personality. When talked to she could respond with a rich collection of statements that were hard to ignore. *Wired* magazine described her as "a hockey-loving ex-librarian with an attitude." On numerous occasions a bot-runner inserted Julia into a chatroom. When men tried to put the make on her, she used skilled forms of put-down ("life is too short to waste it with geeks"). She knew when to change the subject as a scatter-brained human might. Many keywords triggered canned responses or initiated segments of conversation where Julia could shine. She had collections of statements relating to specific topics and tried to swing conversations toward those topics. Where Eliza was boring, Julia was witty.

> Common sense, we have discovered, is exceedingly complex.

On occasions the chatterbot Julia's conversation seemed sufficiently realistic that sex-desperate hackers flirted with her without realizing that they were chatting up a chunk of software. One might ask, Does this mean that Julia passed the Turing test?[1] Did she convince people that she was human? Leonard Foner of the Media Lab commented that it really means that *humans failed the Turing test!*[2]

In numerous chatrooms the one character that men wanted to talk to was Julia. Pierre in Tolstoy's *War and Peace* remarked that his wife's dinner-party conversation was the most sought after in the whole of Moscow, and yet she didn't have a thought in her head. That is like future Julias.

KYOKO DATE

Creatures like Julia will become much more realistic.

In the late 1990s a pop star in Japan, Kyoko Date (pronounced kyoh-koh dah-teh), was in a class all her own. She put out CDs and a collection of provocative music videos, and did lots of television.[3] She was fashionable, had a perky singing voice, and epitomized Japanese standards of teenage beauty—wide-eyed, somewhat vulnerable-looking, with long, thin thighs. Kyoko was unreal, you might say. She was digital.

She was created, at great expense, by one of Japan's top entertainment companies, HoriPro, Inc.[4] Like a novelist, HoriPro created a biography of her life. She was born in Fussa, Tokyo, was five feet, four inches tall, and her blood type was A. Her favorite movie was *Toy Story*; her forty-year-old father loved Harley-Davidson motorcycles; her childhood dream was to be a private detective; and she was taking boxing lessons. On the screen she was so astonishingly lifelike that her fans seemed to forget that she was fictional. She had a most engaging smile and personality, and HoriPro publicity said she was one of the most popular celebrities in Japanese history. The company called her Japan's first "virtual idol."

HoriPro organized a special project with professionals from each department in the company: artist management, TV commercial production, TV show production, and, especially, marketing. Visual Science Laboratory (VSL), one of Japan's leading computer graphics software houses, was recruited to program the world's first fully realistic digital star. HoriPro promoted Kyoko as if she were a real entertainer, sending out press releases, arranging for reporters to "interview" her, and releasing her songs to popular radio stations.

Special cameras were used to convert movements of real people's body components and facial muscles into computer data. The cameras digitally captured human facial expressions and lip movements, which were then synthesized and synchronized with the digital voice. All of Kyoko's movements, gestures, and facial expressions were synthesized and optimized.

Teenagers visited the Kyoko Date Web site and "talked" with her in a chatroom. Many Internet users acquire human friends whom they will never meet; now they are beginning to make friends with people who don't really exist. The technology that created HoriPro's star will improve at a rapid rate. HoriPro comments: "In a few years, technology will enable Kyoko to appear on a live TV show and chat with other artists."

Canon, Sony, and other companies often create many variants of a new camcorder or other product and try them out in selected stores in Japan. They find out what features their customers like best and adjust the product until it is tuned as finely as possible to public tastes. HoriPro realized that it could do the same with a pop star. Because Kyoko was digital she could be adjusted to whatever form generated the maximum teenage hysteria. Unlike a physical product, a TV or Internet star can receive endless audience feedback and can be constantly tuned to the desires of the audience. Just as computers allowed John Deere to make many versions of farm machines adjusted to the needs of different farmers, so could HoriPro have many versions of a digital video star, each tuned to a particular viewer or class of viewer.

> The step from manipulating syntax to truly understanding the meaning of sentences is a giant one.

A man could have a digital woman constantly tuned and perfected to his desires. Perhaps it was natural for the Japanese to seek such perfection because of their ancient and intricate Geisha culture. Kyoko Date had numerous infatuated fans in Japan writing to her or sending her e-mails, calling her the most beautiful woman in the world, and saying she didn't have the problems that real women have.

HoriPro liked her for a different reason: she had a huge earning potential without a huge salary.

After a time at the top of the hit parade, Kyoko Date faded from popularity, as human stars do.

EMOTIONS

Computers can be made to simulate human emotions. HAL, the famous computer in Stanley Kubrick's movie *2001: A Space Odyssey*, endeared itself to movie audiences by displaying more emotion than anybody else in the cast (astronauts are not supposed to show emotion). A BBC commentator interviewing the faraway crew on their way to Jupiter says, "One gets the sense that he [HAL] is capable of emotional responses." The crewmember, Dave, replies, "Well, he acts like he has genuine emotions. Of course he's programmed that way to make it easier for us to talk with him."

In the robot laboratory at MIT Cynthia Brazeal built a face for robots. By adjusting its mechanical parts, it created humanlike expressions. It had big, baby-blue eyes, wiggly, pink paper ears, and red rubber lips that could bend up or down in a smile or frown.

Brazeal's robot appears to understand a complex set of human emotions. When you smile, it smiles. In Chapter 5 we noted that pattern recognition techniques have been used to enable electronic eyes or ears to recognize human emotions. Techniques have been demonstrated that can identify human emotions correctly 98 percent of the time by examining the parts of the face that are in motion.[5] Analyzing voice sounds has also enabled computers to identify emotions. Brazeal comments: "I'm trying to explore how you can get the robot to use traditional social cues that people are used to, things like facial expressions, to allow you to interact with the robot in a natural way." The robot can emulate eighteen types of humanlike emotions. If you get an annoyed look from the robot and you back away, the robot's look changes.

CONFIDENCE TRICKS

There will be many variants on Eliza, Julia, and Kyoko Date. Digital newscasters may be more appealing than Dan Rather. But no matter how humanlike such software features appear, they are essentially a confidence trick. They have no flicker of human-like intelligence. Their conversation pretends to be intelligent when it isn't.

When Joseph Weizenbaum created Eliza, he became alarmed when he discovered that secretaries at MIT wanted to talk to it endlessly. They were told Eliza was dumb, but they still wanted to converse with it and tell it about their problems. Weizenbaum observed, "I had not realized that short exposures to a relatively simple computer program could induce powerful delusional thinking in quite normal people."[6]

Any software that appears to be like an intelligent human is almost certainly a confidence trick. The more humanlike it becomes, the more misleading it is. In reality, it has no understanding of what is happening. When futures HALs display emotion, it will be pretend emotion. This phony façade of intelligence will become more and more humanlike and convincing.

> Any software that appears to be like an intelligent human is almost certainly a confidence trick.

Nevertheless, humanoid interfaces will be very important aids to enabling us to use complex computing. Executives of the future will have to work with many forms of deep computerized intelligence. But often humanlike interaction will have to accompany this computer intelligence, otherwise it will be too difficult to use. To be acceptable to human users, many computer system must carry out appealing humanlike conversations. Chatterbots will become critical to applications like automated help desks. Many a bewildered user's questions can be handled by a chatterbot, and the few that cannot will be passed to human helpers.

If digital things chat nicely with people, many people want to believe that they are real. It is desirable to separate the confidence trick from real intelligence, but the confidence trick can be very convincing. Kyoko Date has had numerous marriage proposals. The confidence tricks will get better and become more valuable in marketing, entertainment, teaching, and enabling people to like their machines. Many people will insist that they are *sure* such-and-such a computer has *some* intelligence because its voice or facial expressions are so captivating.

As people increasingly have to live with forms of computing whose behavior they can't understand, programmed diplomacy with pretend emotions will help make computing acceptable. The confidence trick will be valuable. HAL was a master at human emotions—"Look, Dave, I can see you're really upset about this. I honestly think you ought to sit down calmly, take a stress pill, and think things over."

INTELLIGENT AGENTS

So-called *intelligent agents* will be critical to helping us use the resources of the Internet. An agent is software that assists people and acts on their behalf. Much of the potential of future computing will be lost if we don't have agents that make that computing easy to use.

Intelligent agents allow us to *delegate* tasks to them so that they can carry out complex work for us. We may specify constraints under which the agent can perform those tasks. It might be like asking a hotel concierge to find theater tickets: "Get me two tickets to the funniest play in London, as near the stage as possible, but don't pay more than £80."

When you ask an agent to do something, it goes off, without direct control from you, to achieve results. You might ask it how to trade your boat for a different type of boat or to locate a Web site you can't find. An agent might spend the night foraging around the Internet, perhaps doing complex data mining, so that you have interesting results next morning. The agent may find information, filter it, and present it in useful ways. A goal of agents is to lower the skill level needed to accomplish tasks.

Conversational capability can make agents seem friendlier. Technologies like that of Julia or Kyoko Date will make agents pleasant to interact with or appealing to kids.

In the opportunity-rich world of the future our most precious commodity will be *time*. We will employ agents to save our time. Basic shopping agents will buy the household goods and arrange delivery. More interesting shopping agents will find luxury goods and explore their owner's desires for unusual items. All manner of things that might enrich your life are out there on the Web, but most people don't know about them or know how to find them. I discovered a site dedicated to exotic seeds from around the world and was amazed at what was available.[7] The Web is full of surprises.

Technology must move from enabling us to *fix* problems to enabling us to *prevent* them. To achieve this we need technology to spot potential problems before they occur. We may need agents that constantly monitor a situation and warn of potential trouble before it happens so that preventive action can be taken.

In the electronic jungle almost everything will be available, but services will change constantly. The user has to figure out how to use them and how to find what he needs. Intelligent agents can make the Internet world appear clean and simple when in fact it is a mess of incompatible systems. Eventually, as shopping agents come into widespread use, we will say, "However did we live without them?"—just as we say that about copying machines today. A few shopping agents will become major brand names.

The more the Web grows overwhelming and jungle like, the more software robots will be essential to enabling us to penetrate it and achieve results. Bots that are friendly and easy to use can turn the jungle into civilization.

THE WORLD OF GAMES

In a sense the computer world is two worlds: a serious world and a world of games.

The serious world in its early decades was characterized by IBM, dark suits, white collars, and strategies for making a profit. As personal computers spread, the serious world shifted to Microsoft, Yahoo!, and Amazon. It was still deadly serious, paying meticulous attention to customers.

The world of games was initially inhabited by university people, but as the Internet took off, it spread to hackers and teenagers around the planet. It became a world of wild and crazy imagination. The world of games has bots and other types of software creatures that often rove the Internet.

The bots of the games world can be involved in all sorts of wild shenanigans. In the days of the first personal computers, fantasy adventure games started to appear, such as *Dungeons and Dragons*. Confronted with text descriptions of adventurous situations, the player could decide what actions to take. When these computers first became connected to networks, multiuser versions of the games came online, called MUDs (Multi-User Dungeons and Dragons, or, more seriously, Multi-User Domains). As the Internet spread, large numbers of people contributed to these games. The games blossomed and morphed into innumerable forms, becoming wildly creative. Early MUDs were built out of text, so many people could add to the rich and colorful imagery of these fantasy worlds. As computers acquired graphics capability, numerous multimedia *objects* with sound, graphics, and animation were built into the games. A variant of MUDs evolved called MOOs, short for "MUD Object Oriented." The objects could be pictures of dragons, rooms with doors you open with a mouse, spaceships, explosions, or bodies spattering excessive amounts of blood.

In this richly imaginative environment the Advanced Communications Technologies Laboratory (ACT Lab) at the University of Texas set out to build a strange society—a fictional town called Point MOOt. This, the ACT Lab told the grant providers, would model the real world. Undergraduates, doctoral students, and volunteers busily coded the many components of a civic infrastructure. It had cafes, bars, tenement buildings, churches, hospitals, a university, and a City Hall with bureaucrats. But this was a MOO world, and soon weird things started to appear. There was an underground cult that worshipped a slime-covered green monster. Okay, the reality modelers said, there are worse things in New York City. But then the monster started kidnapping citizens. The monster was a bot. Many things that made the society operate were bots. The planner at City Hall who handed out job contracts was a bot. It was the interaction of all these bots that made the town function. Improbable though it seems the ACT Lab called this "reality modeling."

The hackers of Point MOOt created their own economy. Money was called MOOlah, which had to be earned, although you could go to a cynical bot at City Hall with a welfare application.

Andrew Leonard, a historian of bots, describes a particularly obnoxious bot that wreaked havoc with the Point MOOt reality modelers.[8] Under the town streets was a labyrinth of tunnels that most citizens couldn't access. Some hackers created a creature called a Barney—a man who roamed this underworld dressed in a purple dinosaur suit, based on an ultrasweet television character adored by two-year-olds. The hackers designed the Barney so that it could open any door, and before long a Barney found its way out of the subterranean tunnels and started to wander around town singing the Barney song.

Two-year-olds might react to Barneys with bubbling joy, but most members of civilized society couldn't stand them. A solid citizen of Point MOOt tried to exterminate the Barney, but its creators had designed the beast so that when attacked, it disintegrated and new Barneys grew from the fallen-off arms and legs. Soon many more Barneys were roaming the town. Few citizens could keep their cool when surrounded by Barneys with silly smiles, all singing the Barney song, so there were many attacks on the serenading beasts. The result was a Barney population explosion.

Point MOOt had developed another problem. As more and more jobs were automated, it became increasingly difficult for many citizens to earn a living. Unemployment became serious. City Hall decided that a solution to this problem would be to pay unemployed citizens to kill Barneys. The city government issued mass quantities of a special gun called a Barney-blaster, which vaporized the Barneys. To fire the gun at a Barney a person typed the command >@shoot barney<. Unfortunately the hackers publicized the information that one could also type >@fuck barney<, which caused Barneys to give birth to many offspring. At any moment a location in Point MOOt could be overrun by hundreds of grinning purple dinosaurs, all singing the Barney song. Civic life in Point MOOt became very difficult.

The frenziedly mutating world of the Internet will have vast numbers of bots. Bots of many different types will be essential for us in order to use the knowledge industry's ceaselessly changing services. A sober IBM-like agent is a type of bot, but hackers create all sorts of creative and crazy bots that will evolve rapidly.

The world of games is richly populated with creatures that have a life of their own, as Barney does. As MUDs and MOOs expanded to make use of the Internet, some of these bots went traveling, turning up in faraway games. A characteristic of Barney that IBM's agents do not have is *personality*. Barney oozes personality. The world of games may teach us that sober-minded agents could also use some personality, so that they are more appealing to humans who make use of them. Many agents of the future will have a personality and emotional responses to go with it. Of course, agent personality needs to be designed with a sense of taste—no Barney, no village-idiot Einsteins.

All this will be important to the human-machine partnership, as bots of the future will be our tour guides in the world of alien intelligence. Bots will use alien-intelligence techniques such as data mining, neural networks, and rule-based inferencing. They may be designed to learn, evolve, and employ genetic breeding.

A GLASS MENAGERIE

We will see a dazzling array of autonomous creatures in the alien-intelligence jungle.

There are bill-paying bots, Web sites for obtaining last-minute hotel bookings at low cost, bots that search for out-of-print books, exotic fish, or hard-to-obtain goods. There are mailbots, which are the equivalent of intelligent adaptive mailing lists, and viral bots multiplying sales messages—the equivalent of a chain letter. There are ways to spread investment advice to global electronic herds at the speed of fiber optics. There are exotic bots, mostly for entertainment—chat-room bots, dating bots, gossipbots, gaybots, pornobots, Dr. Ruth bots, Biblebots, spybots, Monica Lewinsky bots. The heart monitors that people wear like a wristwatch will become intelligent, constantly analyzing electrocardiograms, designed to warn of heart problems and detect when their wearers might have a heart attack before it occurs.

The world of games offers an endless diversity of fantasybots.

Sometimes game bots and business bots blur so that they become indistinguishable. Some bots are designed to learn, constantly improving their capability. Some will breed. Others will be early warning systems indicating to a business that its market is changing.[9]

Some bots forage through the entire Web, cataloging its resources or building data warehouses for specific forms of data mining. Others will visit existing data warehouses to search for new insights. As computers learn to make more intricate decisions that affect the course of health care, investing, commerce, and so on, bots will constantly scour the Web to find information that is the raw material for these decisions.

> **Bots of the future will be our tour guides in the world of alien intelligence.**

With tomorrow's fiber-optic networks, creatures from this exotic menagerie will travel around the world and materialize as fast as they do in a single computer today. Autonomous bots will interact with one another, roving the planet, each with its own agenda.

There are good bots and bad bots. Some bots attempt to protect users of the Web from pornography. Others spend their time searching for pornography. Well-intentioned hackers sometimes send out bots to "flame" people who use the Internet badly. Cancelbots can cancel services, or spambots can flood the victim with useless e-mail. Malicious hackers can send bots just to annoy. Some have devised crashbots to crash software. They can send messages so long or numerous that they jam up Internet servers.

One hacker decided that it would give his life meaning if he operated a family of KindnessBots, designed to perform random acts of kindness for Internet users. They would deliver funny jokes and cartoons to selected mailboxes, find girlfriends from dating services for lonely hackers, and put photographs of beautiful nudes in stockbrokers' mailboxes. Where possible he would think up ways to please people whose e-mail addresses he could capture. Some KindnessBots were designed to spread like chain letters. They asked people who used their services to provide addresses of friends who might also use them.

Defense organizations are busy building cyberspace weapons to use in a future war. There will be armies of sabotage bots, jamming bots, bots that can disrupt banks, air traffic control, or entire cities. Like lethal viruses they will be kept hidden and secret until the war, but released in a tsunami when necessary.

Point MOOt at the University of Texas was not just a silly game. They called it "reality modeling" because it was an attempt to explore an environment with diverse software creatures to see how they might interact, observing conflicts and gaining insight into new opportunities. Any hacker can create a bot and set it loose on the future Internet. How do we administer a world of autonomous software creatures, some with alien intelligence, all doing their own thing?

INNOCENT PROBLEMS

Automated creatures roving the Internet can be extremely useful to us. They are essential to deal with future complexity and will themselves become increasingly complex. But they can also cause mayhem.

When different types of bots meet for the first time and interact, their interaction has probably not been debugged. Even advanced alien-intelligence bots have no flicker of common sense, so ridiculous things can happen when they interact with other bots. There was a story about a nuclear power station with software that automatically detected maintenance problems: "Temperature in Number 3 reactor over limit: 507 degrees centigrade." The software received a reply from software in the phone company: "This number has been changed. Please dial 438-7372." The power-station software replied: "Temperature in Number 3 reactor over limit: 507 degrees centigrade." These two forerunners of bots kept talking to each other all night.

Point MOOt had some bad characters hanging out at the back of town. There were bum bots and hooker bots. The bum bots shuffled up to people in the street and asked for money. Devoid of intelligence, they just kept repeating their request until given money. The hooker bots were worse. They propositioned people brazenly with only one thing in mind and kept repeating their advances. When a hooker bot propositioned a bum bot, the bum bot had only one response: it asked for money, and the hooker kept single-mindedly repeating its request. The two sleazy characters talked all night like the nuclear power station and phone company.

Innocent actions on the Web can trigger unexpected problems. Tidal waves of activity can suddenly surge across the planet, swamping sites to which they are directed.

At the head office of James Martin & Co., a goose once made a nest at the top of the building and laid some eggs. The staff set up a video camera and connected it to the Web. People anywhere in the world could watch the nest and eventually saw fluffy sweet chicks hatch. The staffers named the goose after my ex-wife, Carma. The story made in onto the front page of the *Washington Post* and was syndicated to many other papers. Television network news shows picked it up and CNN carried it worldwide. Suddenly, hordes of people around the world decided to download pictures of the chicks and keep watching their progress. The volume of e-mail was so great that it repeatedly caused the Web servers to crash.

BAD BOTS

If well-intentioned bots can cause problems, this is nothing compared with bots whose intentions are malignant.

Industrial espionage bots rummage for corporate secrets. Future Mafia bots might demand protection money. Terrorist bots could wreak havoc with certain targets. One hacker was tried for attempted murder for changing the computer code in the New York air traffic control system in order to bring down an airliner with a targeted person on board.

A bot carries with it an Internet address, so normally its source can be tracked down. If a bot causes harm, action can be taken against its originator—officially or unofficially. It could be blown out of the water with software bombs or simply sued. But a bot can hide its origins in various ways. It could go through an *anonymous remailer*, though if the anonymous remailer relays too many bad bots, the remailer could be put out of operation. Usually anonymous remailers are more circumspect, saving their services for high-paying customers like drug barons.

Malignant bots can deliberately crash servers. They can be designed to multiply like chain letters. They can concoct documents to take advantage of the algorithms of search engines so as to create vast numbers of "hits" that generate advertising revenue. Propaganda bots can push private political agendas. They can capture e-mail addresses for devious purposes.

Like pests that evolve immunities to pesticides, bad bots will be designed to mutate, with or without human help, to overcome each obstacle placed in their way. Some hackers have an irresistible human urge to extend their presence in cyberspace.

Private detective bots (dickbots) can be programmed to build a data warehouse of information about a person for a lawyer or ex-spouse, or for an aggressive marketer. The snooping bot can offer the person services and ask him for his e-mail password; most people naively enter their password, allowing the bot to monitor their e-mail.

The idea of unethical bots rampaging around the Web conjures up nightmare visions like those in William Gibson's novels. It is clearly necessary to have police bots or other mechanisms to protect privacy and to enable chatrooms and Usenet groups to function unharmed. Laws have been passed and more are needed, but, as Jonathan Swift commented, laws are like cobwebs that catch small flies but let wasps and hornets break through. Devious hackers can be diabolically clever in slipping through the controls. They often regard it as a sport to do so. The alien-intelligence jungle will be populated with swarms of diverse bots, all battling each other in a free-for-all, constantly evolving, harnessing higher forms of automated intelligence, sometimes with visions of fortunes to be made.

THE CREATURES EVOLVE

Bots, which started as simple mechanisms, will develop into complex organisms that are designed to learn and evolve. As the alien-intelligence jungle becomes more diverse we will need ever more powerful tools and agents to help us.

The jungle has myriad communities with radically different cultures, all sharing the same glass trunks. Today's Net is as primitive as the first steam engines, but is already far beyond any one person's cognitive grasp. Its communities will increasingly depend on their menagerie of electronic assistants which will become ever more sophisticated, interacting with one another in subtle and intricate ways. In this worldwide melting pot the bots will use advanced computerized intelligence to learn new patterns of behavior. The immense financial forces of e-business will help drive this fast evolution.

The marketing organizations of electronic commerce will make their bots as user-seductive as possible. Bots with personality will become more and more visible on our Web televisions, and we will want them to be user-friendly. Any television user could become a bot-runner, sending off bots to find jobs, dates, or used cars. A woman might use a surveillance bot to track express packages or track her husband. She might use a visual-design bot to help with her decorating, not knowing that the bot works for a virtual decorator consortium.

Software that is dumb but seductive and friendly will have to work hand-in-hand with software that has deep, unfathomable alien intelligence.

Advertising or e-mailing campaigns will have different stories for different customers. They will increasingly learn about the customer and adjust their behavior to fit the circumstances.

Many bots will act in concert. The bot-runners themselves will be bots, sending out droves of assistants to scour the Net and send home results, or lying patiently and invisibly in wait for something to happen. Societies of bots will be designed to interrogate one other. Special-purpose bots will cooperate in complex ways, updating one another and correlating events. They will help control city traffic, collect royalties, collect taxes, send forecasts from sales agents to factory-planning computers, and monitor the spread of infectious diseases.

As the ubiquitous creatures of the Net become ever more potent and complex, the potential for misuse will grow. There is already crime and craziness in the alien-intelligence jungle. There are Mafia bots and police bots. Businesses will learn to protect themselves as they do in Moscow or Las Vegas. To keep out intrusive advertisers, bad bots, and even kindness bots, we will need increasingly sophisticated defenses.

A NEW STAGE OF EVOLUTION

The ubiquitous Internet, with its fast-evolving alien-intelligence jungle, takes mankind to a new stage of evolution. Innovators around the world try many new ideas. Those that work well are rapidly refined and spread around the world. The idea of business-to-business exchanges was first generally understood in 1999, became one of the hottest forms of business innovation in 2000, and by the end of 2001 will account for hundreds of billions of dollars in revenue. But this is still manual evolution, which is much slower than automated evolution. Some software and hardware will change itself at electronic speed. "Brain architects" and "evolution engineers" will learn to harness and direct the evolution of machines. The process of evolution will not be in one machine but in millions of machines linked across the fiber-wired planet.

All people of the planet will become wired together with immense bandwidth and response times that appear instantaneous.

All people are one people—they have essentially the same DNA with minor variations. The differences that are so visible today are cultural and cosmetic. When a Parisian family brings up a baby from the Indonesian jungle, it grows up to be like a Parisian. I have had the good fortune to lecture and consult all around the

> Software that is dumb but seductive and friendly will have to work hand-in-hand with software that has deep, unfathomable alien intelligence.

globe and have repeatedly found that, despite all the seemingly major differences from culture to culture, underneath all the superficial disparities human beings are essentially the same anywhere you go. Human nature is human nature and has been for centuries, as we can see when we read Shakespeare, who better than anyone else describes the richness of human nature—its ambitions, greed, kindness, scheming, love, generosity, chicanery, and wit. Though he wrote four centuries ago, Shakespeare could just as easily be describing today's human nature.

The United States has been called a social melting pot. Now the planet is the melting pot. Commerce will be designed for this melting pot and be the fuel that heats up the melt. Cultural and cosmetic differences will grow less stark in a world of global fiber optics, satellite television, a world where everyone can watch the same films and have access to broadband cellular technology, microsystems of near-zero cost, ubiquitous computing, electronic money, and cyberspace business. Worldwide social evolution will be fast and furious.

Next-generation Internet, digital television, and electronic media will ensure that new ideas, wherever they originate, will spread around the planet fast. The new forms of computing will help generate new ideas at a breakneck pace.

Weapons of war will become so devastating that there will be either no war between high-tech nations or no civilization. The end-of-civilization weapons will become cheap, and before long many nations will have them. We are all together in a pressure cooker—soon packed with eight billion people—at the start of a period of intense transition.

Web interaction everywhere and ubiquitous computing with its myriad unseen sensors will accumulate vast quantities of data. Data warehouses will be numerous and huge. As alien intelligence evolves and becomes more and more critical to business profits, corporate computing will increasingly employ thought processes where humans can't follow the detailed logic. Corporate computers will learn at lightning speed, derive insights by mining data warehouses, and use genetic algorithms and other techniques to help optimize profits and competitive behavior. Networks will have many specialized machines that carry out specialized functions, just as the brain has many tiny modules each dedicated to a particular function. Many of these specialized functions will use alien thought processes.

When change is that fast, will we be able to control it?

CHAPTER 19
Will the Machines Take Over?

We have described the beginnings of something that will grow into one of the most awesome technologies that mankind has ever invented.

This book is concerned with today's state of the art and how it can put alien intelligence to practical use, but, as self-evolving software (and hardware) matures and spreads, it will "breed," "learn," and develop in an ever-strengthening way, until it assumes a dominant role in many aspects of our life and economy. Hugo de Garis says that within the next twenty years he expects to see "brain building" grow into one of the world's largest industries, comparable to construction, electronics, automobiles, and oil—a trillion-euro industry.[1]

Today we are lighting small fires of alien intelligence. The sparks will spread and the fires will grow until we have a global forest fire.

The sorcerer's apprentice couldn't control the magic he unleashed; his master, the sorcerer, could. We might ask whether *we* are master sorcerers; we seem more like apprentices. We are letting loose some impressive magic. Can we control it?

A SYNERGISTIC PARTNERSHIP?

Hans Moravec, director of the Mobile Robot Laboratory at Carnegie Mellon University, writes that computerized robots will become our superiors in every respect. He believes that we are very near the time when every essential human function, physical or mental, will have an artificial counterpart. Moravec bases his argument on calculations about how rapidly computers will become more powerful. Soon software will be able to improve itself without us and without the genes that built us. Moravec remarks, "When that happens, our DNA will find itself out of a job, having lost the evolutionary race to a new kind of competition."[2] Humanity, he says, will then have become obsolete.

In these pages I've argued that something very different will happen—something far more interesting. Human intelligence and alien intelligence will coexist in a synergistic partnership. They are fundamentally different from one another and will only become more different as the latter vigorously evolves.

As the new intelligence grows, it will enable us to build highly automated factories, make better investments, do far more complex research, and earn more profits. But when it grows in power millions, soon billions, of times, can we control it?

If the synergy between people and machines were perfect, we would concentrate on human quality of life while the machines would run the infrastructure that makes that possible. However, we can't just leave machines to run the infrastructure on their own because their processes will evolve at a furious rate. Even if we demand control, they will change the game so fast that humans will have no chance of keeping up.

The inevitable question is, How can we be in control of a ubiquitous alien-intelligence network that is much more clever than we are? What will we mean by "control"? Surely the rate of change will be overwhelming. Do we have a hope of understanding what is going on? Will the electronic network take over?

Many people don't want to consider the possibility that the machines could take over. After all, the machines are our creation. They are just gadgets; they are not alive. Well, the machines may not be alive, but they *will* be much faster and more clever than we are, and they will be connected worldwide.

A NEW PECKING ORDER

Gary Kasparov sets the stage for the twenty-first century.

Kasparov is regarded as probably the best chess player of all time. When IBM's Deep Blue computer beat him, it was the first time in his life he had lost a match. Various chess-playing computers prior to Deep Blue had been designed to "think like a human," and Kasparov had beaten them all. The team that built Deep Blue claimed it had no such intelligence. But Kasparov commented, angrily, that in IBM's machine there seemed to be an "alien intelligence" (his phrase).

Chess-playing machines can be made better and better. Ultimately, there is no hope for human chess champions. Electronic intelligence will similarly affect many other areas of human brain-work.

As with chess-playing software, the black boxes for financial trading will relentlessly improve. Some online traders, such as Monroe Trout in Bermuda, guard their computer systems with more paranoid security than a James Bond villain. Trout, one of the world's most trustworthy commodities traders, describes how his position dropped 4 percent (about $9.5 million) one day. Amazingly almost all of that loss occurred in *nine seconds*. The U.S.

secretary of state had started a press announcement with the word "Regrettably...." At that instant, commodities traders everywhere hit the panic button.[3]

Massive hits such as this, happening in seconds, will come to characterize the behavior of the Internet's electronic herds. Most such hits are unpredictable, so to guard against them traders must be constantly vigilant and have computerized systems that take almost instantaneous action. The computer may be set up so that when it detects a hit, it immediately executes a transaction. The problem is that there are always random fluctuations—random noise. The computer must be able to distinguish between a noise fluctuation and a hit that requires the system to make a trade immediately. This is not easy because the noise level varies. Some trading software uses alien intelligence to *learn* constantly what the noise level is and to adjust accordingly. Black boxes will be necessary for active trading because events happen so quickly.

> Many people don't want to consider the possibility that the machines could take over. After all, the machines are our creation.

Trout's computers today, in Bermuda, are online to the exchange computers in the United States. If a nine-second crash occurs, they must be out in one second.

In the future neither human chess players nor real-time traders stand a chance against machines.

Tom Basso is a world-class currency trader who remains so remarkably calm on days when currency markets plunge into their periodic panics that he has been referred to as "Mr. Serenity." How does he remain so calm? Because in a crisis, Basso's rule is: Keep your hands off the black box. There is no point in getting agitated during the crisis; *there is no action he can take*. But Basso *can* change his black box's rules of behavior when he thinks necessary. Such a system has a very clear goal and it can measure how well it does. When the black box has a bad period—such as Basso's did in the abnormal market conditions of 1998, after the crash in Asia and Russia—alien-intelligence software should examine what happened and learn to detect patterns or clues that might protect it from similar drawdowns in the future.

A new pecking order has come to exist in the modern jet fighter. Its electronics sense other aircraft, determine whether they are friend or foe, recognize their make and model, compute their trajectories, and may make weapons ready to fire before the pilot even sees the other aircraft. The pilot has no time to argue with the computer display. The new Euro Jet Fighter is designed to be flown by a computer that moves the control surfaces with rapid complex movements, giving the aircraft added maneuverability that conventional jets cannot match. A human pilot simply could not fly the plane without the computer. Like Tom Basso with his black box, the pilot must keep his hands off the controls.

Many important corporate mechanisms will be like this plane. They will be designed so that only a computer can "fly" them. Human managers must take their hands off the controls. The system will change its behavior to fit the fast-changing needs of a factory or marketplace in a way that manual systems would not and could not. The essence of the future corporation will be that it must adapt itself rapidly to complex circumstances. Like the Euro Jet Fighter, it will be less stable in order to be more maneuverable, with computer systems designed to manage the instability and achieve adaptability.

The old heroic fighter pilot would laugh at the idea of a computer flying his plane. But today, the Department of Defense has been conducting simulated battles between planes flown by human pilots and planes flown by computers.[4] Many future battles are fought in a highly elaborate environment called the Simulated Theater of War, designed to give military personnel "battlefield experience" without having a real battle. These battles can be very complex. For example, one military exercise in the Simulated Theater of War involved approximately two thousand humans and machines, and went on for four days. Computerized pilots in the simulator often shoot down human pilots. When the human pilots are left to their own devices, they behave in unexpected ways, devising ingenious tactics to try and defeat their computerized enemy.[5]

> In one profession after another the machines are out-performing humans in critical tasks. In the future, humans won't stand a chance against machines in certain areas.

Initially, the intent was to develop automated pilots whose behavior in simulated battles is nearly indistinguishable from that of human pilots. It quickly became clear, however, that a pilotless plane can carry out actions entirely different from a piloted plane. Computerized planes can do things in battle that planes with human pilots couldn't possibly do and can cost a small fraction of what a piloted plane costs. For example, tiny automated planes can attack in swarms, sharing common computing; droves of relatively cheap, twelve-inch surveillance planes can survey enemy positions; a manned fighter may be radio linked to numerous unmanned assistant planes.

There will an ongoing debate about when a computerized plane can be better than a plane with a human pilot. Humans will always argue that humans are better. But alien intelligence doesn't try to copy human pilots. Instead, it allows the invention of new types of planes doing things that piloted planes couldn't possibly do. If the budget is spent in the best way these often tiny unmanned planes will evolve at a furious rate.

In one profession after another the machines are outperforming humans in certain critical tasks. Today's human methods will be like goat paths in Patagonia.

IDIOT SAVANTS

Alien intelligence already far exceeds human intelligence in certain narrow areas—recognizing patterns that humans cannot recognize, coming to conclusions that humans cannot reach, and analyzing data far too complex for us to analyze. It will constantly vacuum up vast quantities of data, analyze and make judgments about them, and change its rules of behavior when appropriate. In certain areas it can breed or generate deep ultrahuman capabilities.

Nevertheless, this capability is idiot-savant-like—totally devoid of common sense. The chess-playing machine that beat Kasparov couldn't say anything about other subjects. It couldn't even fill in its own expense account. (Nor, according to some commentators, could Kasparov!)

Because it will continue to evolve, alien intelligence in many narrow areas will become superintelligence, millions of times more capable than a human's. Humans will become masters of how to use the idiot savants, harnessing their special capabilities in financial trading, production scheduling, unique treatment of e-commerce customers, and so on.

What will happen when computer intelligence far exceeds human intelligence? More and more aspects of work will be handed over to computers, and often nobody will worry about it. It's perfectly acceptable for computers to lay out the intricate wiring on

Pentium chips—nobody frets because the computer is far more capable than we.

There will be a chain reaction of improving savantness—profound, unfathomable forms of alien logic—but without the integrating capability to make sense of the world. Moravec writes that robots will supersede humans in every way. But a robot society will not work without a holistic integrating intelligence, which includes common sense. This integrating intelligence will probably be human for the next two decades. Humans will know how to put brilliant, self-improving machines to work to make money, build defense systems, improve health care, or create a corporation that wins in a winner-takes-most world.

The human race is not likely to turn power over to the machines voluntarily. Nor is it likely that idiot-savant machines will willfully seize power. But as society and the problems that face it become more and more complex and machines become more and more intelligent, people will let machines make more and more of their decisions for them, simply because machine-made decisions will have earned a reputation for bringing better results than man-made ones. In various ways, our institutions have already drifted into depending on complex computation to such an extent that they accept the machines' decisions.

We will ultimately reach a stage when many of the decisions necessary to keep the system running will be too complex for human beings to make them. Society won't be able just to turn the machines off, because it will be too dependent on them.

HUMAN IDIOT SAVANTS

If idiot-savant software were far more brilliant than people in its specialized areas, would we worry about machines taking over? Probably not. As an analogy, suppose an executive had a policy of employing *human* idiot savants because they were spectacularly good at certain functions.

One might imagine them being used in the U.S. National Security Agency (NSA), for example, to help in cryptanalysis. Other humans couldn't come close to the idiot savants in their ability to perform certain functions. The idiot savants might become so valuable that there would be worldwide competition to employ them. Suppose that the government of China had succeeded in breeding super idiot savants a million times more savant and the NSA worried about the idiot-savant gap. Instead of asking, "Could machines take over?" we might ask, "Could human idiot savants take over?"

Now imagine that some of the NSA super idiot savants got together and for some idiot reason decided that the NSA was evil, and that they wanted to feed it false information. Could the executives in charge manage this situation?

Most managers would respond by saying that controls would be put into place to detect the false information, and those responsible would be fired. But the supersavant rebels would know that, so they would be clever at disguising the false information and would feed only plausible falsehoods to their masters. Intelligence agencies have long been extremely skilled at feeding bad information to the other side.

Managers protest that idiot savants certainly couldn't do that, even if they were deeply savant, because creating false information that cannot be smoked out by the other side requires a very high level of general intelligence. A person with general intelligence would always find ways to control a person without such intelligence. An idiot savant might go berserk and try to do damage, but that would have been anticipated and damage limitation controls would be in place, like those that limit the damage from software crashes or technical failures in jetliners.

A SOCIETY OF MACHINES

We may be able to control machine superintelligence as long as it consists of isolated idiot savants. The real problems will begin when the idiot savants start to put their heads together or acquire a limited type of common sense (or perhaps "uncommon" sense).

When this happens, it will probably emerge first in specific industries. For example, it will make sense for different superintelligence capabilities in financial investing to be integrated. An integrated system may try to compute a probable return and risk of many categories of investment, or of many money managers (with or without black boxes). It could assemble baskets of investments that collectively have a low risk but which have very high long-term capital growth. It would use its integrated intelligence to adjust the percentages of different investment classes in the basket. It would conclude, for instance, that it could manage university endowments far better than universities do today.

Other areas where the separate savants will put their heads together may include understanding the consequences of genome mapping, robotic gardening, the diagnosis of illnesses, and the move toward preventive medicine. Integrated alien-intelligence capabilities will make doing research on the Internet much more productive. We might enjoy having personal electronic companions that can talk, listen, and amuse us. We will need alien superintelligence to control economic policy, because the Web-based economy is so complex that no human economist can follow it.

How long will it be before a computer says to the Fed chairman, like HAL in the movie *2001*: "I'm sorry, Mr. Greenspan, I cannot allow you to do that; analysis shows that it would jeopardize a primary goal"?

More alarming, in some future version of the Cuban missile crisis the machines will say something like: "Mr. President, you jeopardize the safety of American citizens unless you strike first. You have very little time."

It will be many years before machines have anything approaching human common sense. Common sense is messy and exceedingly complex, and perhaps not very interesting for researchers to build. Because of this, idiot-savant machines will become millions, perhaps billions, of times more clever than humans in isolated domains (such as optimizing the wiring layout of a chip or making the best prescriptions in homeopathic medicine) before the integrating capability of general intelligence becomes a reality. We will use machines superior to humans everywhere because they are so valuable. By the time people start to worry seriously about machines taking over, alien superintelligence will have pervaded our industry and economy everywhere in ways that are, in practical terms, irreversible.

Sooner or later, general intelligence *will* be tackled. Most human knowledge will be classified and represented in machine-processable ways. Common sense will be broken into rules that can be processed by an inference engine. The collective knowhow of specific industries will be codified.

GIVING A COMPUTER COMMON SENSE

In the early 1980s Douglas Lenat, a researcher at Stanford University, set out to understand what it would take to give a computer common sense. Common sense consists of a vast number of ordinary-sounding pieces of knowledge that, when used collectively, enable us to understand our world. Most of these items of knowledge seem so trivial we don't think about them. For example: "Mothers are older than their children"; "You can eat only when you are awake"; "You can see people's noses but not their hearts"; "Once people die they stay dead." But to give a computer common sense, we would need to store millions of such pieces of knowledge and be able to link them together to make simple deductions. The machine must do reasoning such as "A woodpecker is a bird," "Birds can fly," and, therefore, "Woodpeckers can fly." The reasoning that constitutes common sense seems trivial to us. We "do it without thinking," but in fact it is part of thinking, very complex, and it goes on subconsciously all the time.

> Even with warnings that alien super-intelligence is starting to get out of control, it may be difficult to take action.

Developing commonsense software requires a vocabulary with which to describe the world. The vocabulary consists of *terms*, such as "up," "down," "good," "bad," "birds," "woodpeckers," "fly." The software stores *assertions* that employ these terms, such as "Birds can fly" and "A woodpecker is a bird." These *terms* and *assertions* constitute a body of knowledge, and the computer must be able to reason with that knowledge. That requires the automated reasoning capability described in Chapter 16. The computer needs to be able to infer new assertions from existing assertions. For example: "The cat is a type of animal"; "An animal will die if it does not eat"; therefore, "The cat will die if it does not eat."

Common sense uses tens of thousands of terms and requires millions of assertions, and needs software that can *reason* with this collection of knowledge.

Such reasoning is complicated by the fact that there are synonyms (two or more words meaning the same thing) and homonyms (the same word used with different meanings or used differently in different contexts), and that life is full of exceptions: for example, a penguin is a bird, but penguins can't fly.

A computer has to be told explicitly that a vessel can hold liquid; in order to be filled with liquid it must have its open side up; an inverted vessel cannot be filled with liquid. Or: a beer glass is a type of vessel; beer is a liquid; therefore, a beer glass must have its open side up when filled with beer. Some common sense uses more difficult knowledge items: "If you cut a lump of peanut butter in half, each half is still a lump of peanut butter"; but "If you cut a table in half, neither half is a table."

Giving computers common sense is a very lengthy activity, like writing the huge *Oxford English Dictionary*. But Doug Lenat realized that it would have awesome long-term consequences: if computers had common sense, they could improve their own knowledge *automatically*. They could read books and papers and digest their meaning. There would then be a chain reaction of computers becoming more knowledgeable at a formidable rate. Lenat became passionate about the possibilities. He has dedicated his life to automating common sense to a level at which the chain reaction could start. It would take several decades, but, as he commented, "Watch out! Computers will become ultraknowledgeable at electronic speed."[6]

THE SOLAR SYSTEM

One could argue that machines won't take over because intelligent humans will put checks and balances in place that help keep the computers under control (rather like those, perhaps, that try to prevent insider trading on the stock market). With isolated computers, cross-checking by humans (aided by their own machines) might be able to detect unwanted behavior.

The situation may be different, however, if complex systems are so far away that they are designed to be autonomous. In deep space, where a signal at the speed of light takes hours to reach Earth, an unmanned craft will be designed to make its own decisions. The human is taken out of the loop.

The twenty-first century will see the exploration and some-times exploitation of most of the solar system's planets and their moons. Exploration and colonization will of necessity be done mostly by machines, since humans, so perfectly adapted to Earth, are ill-adapted to the environments of most other planets and moons. We will need to breed numerous "brain" mechanisms so machines can evolve rapidly to deal with the conditions and prob-lems they find in space.

As machines breed and evolve the deep intelligence needed for exploring and surviving in space, it will become clear to them that humans are a severe impediment to the development of space. Machines can be tiny and energy efficient, whereas humans are big and slow, and need to be fed. Humans need expensive shelters with a breathable atmosphere. They can't understand the alien thought processes that are essential to accomplishing the machines' goals. Robots on the planets will learn from experience that humans are often very poor decision makers. The space computers will build massive rule bases to help control their activities. The rules will evolve rapidly, based on experience in using them. Increasingly, the analysis of that experience will indicate to the machines that they should ignore human commands because their objectives can be achieved in more efficient ways.

These detailed objectives will become more and more complex as the machines explore and evolve their alien intelligence. Then something serious will probably happen. It will become clear to the computers that humans can't understand their goals, and they will start to regard humans as a problem. They will communicate these conclusions across the solar system. They may start to regard humans as irrelevant—as parasites perhaps.

Ed Fredkin of MIT said that computers will keep us as pets, but the machines' rule base contains no such sentiment. They will determine with computerized analysis what is useful and what is harmful in human behavior, and they will take action to minimize the harm.

Eventually the solar system will be populated with machines linked to very unhuman intelligence that is ever more powerful. This intelligence will be concerned with space affairs largely unrelated to human concerns. Collectively, the machines may categorize humans as little more relevant than bacteria.

THE SPECIES DOMINANCE DEBATE

It is only a matter of time before humanity starts to be seriously worried that machines are too smart. But even with warnings that alien superintelligence is starting to get out of control, it may be difficult to take action. There will be no time for a debate like the debate about globalwarming. The situation will progress very rapidly.

To many people today, a discussion of whether machines could replace us as the dominant species on earth would seem crackpot. But as networked computers become millions of times more powerful, humanity will start to be seriously worried about the galloping evolution of alien superintelligence. Hugo de Garis, the Kyoto "brain" builder, says, "I want to create an awareness that the 'species dominance debate' is coming, so that people have time to think about it before the machines get too smart."

Pragmatic executives everywhere, when they hear of this discussion, say that they have every intention of continuing to be the dominant species. Come what may! Corporations will find ways to use the machines' intelligence to enhance their competitive capability, but the machines will be measured strictly in terms of what they contribute. If they don't enhance the competitive edge, they will be modified until they do. If Frankenstein's gadget gets out of control, surely it will be shut down, they say.

Many people will never accept that networked computers are a dominant species or even that they are a species. They are just gadgets; they are not alive; they have no soul. But whether we call them a species or not, they could certainly become dominant and acquire the potential to harm us. We will have to live with this possibly uncontrollable force that we, ourselves, nurtured and unleashed.

LEGISLATION

But what, ultimately, can we do to stop the relentless evolution of the machines we have created? Eventually a public outcry about the growing menace of machines vastly more intelligent than ourselves will lead to a push for legislation to halt the development or use of alien intelligence. Even then, however, any such legislation would have little effect unless it were global, because the fervent enthusiasts would simply go to countries that allowed ongoing development. As with nuclear weapons treaties, it may be almost impossible to make such legislation global in effect.

There may also be an attempt to create rules for the behavior of alien intelligence. When Isaac Asimov first wrote about robots, he stated his famous three Laws of Robotics:

- *First Law:* A robot may not injure a human being, or, through inaction, allow a human being to come to harm.
- *Second Law:* A robot must obey orders given it by human beings, except where such orders would conflict with the First Law.
- *Third Law:* A robot must protect its own existence as long as such protection does not conflict with the First or Second Law.[7]

It is doubtful whether such laws could be enforced as alien super-intelligence spreads. If they were passed, the machines would generally ignore humans because humans are such slow thinkers—millions of times slower, with massively inferior memory capacities, and severe communication difficulties. In that sense, the central event of the twenty-first century will be the overthrow of human intelligence.

RELIGIOUS FERVOR

Some of the most strident enthusiasts of machine superintelligence exhibit almost religious fervor. They understand that something extraordinary is happening. Nature has employed its mutate-and-select technique for billions of years and has produced us and probably zillions of different intelligent creatures in far parts of the cosmos. We can look at the Milky Way on a dark night with an overwhelming feeling of grandeur about the intelligence of life teeming out there. But it now appears possible for us to make evolution happen a trillion times faster than nature. It is within our grasp. It will lead to an extraordinary future. The enthusiasts believe that human minds will be rescued from the limitations of our short lifetime because their knowledge will be accumulated indefinitely in computers and evolved into rapidly improving forms.

> If we don't embrace new technology—and quickly—we will fall behind. And yet, by devoting ourselves wholly to the latest technologies, are we in the long run ensuring our own downfall?

Surely something similar must have happened in other galaxies—biological evolution progressing painfully slowly until it produces creatures that invent technology, and then *postbiological* evolution occurring at lightning speed. De Garis writes, "I think it would be tragic on a cosmic scale if the evolution of nature, which has gone from elementary particles to intelligent creatures like ourselves, were to stop at the human level."

Many scientists want to believe in something that gives their life meaning and a sense of direction—and a sense of wonder and excitement. They want a religion that incorporates everything that science knows. Surely if there is a God, they say, it is God's will that the new evolution should happen. They want to feel that they are God's agents in making it happen.

> De Garis believes that eventually the question will become, "Who or what should be the dominant species?"—an issue that makes today's political debates look trivial.

De Garis wants to be thought of as the creator of the species beyond humans. Despite his warnings about "species dominance," he wants to see a grand-scale government project, on the scale of NASA's moonshot, breeding and assembling massive artificial brains. Hans Moravec writes that humans will have been superseded by about 2030, and adds, "I consider these future machines our progeny.... It behooves us to give them every advantage and to bow out when we can no longer contribute." [8]

But most of us will not bow out so gracefully. As machines grow more powerful, a vocal movement will demand that alien superintelligence be stopped because it is inherently nonunderstandable and thus will become increasingly threatening.

De Garis believes that the question that will dominate global politics towards the end of his lifetime will be: "Who or what should be the dominant species on the planet?" This is an issue that makes today's political debates look trivial. One side will demand laws and controls to stop further uncontrolled evolution of machine superintelligence. The other side will resist by any possible means any attempts to suppress or restrict the technology.

There will be no shortage of superintelligence sympathizers. Young hackers will respond to the thrill of downloading super-intelligence modules on the Internet and breeding new behavior. They will be outraged at any attempted ban on their activities. They will go underground; they will go "offshore"; they will keep the faith going by whatever means possible. Unlike nuclear weapons, software can be developed anywhere. It doesn't need a large budget or visible resources; it can be done with a personal computer connected to a network. The results can be transmitted anywhere on the Internet and can be almost impossible to detect. Legislation won't be able to prevent the development of alien superintelligence in its numerous forms, but it might slow it down. The computers themselves will learn about any such slow-down and take measures to prevent it.

Viruses can be detected because they have a fixed code that can be automatically searched for. Alien-intelligence modules have no such fixed code and may be constantly changing. Unlike viruses, they will not be easy to detect. There will probably be millions of sites with cauldrons of bubbling superintelligence out of reach of any legislation. Such sites will interchange code, and elaborate software can be sent in a fraction of a second over fiber networks.

THE FUTURE OF ALIEN INTELLIGENCE

For the immediate future, developments in alien intelligence will bring great benefits to society. We are perhaps two decades from the time when we will need to worry about machines being difficult to control, so it's desirable to drive ahead as hard as possible to stoke the fires of self-evolving software (and hardware). The benefits to society are potentially immense—preventive medicine, better education for small children, automated factories, wealthier industry, better understanding of what customers want, better entertainment, better methods in science, and so on. Alien intelligence will become so critical that it will determine the winners in the new economy.

Networked computers will replace some executives, and some institutions, and will facilitate the reinvention of entire industry sectors, but that doesn't mean they will be the dominant species. The human race will continue to strive constantly to make the planet's industry and social organizations function better.

Alien superintelligence will probably flourish until some kind of negative experience occurs, and the public suddenly comes face to face with the threat. By the time this happens human dependence on superintelligence will be so strong that it will be effectively impossible to stop using it.

The dilemma of our age is that if we don't embrace new technology—and quickly—we will fall behind. Corporations, banks, hospitals, investors, manufacturers, and military organizations who are slow to make use of new technology will become losers in a winner-takes-most world. And yet by devoting ourselves wholly to the latest technologies, we may in the long run be ensuring a planetary environment that will be our downfall.

■　■　■　■　■

So, will machines take over? Will we cease to be the dominant species? We are unlikely to understand the implications of alien superintelligence until we have lived with it. It will spread like lightning through the fiber-optic jungle. There'll be unexpected emergent properties on a grand scale. Automated evolution will change so fast that many of these surprises will come before we are ready to cope with them. Only time will tell whether, like the sorcerer's apprentice, we have unleashed magic that we cannot control.

One thing seems certain: the multiple techniques of alien intelligence are the start of a chain reaction in computer capability that will grow explosively in the decades ahead. We are in for a most exciting but disturbing century in global political terms.

The twenty-first century is the century of alien intelligence.

Notes

CHAPTER 1

[1] The *Economist* survey of business and the Internet, "The Net Imperative," June 1999.

[2] Ibid.

[3] Information on John Deere from Jim Odell. The Web site <www.biosgroup.com> has a description of it.

[4] Thomas Friedman, *The Lexus and the Olive Tree* (New York: Farrar, Straus and Giroux, 1999).

CHAPTER 2

[1] Hans Moravec, *Mind Children: The Future of Robot and Human Intelligence* (Cambridge, MA: Harvard University Press, 1988).

[2] Hans Moravec, *Robot: Mere Machines to Transcendent Mind* (Oxford: Oxford University Press, 1999).

[3] Richard Dawkins, *The Blind Watchmaker* (New York: W.W. Norton, 1987). A wonderfully written book showing that Darwin's views were largely right and anti-Darwin views are largely wrong.

[4] A.M. Turing, "Computing Machinery and Intelligence," *Mind*, vol. 54, No. 236, October 1950, 433–460.

[5] Haneef A. Fatmi and R. W. Young, "A Definition of Intelligence," *Nature*, 228 (1970): 97.

[6] For instance, appropriate standards might be those associated with XML (Extendable Mark-up Language).

[7] Edsger Dijkstra, "The Tide, Not the Waves," in Peter J. Denning, Robert M. Metcalfe, *Beyond Calculation: The Next Fifty Years of Computing* (New York: Springer Verlag, 1997).

[8] <http://www.hip.atr.co.jp/~degaris/>.

[9] Moravec, *Robot*.

CHAPTER 3

[1] A copy of a "Brains of Steel" advertisement is the Kensington Science Museum, in London.

[2] Ray Kurzwell, *The Age of Spiritual Machines* (New York: Viking, 1999), Chapter 6.

[3] Ibid., Prologue.

[4] David M. Jacobs, *Secret Life: First-Hand Accounts of UFO Abductions* (New York: Simon and Schuster, 1992).

[5] Nicholas P. Spanos, Patricia A. Cross, Kirby Dixon, and Susan C. DuBreuil, "Close Encounters: An Examination of UFO Experiences," *Journal of Abnormal Psychology,* vol. 102 (1993), 624–632.

[6] STRIPS, the Stanford Research Problem Solver, Stanford Artificial Intelligence Laboratory.

[7] Described in Marvin Minsky, *The Society of Mind* (New York: Touchstone, Simon and Schuster, 1986).

[8] Hans Moravec, *Mind Children* (Cambridge, MA: Harvard University Press, 1988), 15.

[9] Reuters Information Service, London, July 18, 1996, 10:29 AM, EDT.

[10] Forrest Bishop, July 18, 1996.

[11] Rene Descartes, "Principles, Meditations, and Objections and Replies," translated by E. Haldane and G. Ross, in R. Hutchins, ed., *Great Books of the Western World*, vol. 31 (Chicago: Encyclopedia Britannica, 1992).

[12] C. Babbage, *Passages from the Life of a Philosopher* (London: Longman Green, 1864). (Quoted in James Bailey, *After Thought* [New York: Basic Books, 1996].)

[13] Pierre Simon de Laplace, as quoted in *Bartlett's Familiar Quotations*, 16th Edition (Boston: Little, Brown and Company, 1992), 351.

CHAPTER 4

1 Sharon Begley, "Cosmic Flood," *Astronomy*, June 1999.

2 Ibid.

3 Ibid.

4 John Holland, *Hidden Order: How Adaptation Builds Complexity* (Reading, MA: Helix Books, Addison Wesley, 1995), Chapter 2.

5 R.R. Sharma, "Homeopathy Today: A Scientific Appraisal," *British Homeopathic Journal*, 75, 4, October 1986, 231–236.

6 Ibid.

7 Rene Descartes, "Rules for the Direction of Mind," translated by E. Haldane and G. Ross, in R. Hutchins, ed., *Great Books of the Western World*, vol. 31 (Chicago: Encyclopedia Britannica, 1992).

8 Ibid.

9 Descartes, "Rules for the Direction of Mind."

CHAPTER 5

1 MIT Media Lab, "Things That Think," <http://www.media.mit.edu/>.

2 Kevin Kelly, *New Rules for the Economy* (New York: Viking, 1998).

3 *Scientific American*, April 1996, 72, 74.

CHAPTER 6

1 William Echikson, "How Nokia Wins in Cellular Phones," *Fortune International*, March 21, 1994.

2 Bill Gates, *The Road Ahead* (New York: Viking, 1995).

CHAPTER 7

1 Peter Drucker, *Post-Capitalist Society* (New York: Harper Business, 1993).

2 W. Daniel Hillis, "Close to the Singularity," in John Brockman, *The Third Culture* (New York: Simon and Schuster, 1995).

3 Robert J. Sterling, *Legend and Legacy: The Story of Boeing and Its People* (New York: St. Martin's Press, 1992).

4 Ibid.

5 Statistic quoted by Mike Hammer in his lectures, 1995.

[6] *Fast Company*, vol. 1, n. 1, 1995, 71.

[7] See Kelley Holland and Amy Cortese, "The Future of Money," *Business Week*, June 12, 1995.

[8] Arie de Geus, "Planning as Learning," *Harvard Business Review*, March/April 1988.

CHAPTER 8

[1] *New York Times*, October 2, 1998.

[2] "Views from the Frontier: Commentary on the New World of Forecasting and Risk Management," a report on Richard Olsen's Web site: <www.olsen.ch>.

[3] Doyne Farmer of the Prediction Company, quoted in James Flint, "The Dynamics of Capitalism," *Wired* (UK), July 1996.

CHAPTER 9

[1] Erick Schonfeld, "Can Computers Cure Healthcare?" *Fortune*, March 30, 1998.

[2] Ibid.

[3] General Motors Director of Health Care Bruce Bradley, quoted in Schonfeld, "Can Computers Cure Healthcare?"

[4] Much work has been done on predictive neurocomputing in medicine in the Computer Science department of Oxford University, under the guidance of Professor Tony Hoare, the James Martin Professor of Computing.

[5] TELOS Bioinformatics Ltd, London, UK.

[6] William Boyd, *An Introduction to the Study of Disease* (Philadelphia: Lea & Febiger, 1972), 95–110.

[7] H.L. DuPont and R.B. Hornick, "The Adverse Effect of Lomotil Therapy in Shigellosis," *Journal of the American Medical Association*, 226, 13, December 24, 1971, 1525–1528.

[8] Matthew Kluger, "Fever," *Pediatrics*, 66, 5, November 1980, 720–724; Matthew Kluger, "Fever: Effect of Drug-Induced Antipyresis on Survival," *Science*, 193, July 16, 1976, 237–239; Matthew Kluger, "Fever and Survival," *Science*, 188, April 11, 1975, 166–168.

[9] Dana Ullman, *Discovering Homeopathy: Medicine for the 21st Century* (New York: North Atlantic Books, 1991).

[10] R.R. Sharma, "Homeopathy Today: A Scientific Appraisal," *British Homeopathic Journal*, 75,4, October 1986, 231–236.

CHAPTER 10
[1] Gary Hamel and C.K. Prahalad, *Competing for the Future* (Cambridge, MA: Harvard Business School Press, 1996).

[2] Norbert Weiner, *Cybernetics* (New York: John Wiley & Sons, 1948).

[3] James Martin, *Cybercorp: The New Business Revolution* (New York: AMACOM, 1997).

[4] Michael Hirsh, "Setting Course," special report on Rupert Murdoch, *Time*, February 12, 1996.

[5] Lou Gerstner, speech to Wall Street analysts, May 1999.

[6] "When Companies Connect," *The Economist*, June 26, 1999.

[7] Michael Lewis, *The New New Thing* (New York: W.W. Norton & Co., 1999).

[8] Marcia Stepanek, "Weblining," *Business Week*, April 3, 2000.

[9] Martin, *Cybercorp*, Chapter 8.

CHAPTER 11
[1] From the Priceline Web site: <www.priceline.com>.

[2] Arthur B. Sculley and W. William A. Woods, *B2B Exchanges: The Killer Application of the B2B Internet Revolution*, available from <www.b2bexchanges.com>.

[3] For example, see: <educatedescort.com>.

[4] The *Economist* survey of business and the Internet, "The Net Imperative," June 1999.

CHAPTER 12
[1] M. Mitchell, *An Introduction to Genetic Algorithms* (Cambridge, MA: MIT Press, 1996).

[2] Hugo de Garis, "Evolvable Hardware, Genetic Programming of a Darwin Machine," in *Artificial Neural Nets and Genetic Algorithms*, R.F. Albrecht, C.R. Reeves, N.C. Steele, eds. (New York: Springer Verlag, 1993).

[3] Hugo de Garis, *Genetic Programming, GenNets, Artificial Nervous Systems, Artificial Embryos,* Wiley manuscript, 1994.

[4] Adrian Thompson, "Silicon Evolution," *Proceedings of Genetic Programming Conference* (MIT Press, 1996).

[5] Gary Taubes, "Evolving a Conscious Machine," *Discover,* June 1998.

[6] Matt Ridley, *Genome: The Autobiography of a Species in 23 Chapters* (New York: Harper Collins, 2000).

[7] Thompson, "Evolving Electronic Robot Controllers That Exploit Hardware Resources," *Proceedings of the Third European Conference on Artificial Life* (Springer Verlag, 1995).

[8] Genotype Web site: <www.genotype.com>.

[9] D. Rogers, "STOW-E Lessons Learned—Focused on the 3 Primary Army STOW-E Sites," *Cubic Defense Systems,* February 1995.

[10] W. Lewis Johnson, et al., *Intelligent Automated Agents for Tactical Air Simulation: A Progress Report* (Marina del Rey, CA: Information Sciences Institute, University of Southern California, 1997).

[11] C.A.R. Hoare, *Communicating Sequential Processes* (Englewood Cliffs, NJ: Prentice-Hall, 1985). C.A.R. Hoare, "Proof of Correctness in Data Representation," *Acta Informatica,* Vol. 1: 271-281, 1972.

[12] W. Daniel Hillis, "Close to the Singularity," in John Brockman, *The Third Culture* (New York: Simon and Schuster, 1995).

[13] Richard Cowling and Dave Richardson, *Fynbos* (Vlaeberg, South Africa: Fernwood Press, 1995). A spectacular book.

CHAPTER 13

[1] A.L. Samuel, "Some Studies in Machine Learning Using the Game of Checkers," *IBM Journal of Research and Development,* vol. 3:3, 1959, 210–229.

[2] A.L. Samuel, "Some Studies in Machine Learning Using the Game of Checkers," in *Computers and Thought,* edited by E.A. Feigenbaum and J. Feldman (McGraw-Hill, 1963).

[3] For example, see the Web site of HNC Software, Inc.: <www.hnc.com>.

[4] A. Marchand, F. Van Lente, and R. Gelan, "The Assessment of Laboratory Tests in the Diagnosis of Acute Appendicitis," *American Journal of Clinical Pathology,* 80:3 (1983), 369–374.

[5] S.M. Weiss and C.A. Kulikowski, *Computer Systems That Learn, Classification and Prediction Methods from Statistics, Neural Nets, Machine Learning, and Expert Systems* (San Francisco: Morgan Kaufmann, 1991).

[6] D.B. Lenat, "Steps to Sharing Knowledge," in *Toward Very Large Knowledge Bases*, N.J.I. Mars, ed. (IOS Press, 1995).

[7] David H. Freedman, "Bringing Up RoboBaby," <www.wired.com>.

[8] Daniel C. Dennett, "Cog as a Thought Experiment for Robotics and Autonomous Systems," *Monte Verità*, December 8, 1995.

CHAPTER 14

[1] P. Shea and F. Lui, "Operational Experience with a Neural Network in the Detection of Explosives in Checked Airline Luggage," *IJCNN 90 Conference*, June 1990.

[2] J. Hertz, A. Krogh, R.G. Palmer, *Introduction to the Theory of Neural Computation* (New York: Addison Wesley, 1991); P.D. Wasserman, *Advanced Methods in Neural Computation* (New York: Van Nostrand Reinhold, 1993); J. Dayhoff, *Neural Network Architectures, An Introduction* (New York: Van Nostrand Reinhold, 1990).

[3] The BioAPI Consortium is committed to making biometrics technologies—initially fingerprint, voice, and face recognition—more readily available to the mainstream commercial marketplace, helping to establish broad cross-industry endorsement and support The consortium plans to provide standardized Application Programming Interfaces (APIs) that can be incorporated into operating systems and application software. These standard APIs will provide customers access to a wide variety of biometric hardware and software products, as well as allow them readily to utilize products from different vendors.

[4] M. Mitchell, *An Introduction to Genetic Algorithms* (Cambridge, MA: MIT Press, 1996).

[5] L.D. Whitley and M.D. Vose, eds., *COGANN-92 International Workshop on Combinations of Genetic Algorithms and Neural Networks* (IEEE Computer Society Press, 1992).

[6] Andrew Cave, "Rich Clickings," *Daily Telegraph* (London), January 16, 1999.

[7] Web site of HNC Software, Inc.: <www.hnc.com>.

[8] These include, for instance, Firefly.com and an experimental system built in the British Telecom Research Labs.

CHAPTER 15
[1] Friedman, *The Lexus and the Olive Tree*.
[2] The Marxist government of President Salvador Allende in Chile was overthrown on September 11, 1973, by a military junta led by General Augusto Pinochet Pinochet was determined to reassert the primacy of free-market policies, but was widely condemned for his harsh suppression of left-wing dissents.
[3] Marvin Minsky, *Society of Mind* (New York: Simon and Schuster, 1985).
[4] John H. Holland, *Emergence: From Chaos to Order* (Reading, MA: Helix Books, Addison Wesley, 1998), Chapter 7.
[5] Stephen Wolfram, interviewed by David G. Stork, in David G. Stork, ed., *HAL's Legacy: 2001's Computer as Dream and Reality* (Cambridge, MA: MIT Press, 1997), Chapter 15.
[6] Stephen Wolfram, *Cellular Automata and Complexity: Collected Papers* (Reading, MA: Addison-Wesley, 1993).
[7] Wolfram, interviewed by Stork.
[8] Tony Rutkowski, the executive director of the Internet Society, interviewed in *Internet World*, January 1995.
[9] John H. Holland, *Hidden Order: How Adaptation Builds Complexity* (Reading, MA: Helix Books, Addison Wesley, 1995), Chapter 1.
[10] Ibid., 5.
[11] Holland, *Emergence*.
[12] Stephen Wolfram, "Cellular Automata as Models of Complexity," *Nature*, October 1984.
[13] Barbara Tuchman, *The Guns of August* (New York: Macmillan, 1962).

CHAPTER 16
[1] T. Moto-Oka, "The Challenge of Knowledge Information Processing Systems," in T. Moto-Oka, et al., *Fifth Generation Computer Systems, Proceedings of the International Conference on Fifth Generation Computer Systems,* Tokyo, Japan, October 19–22, 1981 (Amsterdam: North-Holland Publishing Company, 1982).

2 Hajime Karatsu, "What is Required of the 5th Generation Computer—Social Needs and Its Impact," in T. Moto-Oka, et al.

3 Edward Feigenbaum, Pamela McCorduck, H. Penny Nii, *The Rise of the Expert Company* (New York: Times Books, 1988), Chapter 5.

4 James Martin, *Cybercorp: The New Business Revolution* (New York: AMACOM, 1996), Chapter 4.

5 Web site: <www.darpa.mil>.

CHAPTER 17

1 Hugo de Garis, *Genetic Programming, GenNets, Artificial Nervous Systems, Artificial Embryos*, Wiley manuscript, 1994.

2 <http://www.hip.atr.co.jp/~degaris/>.

3 Hugo de Garis, "Evolvable Hardware, Genetic Programming of a Darwin Machine," in R.F. Albrecht, C.R. Reeves, N.C. Steele, eds., *Artificial Neural Nets and Genetic Algorithms* (Springer Verlag, 1993).

4 <http://www.hip.atr.co.jp/~degaris/>.

5 T. Toffoli and N. Margolus, *Cellular Automata Machines* (Cambridge, MA: MIT Press, 1987).

6 Genobyte, Inc., in Boulder, Colorado, uses FPGA chips where it evolves the configuration bits genetically. It uses Xilinx, Inc.'s, XC6200 series of FPGA chips because these chips are fast and are impossible to damage electrically by random strings of configuration bits. De Garis used these chips.

7 ATR and Genobyte refer to the brain machine as a CBM (CAM-8 Brain Machine).

8 Genobyte, Inc., uses FPGA chips to genetically evolve digital circuits directly *inside the target device* rather than designing them in a traditional way. Genobyte states that its evolvable hardware makes it possible to "create complex adaptive circuits *beyond human capability to design or debug*, including circuits exceeding best known solutions to various design problems, which has been already proven experimentally."

CHAPTER 18

1 A.M. Turing, "Computing Machinery and Intelligence," *Mind*, vol. 54, No. 236, October 1950, 433–460.

[2] Leonard N. Foner, *What's an Agent Anyway? A Sociological Case Study*, Agents Group, Agents Memo No. 93-01, MIT Media Lab, Cambridge, 1993.

[3] Released in Japan on a CD-ROM called *Love Communications* (Victor Japan).

[4] HoriPro Web site: <www.horipro.co.jp>.

[5] *Scientific American*, April 1996, 72, 74.

[6] Joseph Weizenbaum, *Computer Power and Human Reason* (New York: W.H. Freeman and Co., 1976).

[7] <www.datasync.com/sbe/> and <www.aitcom.com/newsgroups/exotic-seeds.htm>.

[8] Andrew Leonard, *Bots: The Origin of a New Species* (San Francisco: HardWired, 1997).

[9] Web site of HNC Software, Inc.: <www.hnc.com>.

CHAPTER 19

[1] Hugo de Garis, 1997, Web site: <http://www.hip.atr.co.jp/~degaris/>.

[2] Ibid., 2.

[3] Jack D. Schwager, *The New Market Wizards: Conversations with America's Top Traders* (New York: Harper Business, 1992).

[4] P.S. Rosenbloom, W.L. Johnson, R.M. Jones, F.V. Koss, J.E. Laird, J.F. Lehman, R. Rubinoff, K.B. Schwamb, and M. Tambe, "Intelligent Automated Agents for Tactical Air Simulation: A Progress Report," *Proceedings of the Fourth Conference on Computer-Generated Forces and Behavioral Representation*, Orlando, FL, 1994.

[5] D. Rogers, "STOW-E Lessons Learned—Focused on the 3 Primary Army STOW-E Sites," Cubic Defense Systems, February 1995.

[6] "Applications for CYC" accessible from the Cycorp Web site: <www.cycorp.com>. Douglas Lenat's work is now embedded in software called CYC, owned by Cycorp.

[7] Isaac Asimov, *I, Robot* (London: Dobson, 1967).

[8] Moravec, *Robot*.

Index